BL ... **ION**

BLACK SELF-DETERMINATION

A Cultural History Of African-American Resistance

V. P. FRANKLIN

LAWRENCE HILL BOOKS

Library of Congress Cataloging-in-Publication Data

Franklin, V. P.
    Black self-determination : a cultural history of African-American resis-
tance / V.P. Franklin.—2nd ed.
        p.   cm.
    Includes bibliographical references and index.
    ISBN 1-55652-168-5: $14.95
    1. Afro-Americans—History.   2. Afro-Americans—Race identity.
3. Black nationalism—United States—History.   I. Title.
E185.F827 1992
973'.0496073—dc20   92-17889
                                                             CIP

Printed in the United States of America
Second Edition
Published by Lawrence Hill Books, Brooklyn, New York
An imprint of Chicago Review Press, Incorporated
814 North Franklin Street
Chicago, Illinois 60610
5 4 3 2 1

To the memory of
Charles T. Davis
Gentleman—Scholar—Friend

CONTENTS

FOREWORD

SINCE 1984 WHEN V.P. FRANKLIN'S *Black Self-Determination* was first published, one of the most significant political changes that has occurred worldwide has been the increased demand for self-determination by peoples and nations dominated and oppressed by political and military forces not of their own choosing. We have witnessed the successful liberation movement in Namibia and the breakup of the Soviet Union's empire in Eastern Europe leading to the creation of independent states in Poland, Czechoslovakia, and Hungary. The reunification of Germany in 1991 has kept the issue of self-determination on television and in the headlines of newspapers and magazines all over the world. The demand for self-determination in the Soviet Union was so strong that it eventually resulted in its dissolution and the emergence of independent republics in Russia, the Baltic States, the Ukraine, Georgia, and Central Asia. While the down side has been the increasing violence or threats of violence in Yugoslavia, the Baltic republics, and several other newly-independent nations, the larger trend toward increased autonomy for culturally distinct groups victimized by various forms of overt and covert discrimination will very likely continue into the twenty-first century.

V. P. Franklin's *Black Self-Determination* is one of the most important works in the area of African-American cultural history because it shows that the same historical factors that led to the development of self-determinist values among oppressed peoples in Europe, Africa, Asia, and South America were also operating among the people of African descent who were enslaved and oppressed in the United States. Drawing on the testimonies of hundreds of African Americans from the early nineteenth to the late twentieth century, Franklin provides a vivid account of how and why freedom, resistance, education, and self-determination became the most important cultural objectives for black Americans.

The initial source of oppression for people of African descent in the United States was the institution of slavery. While slavery was an ancient practice and virtually all peoples have slave ancestors, for the African populations of North and South America and the Caribbean, who were enslaved from the sixteenth to the nineteenth century, slavery was not something in the distant past. Indeed, throughout that period it was a determining force in their daily lives, and it served as the crucible for forging a cultural value system that could serve as the basis for survival and advancement for future generations.

While there were important similarities in the history and experiences of African peoples throughout the New World, there were also important differences and Franklin's *Black Self-Determination* provides the historical background and information to explain the development of distinct African-American cultural beliefs and practices in the United States. The fact that African Americans were the numerical majority in only a few areas of the United States helps explain why there were fewer large-scale rebellions and revolts during the period of slavery in the United States than in other parts of the New World. And unlike the situation on many of the Caribbean islands and in South America, only a few areas in the United States were sufficiently inaccessible to sustain large communities of runaway slaves or "maroons" over long periods or time.

However, enslaved African Americans in the United States engaged in resistance other than massive rebellions, including arson, poisonings, destruction of property, and flight. Citing letters, autobiographies, interviews, and slave songs, Franklin makes it clear that resistance was a core value among enslaved African Americans and was completely sanctioned by slave religion. The religious beliefs that emerged from the slave community were liberationist, based on the premise that to resist the inhumane practices of the slaveowners was to do the will of God. Although both the masters and the slaves in the ante-bellum South considered themselves "Christians," and many of their outward religious practices were similar, their beliefs and ideals had very little in common.

Religious self-determination became a core value among African Americans in the decades following emancipation not merely because African Americans were removed and banned from Euro-American reli-

gious institutions but because their religious organizations served the social, economic, and educational interests of their communities. Black religious congregations provided literacy training and opened schools; they
purchased property and provided housing for the poor, aged, and infirm;
and, most important, they became the centers for organizing protest activities against the legalized oppression of African Americans in the United
States. Franklin's *Black Self-Determination* explicates the cultural meanings
in African-American liberation theology and documents the role of black
churches in the campaigns to end slavery and to gain "simple justice" for
African Americans.

In 1740, following the Stono Revolt in South Carolina, in which hundreds of enslaved Africans and African Americans rose in rebellion, killing
at least sixty whites, the South Carolina colonial assembly passed a statute
that stated:

> And whereas the having of Slaves taught to write, or suffering them to
> be employed in writing may be attended with great Inconveniences; *be
> it therefore enacted* by the Authority aforesaid, That all and every Person
> and Persons whatsoever, who shall hereafter teach, or cause any Slave
> or Slaves to be taught to write, or shall sue or employ any Slave as a
> Scribe in any manner of Writing whatsoever, . . . every such Person and
> Persons shall, for every such Offense, forfeit the sum of *One Hundred
> Pounds* current Money.

This statute became the model for subsequent laws enacted throughout the
colonial era and later by the slave states during the first half of the nineteenth century. Such prohibitions on slave literacy, however, did not keep
enslaved African Americans from learning to read and write. Franklin cites
slave testimony to explain how and why education in general and literacy
training in particular became one of the most important objectives for
African Americans. Black schools and other educational institutions became
symbols of the advances African Americans had made in their struggle "up
from slavery," and embodied the cultural values of freedom, resistance, and
self-determination.

Franklin's examination of the material conditions for the African-
American population that led to the development of their distinct cultural
value system also provides the important historical background for explaining the success of the civil rights campaigns launched in the 1950s and
1960s. Martin Luther King, Jr., A. Philip Randolph, James Farmer, Bayard
Rustin, and other movement leaders appealed directly to the African-

American core value system to recruit those who participated in the nonviolent direct action protests of this period. The most important accomplishments of the civil rights campaigns were the passage of the 1964 Civil Rights Act and 1965 Voting Rights Act, which brought about first class citizenship rights to African Americans and other oppressed groups in the United States. While this was an extremely significant victory, the circumstances for the black population a quarter century after these triumphs make it very clear that much still remains to be accomplished in the 1990s. The decline in high school and college graduation rates, the increase in violent crime and drug addiction in black communities, and the relentless poverty for African-American families, especially those headed by females, are just a few of the current social problems that undercut the gains made during the civil rights era.

Over the last decade African-American spokespersons have debated the most appropriate strategies for black social and economic advancement in American society. The putative success of capitalist market economics in advanced Western societies and the failures and limitations of countries committed to Socialism and planned economies have not only produced widespread debate and deliberations in non-Western societies over capitalism versus Socialism but have also generated a great deal of argument and contention among African Americans in the United States.

Black conservatives, many of whom benefitted from affirmative action and other programs designed to help break down barriers to power and wealth in American society, now oppose further government intervention in the attempt to bring economic parity to African Americans, women, and other groups previously victimized by legalized discrimination. Thomas Sowell, Glenn Loury, Robert Woodson, among other conservative analysts, contend that it is a matter of "individual initiative" and that government social programs encourage an attitude of dependency and keep African Americans from helping themselves. In addition, while civil rights leaders and black politicians, such as Jesse Jackson, Andrew Young, John Jacobs, and Marian Wright Edelman, argue that the social programs of the 1960s and 1970s were designed to provide an improved quality of life for lower- and working-class Americans, the conservatives insist that only middle-class blacks benefitted from them.

This debate will very likely continue throughout the 1990s, and Franklin's *Black Self-Determination* provides important historical insights and background on current ideological differences among African-American spokespersons. Franklin demonstrates that these differences of opinion have a long history, and he provides an assessment of the mass response in the past to the strategies and programs put forward by black leaders. Franklin shows that those leaders whose programs and objectives most clearly reflected the cultural value system of the African-American masses were more likely to develop a broad-based political movement that ultimately led to the advancement of both the masses and the elite in American society.

Franklin provides the most insightful description and analysis to date of the origins and development of the African-American cultural value system in the United States. His study should be must reading for anyone with a serious interest in current societal trends and African-American history.

Mary Frances Berry
University of Pennsylvania
September 1992

PREFACE

TO THE 1984 EDITION

SELF-DETERMINATION for politically and economically oppressed groups that define themselves as a people or "nation," but do not participate in a meaningful way in decisions affecting their lives and the lives of their children has been one of the most volatile and explosive issues of the late twentieth century. Almost nightly on the evening news we are shocked and confronted by accounts of "armed guerrilla movements" whose primary objective is to wrest control of the political and economic destiny of a particular cultural group from the hands of "outsiders," "aliens," or "infidels." The campaign of the Palestinian Liberation Organization (PLO) for a Palestinian state in the Middle East and the activities of the South-West Africa Peoples Organization (SWAPO) in Namibia and of the Irish Republican Army (IRA) in Northern Ireland are examples of "underground" or guerrilla movements that have as their primary objective self-determination for a culturally distinct group. But so, too, was the "right of self-determination" evoked in 1982 by the British government in its defense of the Falkland Islands (Malvinas), and more recently by most nations of the world in their condemnations of the United States invasion of Grenada. The overwhelming support of the masses of Afro-Americans for the recent presidential bid by Jesse Jackson has been interpreted by some commentators as only the most recent example of black self-determination within the United States.

I was originally attracted to the subject as a result of my interest in documenting the various manifestations of the "New Negro consciousness" of the 1920s. In earlier research in the period I found that black socialists, communists, integrationists, and nationalists were making strong bids for support among the masses of Afro-Americans who had become disenchanted with their chances for social, political, and economic advancement in post-World War I America. Upon closer examination, it became increasingly clear that one group or position, that is, the nationalists, had succeeded in gaining the support of several hundred thousand average black citizens—North and South. While I was engaged in this research, other scholars began publishing numerous books, monographs, and articles on Marcus Garvey and the Universal Negro Improvement Association (UNIA), including the publication of the first two volumes from the Marcus Garvey Editorial Project. All these works demonstrated the strength and expanse of the movement throughout the African diaspora. I came to understand that if I was going to try to delineate the nature and influence of the New Negro consciousness of the 1920s, then I should first have to explain why all those Afro-Americans joined the Garvey movement. Since Marcus Garvey did not arrive in the United States until 1916 and by 1922 had several hundred thousand followers, it was clear to me that he was appealing to a set of cultural values or "value system" that already existed among people of African descent in this country. It was not merely the social, political, and economic rejection of Afro-Americans by the larger white society following black participation in the war to "make the world safe for democracy," but the contemporary reality that Marcus Garvey's program appealed to the interests and self-determinist cultural values that had developed among Afro-Americans from the eighteenth century.

I had to embark upon a journey to discover the "meanings and interpretations" that average blacks attached to significant events in their lives and in the history of "the race." I found that in doing "cultural history" the theories and approaches of anthropologists for understanding cultural phenomena were extremely helpful. In effect, my attempt to document Afro-American cultural meanings in the nineteenth and early twentieth centuries resembled in many ways the ethnographer's task of gathering "native testimony" or "emic perspectives" on particular sacred and secular practices in more traditional societies today. I gathered "mass testimony" (much more than is presented here) that dealt with Afro-American cultural values and objectives from contemporary sources, including folk narratives, songs, autobiographies, addresses, letters, and essays, and compared these statements with the recollections of ex-slaves collected throughout the South in the 1930s by the Federal Writers Project. Many average or "drylongso" Afro-Americans testified before the various congressional investigating committees of the 1860s, 1870s, and 1880s, and this sworn testimony provides important evidence of what they considered good, worthwhile, and meaningful. While some researchers collecting the narratives and life stories of slaves, former slaves, and average black citizens decided to transcribe these testimonies in what they considered a form of "Negro dialect," most did not. The greater part of the evidence from mass sources is written in "standard English," but some was originally published in dialect. I hope that the reader will not be discouraged from trying to understand what these people meant by the way it was transcribed. Indeed, since much of this is "testimony," I would suggest that the longer stories and exchanges be read aloud to gain the full sense of what is being communicated.

This mass testimony is an integral part of the text. I have tried to present a unified story that flows from one value or set of values to another. The objective was *not* to have the Afro-American masses "speak for themselves," for the very selection of statements and excerpts imposes some sort of interpretation on the source materials. But I do believe that these mass voices support an interpretation that better explains mass behavior in the nineteenth and twentieth centuries. Earlier interpretations of Afro-American history have emphasized the gradual movement of the masses of blacks into the political and economic mainstream of American society. In my view, however, these perspectives do not really explain mass movements among Afro-Americans before the 1930s. When we add the cultural component to our understanding of the social, political, and economic situation for the masses of Afro-Americans, we are better able to explain the social movements and institutional development within Afro-America.

A number of agencies and individuals were of great assistance in the preparation of this study. A Fellowship for Independent Research from the National Endowment for the Humanities made it possible for me to conduct the research. Much of the writing was completed while I was a fellow at the National Humanities Center in 1981–82. The excellent research facilities there were only matched by the stimulating intellectual exchanges that allowed me to discuss (and defend) my findings on Afro-American cultural history. I am particularly grateful for the suggestions and observations of William Banks, William Chafe, John Clark, John Hope Franklin, Mary A. Hill, Brenda Murphy, Paul Murphy, Anna Nardo, Kejia Yuan, and Mas'ud Zavarzadeh. A number of members of the staff at the Center were also very helpful, especially Kent Mulligan, Susan Metts, Rebecca Sutton, Alan Tuttle, Ineke Hutchinson, and Madeline Moyer.

Over the last two years other individuals have read either the entire manuscript or sections and provided many suggestions for improvements. I would like to thank Ernest Batchelor, Ronald Batchelor, Maurice J. Bennett, Mary Frances Berry, John W. Blassingame, Malcolm Call, John Brown Childs, John E. Cooper, Gail L. Franklin, Donald J. Davidson, Robert

Harris, Lawrence Hill, Robert Lynch, Sylvia Jacobs, John McGuigan, Genna Rae McNeil, Sigmund Shipp, Sonia Stone, Glenn Taylor, and Earl E. Thorpe. Jan Paxton and Gwen Williams were also very kind and patient in typing the various drafts of the manuscript. The late Charles T. Davis was the Chairman of the Afro-American Studies Program at Yale University when I began this research. Without his assistance and guidance I would not have been able to undertake this project. And finally I want to extend a special thanks to the graduate and undergraduate students at Yale who took my classes and seminars over the last few years. I am sure that their stimulating insights and observations about Afro-American cultural values have found their way into this analysis.

Volumes could be (or have been) written about each of the values examined in this study. I was primarily interested in providing a more satisfactory explanation for the response of the Afro-American masses to the appeals of Marcus Garvey in the post-World War I era. Now that I have a better understanding of why many Afro-Americans joined the Garvey movement, I can get back to my original project—a detailed examination of black life and culture in the 1920s.

V. P. FRANKLIN
New Haven, Connecticut

INTRODUCTION

Thy God hath commanded thy strength:
Strengthen, O God, that which thou
hast wrought for us. . . .
Scatter thou the people that delight in war.
Princes shall come out of Egypt;
Ethiopia shall soon stretch out her
hands unto God.
Sing unto God, ye kingdoms of the earth
O sing Praises unto the Lord.

Psalms 68: 28–32

True liberation can be acquired and maintained only when the
Negro people possess power; and power is the product and flower
of organization . . . of the masses.

A. Philip Randolph, 1937

"WELL, FROM THE START, it should be said that we are a nation. The best of us have said it and everybody feels it." Mrs. Hannah Nelson was sixty-one years old when she agreed to participate in anthropologist John Langston Gwaltney's ethnographic field study of "core black culture," which he defined as the "values, systems of logic and worldview" of Afro-Americans that "are rooted in a lengthy peasant tradition and clandestine theology." In *Drylongso: A Self-Portrait of Black America* (1980) Gwaltney published a generous sampling of "personal narratives" collected in urban areas in the early 1970s at various folk seminars and interviews "devoted to the exchange of views on recurrent themes in personal documents, the evaluation of some main premises of social science and the indigenous definition of core black culture." Gwaltney believed that "from the narratives—these analyses of the heavens, nature and humanity—it is evident that black people are building theory on every conceivable level. An internally derived, representative impression of core black culture can serve as an anthropological link between private pain, indigenous communal expression and the national marketplace of issues and ideas. These people not only know the troubles they've seen, but have profound insight into the meaning of the vicissitudes."[1]

"I know that it will probably bother your white readers, but it is nonetheless true that black people think of themselves as an entity," declared Hannah Nelson. Gwaltney found that "the sense of nationhood among blacks is as old as our abhorrence of slavery. Black nationhood is not rooted in territoriality so much as it is in profound belief in the fitness of core black culture and in the solidarity born of a transgenerational detestation of our subordination." Mrs. Nelson did not like to sing "The Star-Spangled Banner," she preferred "Lift Every Voice," but she really believed "what makes black people a nation has very little to do with formal things like anthems and flags and national days. . . . That's because they mean one thing to us and something else to white people. Most of the things in school that were supposed to arouse national pride in me really made me feel anger, shame or indifference. . . .

We don't really agree with white people about anything important. If we were in power, we would do almost everything differently than they have. We are a nation primarily because we think we are a nation. This ground we have buried our dead in for so long is the only ground most of us have ever stood upon. Africa is mercifully remote to most of us and that is a good thing too. Most of our people are remarkably merciful to Africa, when you consider how Africa has used us.[2]

The experiences of the peoples of African descent in the New World are the bases of the development of the distinct "core black culture" in the United States. While the peoples of western, central, and southern Africa in the seventeenth and eighteenth centuries were diverse in experiences, language, cultural practices, and many other aspects, once these Africans arrived in colonial North America they were treated similarly by the natives and the white settler populations from Europe. The vast majority became slaves, and lived, married, and died in slavery. The fact that the enslaved laborers in the United States were almost all of African descent was extremely significant in the development of many Afro-American cultural expressions—religious practices, music, folklore—but it was the common experience of slavery that served as the foundation for the "cultural value system" that was handed down from the Africans to their American-born offspring, the Afro-Americans. Since more than one generation of Afro-Americans was victimized by enslavement in the United States, certain values remained relevant from one generation to the next and indeed became "core values" of the Afro-American experience.[3]

This book examines the experiential basis for the development of the Afro-American cultural value system in the United States. It utilizes the testimony and narratives of enslaved and free Afro-Americans from the end of the eighteenth century to the beginning of the twentieth, as well as Afro-American folk songs, beliefs, and religious practices, in an attempt to provide a viable explanation of the meaning and significance of self-determination, freedom, resistance, and education in the lives and experiences of the masses of Afro-Americans in this society. Before the General Emancipation and the passage of the Thirteenth Amendment to the U.S. Constitution (1865), the vast majority of Africans and Afro-Americans were enslaved, but even among the half million or more "free blacks" residing in the antebellum North and South, self-determination, resistance, education, and freedom came to be valued and defined as "good" on the basis of what happened to them in American society.

Historians, anthropologists, and political scientists have found that other groups of people who have experienced outside domination, which was generally considered illegitimate by the dominated, have also come to value freedom, resistance, education, and self-determination and passed on these values to their children. The Polish people, the Palestinians, the Irish, and the colonized and dominated peoples of Southern Africa resisted domination by foreign military forces, acquired knowledge of their predicament despite extreme prohibitions from their oppressors, often organized covert "underground" movements to fight for their freedom, and accepted as their ultimate objective control over their own lives and destinies in their native lands. Therefore, these core values of Afro-American culture are not unique, but have a great deal in common with the cultural values of other oppressed peoples around the world. But it was the particular set of circumstances and particular peoples involved that led to the creation of the distinct core black culture in the United States.[4]

The material conditions of the black population in this society, as well as their African background, determined their predominant cultural values. The Afro-American worldview was a product of larger economic and social processes, and the distinct "racial consciousness" of blacks in this country should be considered similar in many respects to the distinct "working class consciousness" that developed among English industrial workers in the early nineteenth century. In *The Making of the English Working Class* (1963), E. P. Thompson argued that "class is a cultural as much as an economic formation" which should be viewed as a "historical relationship" that embodied "real people in a real context." Thompson believed that "class happens when some men, as a result of common experiences (inherited or shared), feel and articulate the identity of their interests as between themselves, and as against other men whose interests are different from (and usually opposed to) theirs. The class experience is largely determined by the productive relations into which men are born—or enter involuntarily." Just as Afro-Americans developed a collective identity and sense of "racial consciousness" as a result of their experiences in an American society dominated by whites; the English working class evolved a sense of "class consciousness" as a result of their experiences in a society dominated by capitalists. "Class consciousness," Thompson declared, "is the way in which these experiences are handled in cultural terms: embodied in traditions, value-systems, ideas, and institutional forms." He believes there is a *logic* in the responses of similar occupational groups undergoing similar experiences, but we cannot predicate any law. Consciousness of class arises in the same way in different times and places, but never in just the same way."[5]

Most Afro-Americans in the United States were "enslaved workers," and it could be argued that they represented a particular "class" in antebellum American society, and following Thompson's lead, the examination of the "making of Afro-American cultural values" could be considered the study of the development of a specific value system and "class consciousness" among the enslaved laborers and their offspring in the United States. But such an argument would have to seriously underplay the inherent "racial" dimension of the cultural consciousness developed among the masses of the people of African descent in this country.

Enslavement came to be a social and economic condition reserved to Africans and Afro-Americans. The "racial" (or "biological" or "physical") basis of slavery meant that for blacks *and* whites, competing with the development of "class consciousness" was some sense of "racial consciousness." George M. Fredrickson, in *White Supremacy* (1981), his prize-winning comparative analysis of white racial attitudes and practices in the United States and South Africa, found that in both the American and the South African situations the development of class consciousness among the white workers was inhibited by the development of capitalist-inspired white racial consciousness. Fredrickson argued that "the degradation of non-whites frequently served to bind together the white population, or some segment of it, to create a sense of community or solidarity that could become a way of life and not simply a cover for economic exploitation." In specific areas and at specific times, white nationalist ideologies were utilized by the more powerful capitalist class to elicit the support of the landless agricultural workers and industrial laborers to help maintain the system of nonwhite economic exploitation from which the white working classes received only limited benefits. Poorer (nonslaveholding) whites generally went along with these white supremacist ideas and practices because they tended to bolster their self-esteem (the rule-of-thumb was: "Let the lowest white man count more than the highest negro") and to restrict the competition at the lower end of the socioeconomic ladder for the limited economic resources. White supremacy became a "core value" that evolved out of the experiences of European peoples in the New World and Africa and to a great extent explains the cultural "traditions, value-systems, ideas, and institutional forms" among the white settler populations in North America and Southern Africa.[6]

At the core of the racial consciousness that developed among Afro-Americans in the United States was the cultural objective of black self-determination, which operated in a dialectical relationship with white supremacy. Oftentimes, resistance and education were valued as strategies to obtain the larger goal of self-determination. Even freedom, which during the antebellum period was considered an important objective among Afro-Americans, became following the end of slavery an important means for obtaining collective self-determination or black control over black life and destiny.[7] Political theorist Dov Ronen in his recent study, *The Quest for Self-Determination* (1979), identified five distinct manifestations of the "value of self-determination" that flow along a historical continuum from the end of the eighteenth century to the present. In Western Europe from the 1780s to the 1880s, the French, German, and Italian nations were engaged in campaigns for "national self-determination," while, at the same time, the English working class was struggling for "class self-determination" within the capitalist political economy of Great Britain. Following the defeat of Germany in World War I, President Woodrow Wilson conceived a program for "minority self-determination" for the various subject peoples in Eastern Europe, including the Poles, Hungarians, Armenians, Finns, and Czechs. The movement for "decolonization" in Africa and Asia after World War II led to a sharp increase in the demands of Africans, Indians, and other "colonized peoples" for self-rule. According to Ronen, "the Indian fight for independence from British rule, Arab awakening against British and French mandatory rule, as well as today's black African fight in South Africa are . . . manifestations of decolonization, the quest for self-determination through the activation of non-European/racial identities." In these situations, the colonizer and the colonized formed the two sides of the dialectic. However, once these former colonial territories became "sovereign states," distinct ethnic groups, possessing separate languages, cultural institutions, and heritages within these societies, oftentimes began to demand "ethnic self-determination." These cultural groups conceived of themselves "as oppressed, discriminated against, or dominated by the central government." Thus, the French in Canada, the Biafrans in Nigeria, the Huttu in Burundi, the Basques in Spain, the Muslims in Lebanon, and other Asian, African, and American ethnic groups are engaged in a "quest for self-determination because as individual human beings they feel oppressed, discriminated against, or dominated in the political system of which they are part."[8]

Within the United States, Ronen identified the activities of Marcus Garvey's Universal Negro Improvement Association and Elijah Muhammud's Nation of Islam as typical of the quest for self-determination among Afro-Americans in this country.[9] Civil rights leader James R. Forman, in a more recent study, *Self-Determination and the African-American People* (1981), described self-determinist activities of Afro-Americans interested in creating a separate black state within the "black belt counties" of the southern United States. Forman argued that Afro-Americans "were moulded into a nation of people through the process of capitalist development inside the United States." He believes that the "shared experiences and history as slaves and free people" helped form the particular "psychological make-up inside the African-American people." However, rather than describe the process that led to the formation of that particular "psychological make-up" of the Afro-American, Forman traced the history of self-determination as a "political concept" that became popular among American Communists primarily in the 1920s and 1930s. He compares the theories of "black belt self-determination" developed by black and white Communists in this country with the theories and practices of "national self-determination" put forward by V. I. Lenin in the Union of Soviet Socialist Republics. Forman is much more concerned with self-determination as a "political objective" than as a "cultural value" among the masses of Afro-Americans in the United States. [10]

When one examines the testimony and narratives of slaves and former slaves and the statements and opinions expressed by black tenant farmers, sharecroppers, and average black agricultural and industrial workers of the nineteenth century, one finds that freedom, resistance, education, as well as self-determination were defined over and over again as "good" and things to be valued. In the antebellum South, enslaved Afro-Americans did not merely sing and talk about freedom, they plotted to gain it for themselves and members of their family. They resisted the oppression of the slaveholders by running away, sabotage, poisonings, and physical violence and worked together to create a sense of community and solidarity on the basis of their shared experiences. When slaveholders refused to allow the Afro-Americans to hold separate religious services, they stole away into the woods at night to hold religious services and praise God amongst themselves. Oftentimes, there was a great risk of persecution attached to such activities, but the enslaved Afro-Americans viewed these religious meetings as "good" or valuable and more important than the rules and regulations of the slaveholders. Thus the belief in black "religious self-determination" developed among the masses of Afro-Americans directly out of the material conditions they faced in the slave South. When slavery ended, the masses of blacks remained in separate black institutions, not merely because they were often unwelcome in predominantely white public and private schools, churches, and other social organizations, but because they believed that it was "good" for blacks to control their own lives and affairs in this country now that they were "free."

Afro-American leaders and spokespersons often shared the same experiences as average or "drylongso" blacks, but this did not mean that they always understood mass cultural objectives or necessarily represented mass economic interests. Frederick Douglass understood and eloquently extolled the values of freedom and resistance, which emerged directly out of the Afro-American slave experience, but time and again he opposed mass migration and emigration as against Afro-American interests in the pre- and post-Civil

War South. Booker T. Washington was also born in slavery and understood the Afro-American value of education for advancement, but he also opposed the mass migrations and espoused other social and political positions that did not reflect the objective interests of the southern black masses at the turn of the century. But Marcus Garvey's Universal Negro Improvement Association appealed to both the self-determinist values and the economic interests of the masses of Afro-Americans, and Garvey led the largest mass movement among Afro-Americans before the coming of the Civil Rights movement.

Although the UNIA was briefly successful in stirring the racial consciousness of the black masses, Marcus Garvey never really appreciated certain aspects of the Afro-American culture that developed in the United States. Oftentimes, in making artistic or literary judgments he relied on European standards, and thus dismissed or denigrated Afro-American cultural forms, such as the spirituals, jazz, and dialect poetry, which did not necessarily conform to European ideals and practices. W. E. B. Du Bois also subscribed to certain European theories and perspectives that sometimes distorted the otherwise brilliant analysis in *The Souls of Black Folk* (1903). Although Du Bois was acutely aware of the relationship between the experiences of Afro-Americans and the emergence of the values of freedom, resistance, and education, he limited his comments to the "talented tenth" when he discussed "self-determination." In Du Bois's case, the problem was not the use of "European" theories to explain Afro-American social and cultural phenomena; the problem (as Du Bois himself later admitted) was the use of the *wrong* European theories.

ONE

The Souls of Black Folk Revisited

In the social production of their life, men enter into definite relations that are indispensable and independent of their will, relations of production which correspond to a definite stage of development of their material productive forces. The sum total of these relations of production constitutes the economic structure of society, the real foundation, on which rises a legal and political superstructure and to which correspond definite forms of social consciousness. The mode of production of material life conditions the social, political and intellectual life processes in general. It is not the consciousness of men that determine their being, but, on the contrary, their social being that determines their consciousness.

KARL MARX, 1859

I painfully regret that in almost every political controversy of the last fifty years the leisured classes, the educated classes, the wealthy classes, the titled classes have been in the wrong. The common people—the responsible toilers, the men of uncommon sense—these have been responsible for nearly all of the social reform measures which the world accepts today.

WILLIAM GLADSTONE, 1884

AT THE TURN OF THE TWENTIETH CENTURY the Harvard and Berlin-trained scholar, William E. B. Du Bois at thirty-two was one of the best known Afro-Americans in the United States. His doctoral dissertation, *The Suppression of the African Slave Trade to the United States, 1638–1870,* had been published in 1896 as the first volume in the prestigious Harvard Historical Studies, and in 1899 he had published the first sociological study of Afro-Americans, *The Philadelphia Negro.* Du Bois had been living in the South and teaching at Atlanta University since 1897, when President Horace Bumstead asked him to join the faculty and take charge of the work in sociology and direct the annual conferences on the "Negro Problem" held each spring at the school. The Atlanta University Studies, most of which were written or edited by Du Bois, were considered at the time the most "thoroughly scientific" studies of black life available.[1]

Du Bois managed to contribute a steady flow of essays and reviews on black life and culture to the leading magazines and journals of the era, including *The Nation, Harper's Weekly, Atlantic Monthly, World's Work, The Independent,* and the *Literary Digest.* In these articles Du Bois attempted to bring to bear his broad knowledge and experience of Afro-American affairs on topics of contemporary significance to "the race." He energetically attacked the stereotypes of black life and behavior that were being disseminated in scholarly and popular publications by whites *and* blacks, and he contributed bold ideas and profound insights into what he considered the "new racial consciousness" emerging among black folk.[2]

In the April 1901 issue of *The Dial,* a literary magazine published in Chicago by A. G. McClurg and Co., Du Bois reviewed a book by William Hannibal Thomas called *The American Negro: What He Was, What He Is, and What He May Become, A Critical and Practical Discussion* (1900). The book was a vicious attack on Afro-Americans by a writer "born of a Negro mother." Du Bois believed that Thomas was one of those northern blacks who came to the South during Reconstruction times, but who later became "embittered and dissatisfied with men." In an earlier pamphlet (1890) on Afro-Americans, Thomas had been hopeful, optimistic; but this new book was a "sinister symptom" that presented "a denunciation of the Negro in America unparalleled in vindictiveness and exaggeration." Du Bois suggested that "his book can only be explained as a rare exhibition of the contempt for themselves which some Negroes still hold as a heritage of the past." In his concluding statement, Du Bois made some favorable and optimistic comparisons between lower-status Europeans and Afro-Americans in the United States.

> All men know that the American Negro is ignorant and poor, with criminal and immoral tendencies. And some of us know why. Nevertheless the Negroes are not as ignorant as the Russians, nor as poor as the Irish, nor as criminal as the English and French workingmen, nor sexually as incontinent as the Italians. If there is hope for Europe there is abundant hope for the Negro. And if there is hope, then in the name of decency let the American people refuse to use their best agencies for publicity in distributing exaggerations and misrepresentations such as *The American Negro*.[3]

A few months later the editors of *The Dial* published Du Bois's review of the recently published autobiography of Booker T. Washington, then the so-called "leader of the race." Du Bois took this opportunity to begin to question Washington's policies and opinions about Afro-American advancement. The review of *Up From Slavery* (1901) was brief. Du Bois merely criticized Washington's leadership as a "throwback" to the colonial era, the period between 1750 and the invention of the cotton gin when "liberalizing tendencies . . . brought the first thought of adjustment and assimilation in the crude and earnest songs of Phillis [Wheatley] and the martyrdom of [Crispus] Attucks and [Peter] Salem." He praised Washington for his successes, but pointed out that "educated and thoughtful Negroes everywhere . . . cannot agree with him" because he represents "the old attitude of adjustment to environment."[4]

Then in the spring of 1902 Francis Fisher Browne and W. R. Browne, the editors at McClurg, urged Du Bois to put together a book of essays that would reflect what he had been saying in their magazine and others over the last few years. Du Bois in his *Autobiography* states that initially he "demurred because books of essays almost always fall so flat. Nevertheless, I got together a number of my fugitive pieces."[5]

What emerged from these "fugitive pieces" is now generally considered a classic of twentieth-century American literature, *The Souls of Black Folk* (1903). As has been noted by virtually all critics and scholars who have studied the work, Du Bois put a great deal of time and effort into making it a smooth, flowing text, which included a much expanded critique "Of Booker T. Washington and Others."[6]

Du Bois was not primarily interested in demonstrating the humanity of the Negro or in dispelling myths of racial inferiority. Arnold Rampersad, in *The Art and Imagination of W. E. B. Du Bois* (1976), notes that "*The Souls of Black Folk* sought to convert and to seduce the American people, white and black, into sharing Du Bois's optimistic view of black culture."[7] Du Bois used as his central metaphor "the Veil," which obscures from the view of the larger society the true existence and spirit of the Afro-American. Thus his book is actually a tour into "the spiritual world in which ten thousand thousand Americans live and strive"—behind the Veil. This image of course comes directly out of Afro-American folk culture, stemming from the generally held belief that a child born with a veil (or a thin covering of skin) over his or her face and eyes has special psychic powers. The Afro-American, according to Du Bois, is a sort of "second son, born with a veil, and gifted with second sight in this American world—a world which yields him no true self-consciousness, but only lets him see himself through the revelation of the other world."

The Afro-American firmly believed in the "promise of democracy"; and as he emerged from the nineteenth century, he was hopeful that it would be possible "for a man to be both a Negro and an American without being cursed and spit upon by his fellows, without having the doors of opportunity closed roughly in his face." There was no discussion or mention by Du Bois of assimilation or "integration." Afro-Americans were to be "co-workers in the Kingdom of culture" because they knew that "Negro blood has a message for the world."

On the basis of the experience of Africans living in the United States, Du Bois posits the existence of certain "Afro-American cultural values," most notably the desire for freedom, the ideal of education and "book-learning," as well as self-development and self-realization or "black self-determination." In the chapter on Booker T. Washington, Du Bois offers as one of his major criticisms of the "Wizard of Tuskegee" that he was out of step with Afro-American culture and with leaders of the past, such as Charles Remond, William Wells Brown, Alexander Crummell, and Frederick Douglass, who adhered to the Afro-American values of resistance, protest, and self-determination.

In reading *The Souls of Black Folk,* however, one finds that, despite the optimism and respectful stance toward Afro-American spirituality and culture, Du Bois is consistently critical of the behavior, and at times the institutions, of the "black masses." He refers for example, to "the black lowly," "Sambo," "the black crowd gaudy and dirty." He believes that no advanced culture will flourish in the South "with the Negro as an ignorant, turbulent proletariat." And typical of these indictments is his summary of the condition of rural black folk at the turn of the century.

> Looking now at the county black population as a whole, it is fair to characterize it as poor and ignorant. Perhaps ten percent compose the well-to-do and the best of the laborers, while at least nine per cent are thoroughly lewd and vicious. The rest, over eighty percent, are poor and ignorant, fairly honest and well meaning, plodding, and to a degree shiftless, with some but not great sexual looseness. Such class lines are by no means fixed; they vary, one might almost say, with the price of cotton. The degree of ignorance cannot easily be expressed. We may say, for instance, that nearly two-thirds of them cannot read or write. This but partially expresses the fact. They are ignorant of the world about them, of modern economic organization, of the function of government, of individual worth and possibilities,—of nearly all those things which slavery in self-defence had to keep them from learning.[8]

Critics who have commented upon Du Bois's "disdain for the unkempt masses" have attributed it to a wide strain of elitism that runs through much of his work during this period. Some have gone so far as to dismiss these views as ramblings of a "black Puritan."[9] But Du Bois's characterizations of the black masses must be viewed in tandem with his explanation of the role and function of the "talented tenth." To label these negatives assessments of the masses as "elitism" without examining the context within which they were written is to distort the meaning and significance of Du Bois's views on Afro-American life, culture, and advancement.

And the Talented Tenth Shall Lead Them

When Du Bois was putting together the ideas contained in *The Souls of Black Folk,* Afro-Americans were less than forty years removed from slavery. Blacks were poor and illiterate, and they were being deprived of political power. But it appears that the Afro-American masses as well as the talented tenth were well aware of their situation, and this is why we find a dogged preoccupation within the black community with the need for "progress," "uplift," "improvement," and "social advancement."[10] Indeed, this is the one important area where Booker T. Washington and W. E. B. Du Bois were in full agreement.[11]

What is more significant, however, were the strenuous disagreements between Du Bois and Washington over the most appropriate means or strategies for bringing about "social advancement." Whereas Washington advocated political withdrawal, agrarian capitalism, and industrial education; Du Bois believed in political organization and participation, the wage-labor system, and higher education, especially for the talented tenth. At the same time, Du Bois took strong exception to one particular characteristic of American life that Washington praised and wanted to instill in the black masses—the materialistic ethos.

In *The Souls of Black Folk* in the essay entitled, "Of the Wings of Atalanta," Du Bois decried the rise of commercialism in the reconstructed South in general and in the city of Atlanta in particular. He expressed his hope that Afro-Americans would not be infected by the American virus of "greed and avarice." "What if the Negro people be wooed from strife for righteousness, from love of knowing, to regard dollars as the be-all and end-all of life? What if to the Mammonism of America be added the rising Mammonism of the re-born South, and the Mammonism of this South be reinforced by the budding Mammonism of its half-wakened black millions?" Du Bois continued with the allusions to Greek mythology.

> Whither, then, is the new-world quest of Goodness and Beauty and Truth gone glimmering? Must this, and that fair flower of Freedom which, despite the jeers of latter-day striplings, spring from our fathers' blood, must that too degenerate into a dusty quest of gold—into lawless lust with Hippomenes?[12]

With the right type of training, however, (in "Righteousness and Truth") Afro-Americans would not become moneygrubbing and greedy, like most Americans; but they would aspire to "truth and beauty" in all things.

> We are training not isolated men but a living group of men—nay, a group within a group. And the final product of our training must be neither a psychologist nor a brickmason, but a man. And to make men, we must have ideals, broad, pure, and inspiring ends of living—not sordid money-getting, not apples of gold. The worker must work for the glory of his handiwork, not simply for pay; the thinker must think for truth, not for fame. And all this is gained only by human strife and longing; by ceaseless training and education; by founding Right on righteousness and Truth on the unhampered search for Truth; by founding the common school on the university; and the industrial school on the common school; and weaving thus a system, not a distortion, and bringing a birth, not an abortion.[13]

It should be pointed out that since the early 1890s Du Bois had been writing about the "role of education in the advancement of the race." In *The College-Bred Negro,* the fifth report of the Atlanta University Conferences, published in 1900, Du Bois noted that the figures on occupational distribution "illustrate vividly the function of the college-bred Negro. He is, as he ought to be, the group leader, the man who sets the ideals of the community where he lives, directs its thought and leads its social movements." In Du Bois's scheme of things, "providing the rudiments of an education for all, industrial training for the many, and a college course for the talented few," he failed to see anything "contradictory or antagonistic." In a somewhat veiled reference to Booker Washington, Du Bois declared that he would "yield to no one in advocacy of the recently popularized notion of Negro industrial training, nor in admiration for the earnest men who emphasize it. At the same time, I insist that its widest realization will but increase the demand for college-bred men—for thinkers to guide the workers."[14]

The phrase "the talented tenth" appears to have been borrowed from Henry L. Morehouse, the executive secretary of the American Baptist Home Mission Society, who used it as the title of an article published in *The Independent* in April 1896. Morehouse believed that his organization was advancing Afro-Americans by opening colleges and universities for the training of the black leadership class.[15] Du Bois's essay of the same title was published in 1903 in *The Negro Problem,* a volume which also contained essays by Booker T. Washington ("Industrial Education for the Negro"), Paul Lawrence Dunbar, Charles Chesnutt, T. Thomas Fortune, and other "representative American Negroes of To-Day." Du Bois begins his essay with the observation: "The Negro race, like all races, is going to be saved by its exceptional men. . . . It is the problem of developing the Best of this race that they may guide the Mass away from the contamination and death of the Worst in their own and other races." He ends with a not-too-subtle threat: "Men of America, the problem is plain before you. Here is a race transplanted through the criminal foolishness of your fathers. Whether you like it or not the millions are here, and here they will remain. If you do not lift them up, they will pull you down."[16]

"Of the Training of Black Men," published in *The Souls of Black Folk,* was an expansion of an essay that Du Bois wrote for the *Atlantic Monthly* in 1902. It is another systematic examination of the most appropriate education for the advancement of the race. "Progress in human affairs is more often a pull than a push," Du Bois declared, "a surging forward of the exceptional man, and the lifting of his duller brethren slowly and painfully to his vantage-ground." Du Bois believed that "it was no accident that gave birth to universities centuries before the common schools, that made fair Harvard the first flower of our wilderness." As a son of "fair Harvard" Du Bois very likely knew that the school traces her beginnings to October 1636, when the General Court of Massachusetts acted to incorporate the school, and that formal instruction began in the summer of 1638. He may not have known that the system of common schools in the Bay Colony, however, originated in April 1635 when the General Court legislated public support for Philemon Pormont, a teacher who was to open a school. Harvard College was started to train the ministers and leaders for the Puritan colony—the talented tenth. The common schools were to provide literacy and religious training so that the lower elements, "the duller brethren," would be equipped to save their souls and participate in the body politic at some level. Both types of schooling, common and collegiate, were considered essential from the beginning of the Puritan experiment. [17]

With regard to the black colleges started by the "missionaries of '68," Fisk University, Spelman Seminary, and Hampton Institute (though at the turn of the century still considered a high school), the original purpose was "to maintain the standards of the lower training by giving teachers and leaders the best practicable training; and above all to furnish the black world with adequate standards of human culture and lofty ideals of life. It was not enough that the teachers of teachers should be trained in technical normal methods," Du Bois felt compelled to add, "they must also, so far as possible, be broad-minded, cultured men and women, to scatter civilization among a people whose ignorance was not simply of letters, but of life itself."

Despite the elitist overtones, Du Bois viewed these proposals as appropriate, given the social and economic status of the black masses. "They are not fools, they have tasted of the Tree of Life, and they will not cease to think, will not cease attempting to read the riddle of the world." Du Bois explicitly stated the threat to southern society from the failure to provide higher training and opportunities for advancement. "No secure civilization can be built in the South with the Negro as an ignorant, turbulent proletariat." The bolder and brighter minds will become dissatisfied, and this will force the masses into "the hands of untrained demogogues." The South itself may at some point want to change its image in the Western world as "simply an armed camp for intimidating black folk." In that instance, the "waste of energy" of its "black third" could not be tolerated, "if the South is to catch up with civilization." And there is also the very real possibility that the "black third" may adopt the "gospel of revolt and revenge" and work against the South's attempts to rise.

In a burst of inspired critical analysis, Du Bois describes the black situation from the perspective of the Afro-American masses.

Even today the masses of the Negroes see all too clearly the anomalies of their position and the moral crookedness of yours. You may marshal strong indictments against them, but their counter-cries, lacking though they be in formal logic, have burning truths within them which you may not wholly ignore, O Southern Gentleman! If you deplore their presence here, they ask, Who brought us? When you cry, Deliver us from the vision of intermarriage, they answer that legal marriage is infinitely better than systematic concubinage and prostitution. And if in just fury you accuse their vagabonds of violating women, they also in fury quite as just may reply: The rape which your gentlemen have done against helpless black women in defiance of your own laws is written on the foreheads of two millions of mulattoes, and written in ineffaceable blood. And finally, when you fasten crime upon this race as its peculiar trait, they answer that slavery was the arch-crime, and lynching and lawlessness its twin abortion; that color and race are not crimes, and yet it is they which in this land receives most unceasing condemnation, North, East, South, and West.

After that very forthright and perceptive statement of the arguments of the black masses, however, Du Bois returned to his central concern—his theory of Afro-American advancement. He had no faith in the ability of larger social and economic forces, such as wars and depressions, to force the masses, the not-so-talented nine-tenths, to act and adopt some program for advancement and liberation, and then drag the talented tenth along. Instead, he argued that the Negro college and university should lead the "social regeneration of the Negro" by maintaining "standards of popular education." More important, even beyond these objectives, Du Bois looked forward to the emergence of the "Negro individual"—the black man or woman of culture who can "sit with Shakespeare" and "move arm in arm with Balzac and Dumas."

> Above our modern socialism, and out of the worship of the mass, must persist and evolve that higher individualism which the centres of culture protect; there must come a loftier respect for the sovereign human soul that seeks to know itself and the world about it; that seeks a freedom for expansion and self-development; that will love and hate and labor in its own way, untrammeled alike by old and new. Such souls aforetime have inspired and guided worlds, and if we be not wholly bewitched by our Rhine-gold, they shall again. [18]

It must be admitted that at this point in his intellectual development Du Bois was an unrepentent idealist. Despite the fact that he was able to diagnose one of the major maladies affecting Euro-American culture—its materialistic ethos—his idealism about the role and purpose of the talented tenth caused him to ignore the very great likelihood that increased participation in the American political economy by the talented tenth could result in many more materialistic Negro individuals! Du Bois presents his hero, Alexander Crummell, as the ideal and model of the educated black man of culture who served his race well. When he first met the great man at a Wilberforce University commencement, "I instinctively bowed before this man, as one bows before the prophets of the world. Some seer he seemed, that came not from the Crimson Past or the gray To-come, but from the pulsing Now—that mocking world which seemed to me at once so light and dark, so splendid and sordid." Du Bois's respect was well-grounded, for Crummell had labored tirelessly as a missionary for twenty-five years "in the wild fever-cursed swamps of West Africa," and returned to the United States to his own people "and brought within his wide influence all that was best of those who walk within the Veil."[19]

Du Bois's idealism, however, obscured the fact that, even though Afro-Americans were isolated and oppressed, they were immersed in the American environment; and there were elements within the black community that accepted many Euro-American materialistic values. Thus, given the objective of the college and university to produce "Negro individuals," it appears more likely that the system of education advocated by Du Bois would generate more Booker T. Washingtons than Alexander Crummells. What Du Bois failed to accept was the contemporary reality that some sectors of the Afro-American community viewed Booker T. Washington as the ideal of the "broad-minded, educated man of culture."[20]

Du Bois was profoundly aware of the relationship between the objective material conditions of the black population and the predominant cultural values within the Afro-American community. The belief in resistance to and protest against discrimination and oppression, the need for literacy, education, and freedom from exploitation Du Bois traced back to the historical reality of the Afro-American experience. He was also aware of the importance of self-realization and self-determination—the need to control those material and spiritual aspects of life that promote survival and advancement. But this latter value Du Bois reserved to the leadership and the talented tenth. Thus, when he discussed the weaknesses of Washington's positions on education and politics, he attacked them primarily as policies and strategies that would not allow the *talented tenth* to move toward greater self-determination—a trend that had been developing throughout the nineteenth century.

Discounting the early movements to form black churches and denominations, as well as "schemes of migration and colonization," Du Bois believed "a new period of self-assertion and self-development dawned" with the participation of Charles Remond, William Nell, and Frederick Douglass in the radical abolitionist movement. "After the war and emancipation, the great form of Frederick Douglass, the greatest of American Negro leaders, still led the host. Self-assertion, especially in political lines, was the main programme, and behind Douglass came Robert Brown Elliot, Blanche Bruce, and John Mercer Langston, and the Reconstruction politicians, and less conspicuous but of greater social significance, Alexander Crummell and Bishop Daniel Payne."

This program of "ultimate assimilation *through* self-assertion" continued until the rise of Booker T. Washington. With his suggestion that Afro-Americans give up political power, civil rights, and "higher education of Negro youth," Washington "represents in Negro thought the old attitude of adjustment and submission, but adjustment at such a peculiar time as to make his programme unique. . . ."

> In other periods of intensified prejudice all the Negro's tendency to self-assertion has been called forth; at this period a policy of submission is advocated. In the history of nearly all other races and peoples the doctrine preached at such crises has been that manly self-respect is worth more than lands and houses, and that a people who voluntarily surrender such respect, or cease striving for it are not worth civilizing.

Washington, in suggesting that "the Negro can survive only through submission," is working against the attainment of "manly self-respect," and the talented tenth has a responsibility to oppose him. "In failing thus to state plainly and unequivocally the legitimate demands of their people, even at the cost of opposing an honored leader, the thinking classes of American Negroes would shirk a heavy responsibility—a responsibility to themselves, a responsibility to the struggling masses, a responsibility to the darker races of men whose future depends so largely on this American experiment, but especially a responsibility to this nation—this common Fatherland."[21]

Du Bois, however, skirts over a major problem that is inherent in his theory of progress as stated: Who will determine what the "legitimate demands" of the people are, the masses or the talented tenth? And if it is to be the talented tenth, which members of the talented tenth? Du Bois in this essay discussed at least three different camps within the talented tenth, each of which claimed to represent the "legitimate demands of their people." He was of course opposed to the Washington camp and to his associates who had received governmental appointments and financial favors through the infamous "Tuskegee Machine." But Du Bois also opposed the camp "spiritually descended from Toussaint the Savior, through Gabriel, Vesey, Turner": "they represent the attitude of revolt and revenge . . . and think that the Negro's only hope lies in emigration beyond the borders of the United States." Given the imperialistic adventures and actions of this country "against darker peoples in the West Indies, Hawaii and the Philippines . . . for where in the world may we go and be safe from lying and brute force?"

The third camp, to which Du Bois belonged, also accepted the responsibility of leadership, but traced its origins back to the activities of James Forten, Robert Purvis, Sojourner Truth, and Frederick Douglass, those who opposed any attacks on black suffrage, civil rights, and higher education. These individuals were degree-carrying members of the talented tenth (Du Bois mentioned the Grimkes, Kelly Miller, J. W. E. Bowen); they believed that their position reflected the "legitimate demands" of the people.[22]

Du Bois's attachment to a theory of the talented tenth reflected his training and experience and the social context. He was a disciple of Thomas Carlyle, the early nineteenth-century British historian, who had popularized the idea that "universal history," or the history of what man has accomplished in the world, was "at bottom the history of Great Men who have worked here." When Carlyle wrote, there was already under way the trend toward "scientific history," which sought to explain social and political changes in terms of broad social movements and economic laws; but Carlyle argued against democratic movements, which exalted "the organized unwisdom of the many" over the "strength and wisdom of the few," and he resisted the influence of the new evolutionary theories of society that treated "the greatest men" as products and expressions of historical circumstances. The "spirit of the times" was determined, according to Carlyle, by the "greatest figures," not by the mode of production, demographic factors, or the power of the ruling classes over the military and police apparatus of the state.[23]

Du Bois accepted and built his theory of Afro-American advancement on Carlyle's theories of human progress. Du Bois later admitted that this decision reflected his education. In his *Autobiography,* he recalled that at Harvard in the 1890s "Karl Marx was mentioned only incidentally and as one whose doubtful theories had long since been refuted." It was not until much later, the 1920s and 1930s, after he had become disenchanted with the artists and writers of the "Harlem Renaissance," that Du Bois began to suggest that the larger trends in Afro-American and world history were determined by the mode of production, material conditions, and mass cultural movements.[24] But what is particularly significant for our purposes is that Du Bois generally associated "self-determination" with the talented tenth and played down the self-determinist values of the black masses.

There should be little doubt that Du Bois was very much in touch with the spirit and form of Afro-American culture in *The Souls of Black Folk*. For example, of the Negro spirituals he observed:

> Through all the sorrow of the Sorrow Songs there breathes a hope—a faith in the ultimate justice of things. The minor cadences of despair change often to triumph and calm confidence. Sometimes it is faith in life, sometimes a faith in death, sometimes assurance of boundless justice in some fair world beyond. But whichever it is, the meaning is always clear: that sometime, somewhere, men will judge men by their souls and not by their skins. Is such a hope justified? Do the Sorrow Songs sing true?[25]

Judging from the overwhelmingly positive response of readers from around the world, Du Bois's interpretation of the Sorrow Songs did indeed sing true of the feelings and emotions of the oppressed.[26] Du Bois had captured a central ethic and value of Afro-American culture, faith in one's ability to triumph over sin and "the wages of sin" in this world. At the level of *mentalité collective,* this meant faith in the collective ability of the emerging Afro-American nation to triumph over oppression and exploitation in order to deliver its particular "message to the world."

Du Bois himself recognized "self-determination" as only one of three possible cultural responses of Afro-Americans to their predicament in the United States. Given a hostile social and political environment, "the attitude of the imprisoned group may take three main forms—a feeling of revolt and revenge; an attempt to adjust all thought and action to the will of the greater group; or finally a determined effort at self-realization and self-development despite environing opinion. The influence of all of these attitudes at various times can be traced in the history of the American Negro, and in the evolution of successive leaders." Du Bois then mentioned the revolts led by Gabriel Prosser in 1800, Denmark Vesey in 1822, and Nat Turner in 1831; and he believed that free blacks in the antebellum North made some sort of bid for "assimilation and amalgamation with the nation on the same terms with other men." This strategy collapsed very quickly because white society "considered them [the free blacks] as one with all despised blacks, and they soon found themselves striving to keep even the rights they formerly had of voting and working and moving as freemen. Schemes of migration and colonization arose among them; but these they refused to entertain, and they eventually turned to the Abolition movement as a final refuge."[27] Although it is not clear when and under what circumstances free blacks in the North supported "assimilation and amalgamation" before the end of slavery in the United States, Du Bois was very likely referring to the tendency of some free blacks not to wish to be associated strictly with organizations and institutions of "people of color." The race institutions were too narrow, too short-sighted, for their purposes; these were broad-minded, cosmopolitan individuals interested in the uplift of all mankind. Clearly, integration or assimilation into predominantly white institutions guaranteed continued white domination, but this action might also bring individual or collective advancement, so demonstrating the potential for conflict between the desire for self-determination and the ethic of advancement within the Afro-American community.

The remainder of Du Bois's discussion of the main responses of the "imprisoned group" of Afro-Americans to subjugation centers on the efforts of the talented tenth to obtain "manhood rights for the Negro." Self-assertion by the leadership generally led to self-improvement and development for the masses, until Booker T. Washington rose and counseled submission. He urged black leadership to accommodate to the dominant white power structures in the South, and advised the masses to "cast down their buckets where they are." For Du Bois this new response by Washington should be opposed because it represented a retrogression in the development of the Afro-American leadership group. Had Du Bois had more faith in the self-determinist values of the Afro-American masses, he very likely would have suggested that the masses would reject Washington's positions (which is indeed what occurred with the coming of the Great Migration).

While it must be admitted that the talented tenth has an important role to play in Afro-American advancement, it is the masses who ultimately determine the ebb and flow of Afro-American social and cultural history. Through their ability to reject or ignore leaders whose programs and strategies do not appear to be in the best interest of "the race"; and, more important, through their support of leaders and social organizations that combine an awareness of Afro-American culture and traditions with a viable program for advancement, the masses are self-determinative.

TWO

The Gospel According to Enslaved Afro-Americans

> We believe slavery to be a sin—always everywhere, and only sin. . . . Sin is the nature of the act which created it, and in the elements which constitute it. Sin, because it converts persons into things; men into property; God's image into merchandise.
>
> AARON, a fugitive slave, 1843

> The idea of a revolution in the conditions of the whites and the blacks, is the corner-stone of the religion of the latter.
>
> CHARLES BELL, a fugitive slave, 1859

W. E. B. Du Bois RECOGNIZED self-determinist values and objectives primarily among the talented tenth, and thus it should be no surprise that he failed to appreciate the self-determinist aspects of the religion of the Afro-American masses. "Of the Faith of the Fathers," the tenth essay in *The Souls of Black Folk,* was an expansion of "The Religion of the American Negro," an essay published in *New World* magazine in December 1900.[1] Du Bois declared that "three things characterized this religion of the slave—the Preacher, the Music and the Frenzy.

> The preacher is the most unique personality developed by the Negro on American soil. A leader, a politician, an orator, a "boss," an intriguer, an idealist,—all these he is, and ever, too, the centre of a group of men, now twenty, now a thousand in number. The combination of a certain adroitness with deep-seated earnestness, of tact with consummate ability, gave him his preeminence, and helps him maintain it.[2]

While the music was plaintive, rhythmic, melodious, and "the most original and beautiful expression of human life and longing yet born on American soil," the "frenzy of shouting" was a common phenomenon in religions throughout the world that required the devotee to demonstrate "true communion with the Invisible" through a "visible manifestation of God." In describing the "successive steps in the social history" of black religion, Du Bois posited his conception of the African influences on Afro-American religious expressions.

> The Negro has already been pointed out many times as a religious animal,—a being of that deep emotional nature which turns instinctively toward the supernatural. Endowed with a rich tropical imagination and a keen, delicate appreciation of Nature, the transplanted African lived in a world animate with gods and devils, elves and witches; full of strange influences,—of Good to be implored, of Evil to be propitiated. Slavery, then, was to him the dark triumph of Evil over him. All the hateful powers of the Under-world were striving against him, and a spirit of revolt and revenge filled his heart. He called up all the resources of heathenism to aid,—exorcism and witchcraft, the mys-

terious Obi worship with its barbarous rites, spells, and blood-sacrifice even, now and then, of human victims. Weird midnight orgies and mystic conjurations were invoked, the witch-woman and the voodoo-priest became the centre of Negro group life, and that vein of vague superstition which characterizes the unlettered Negro even to-day was deepened and strengthened.[3]

Unfortunately, the "mystic conjurations" of the "witch-woman" and "voodoo priest" were ineffective. The "spirit of revolt gradually died away under the untiring energy and superior strength of the slave masters," and the enslaved Afro-American became ripe for the "doctrines of passive submission embodied in the newly learned Christianity." Du Bois believed that the "slave masters cheerfully aided religious propaganda within certain bounds." The unrelenting cruelty and repression of chattel slavery beat the Negro down to a condition of "dumb suffering" where "losing the joy of this world, [he] eagerly seized upon the offered conceptions of the next; the avenging Spirit of the Lord enjoining patience in this world, under sorrow and tribulation until the Great Day when he should lead his dark children home—this became his comforting dream. . . ."

This deep religious fatalism, painted so beautifully in "Uncle Tom," came soon to breed, as all fatalistic faiths will, the sensualist side by side with the martyr. Under the lax moral life of the plantation, where marriage was a farce, laziness a virtue, and property a theft, a religion of resignation and submission degenerated easily, in less strenuous minds, into a philosophy of indulgence and crime. Many of the worst characteristics of the Negro masses of to-day had their seed in this period of the slave's ethical growth. Here it was that the Home was ruined under the very shadow of the Church, white and black; here habits of shiftlessness took root, and sullen hopelessness replaced hopeful strife.[4]

The emphasis on freedom in Afro-American religion and culture, according to Du Bois, was relatively recent, coming with the Abolitionist movement and the growth of a class of blacks who were considered legally "free." The free black became the ethical and social leader, whose "chief characteristic was intense earnestness and deep feeling on the slavery question. Freedom became to him a real thing and not a dream. His religion became darker and more intense, and into his ethics crept a note of revenge, into his songs a day of reckoning close at hand. . . . Through fugitive slaves and irrepressible discussion this desire for freedom seized the black millions still in bondage, and became their one ideal of life." Thus, for Du Bois, the value of freedom, like self-determination, reached the Afro-American masses through a "trickle-down process" from the free blacks.

In the final section of his essay he assessed the "present critical stage of Negro religion." Preoccupation with the civil, political, and economic factors associated with mere survival have "overshadowed and dwarfed" religious issues. In its extreme manifestations, the curse of "double consciousness" was fatal to self-confidence and led to the "peculiar ethical paradox that faces the Negro today and is tingeing and changing his religious life." On the one hand, "conscious of his impotence, and pessimistic, he often becomes bitter and vindictive; and his religion, instead of a worship, is a complaint and a curse, a wail rather than a hope, a sneer rather than a faith. On the other hand, another type of mind, shrewder and keener and more tortuous too, sees in the very strength of the anti-Negro movement its patent weakness, and with Jesuitic casuistry is deterred by no ethical considerations in the endeavor to turn the weakness to the black man's strength." This latter group for Du Bois consisted almost entirely of northern blacks who, though unjust victims of "harsh competition and color discrimination," still managed to raise their political consciousness about their problems through schools, newspapers, and other "race institutions."

> The soul, long pent up and dwarfed, suddenly expands in new-found freedom. What wonder that every tendency is to excess,—radical complaint, radical remedies, bitter denunciation or angry silence. Some sink, some rise. The criminal and the sensualist leave the church for the gambling-hall and the brothel, and fill the slums of Chicago and Baltimore; the better classes segregate themselves from the group-life of both white and black, and form an aristocracy, cultured but pessimistic, whose bitter criticism stings while it points out no way of escape. They despise the submission and subserviency of the Southern Negroes, but offer no other means by which a poor and oppressed minority can exist side by side with its masters.

These Du Bois considered the "extreme positions" within which the mass of northern and southern blacks fell at the turn of the century.

But what did this mean for black religion? Du Bois was not sure. He was uninspired by the religious past and looked to the development of some "new religious ideal" that possibly could spring from the "pent up vigor of ten million souls" in pursuit of the goals of "Liberty, Justice, and Right." And despite his adherence to a theory of advancement through the talented tenth, Du Bois admitted that there was still need for more research into the "meanings of slave religion" and suggested some "attractive lines of inquiry" for future researchers. "What did slavery mean to the African savage? What was his attitude toward the World and Life? What seemed to him good and evil—God and Devil? Whither went his longings and strivings, and wherefore were his heart-burnings and disappointments? Answers to such questions can come only from a study of Negro religion as a development, through its gradual changes from the heathenism of the Gold Coast to the institutional Negro church of Chicago."[5]

These were very significant questions that got to the heart of the issue of the cultural basis for the distinct Afro-American Christianity in the United States. Both Euro-Americans and Afro-Americans started out with the same Holy Book; but how they interpreted the Scriptures was determined by their social situation and the material conditions in this country. Du Bois took a weak stab at interpreting some of the cultural meanings of "Primitive Negro Religion" in the Eighth Report of the Atlanta University Conferences, but these ideas resembled too closely the statements he made in *The Souls of Black Folk,* published in the same year, about "African cults" and other exotic Afro-American religious practices.[6] In 1921 Carter G. Woodson, also a Harvard Ph.D., published *The History of the Negro Church,* but he devoted only a few paragraphs to the cultural meanings in Afro-American religious expressions. Woodson was primarily concerned with the "institutionalized Negro church," rather than the cultural sources for the Negro's religious faith. He did note that "the Negro is conservatively Christian and looks forward to that favorable turn in affairs of man when the wrongs of the oppressed shall be righted without the shedding of blood. . . ."[7]

In 1931 theologians Benjamin Mays and Joseph Nicolson surveyed 609 urban black churches and 591 black ministers, and 185 rural churches and 120 pastors, and provided a great deal of statistical information on the status of the Negro Church. They examined church memberships, buildings, educational programs, and decried the limited financial resources within these communities to support so many churches. "The Negro is over-churched," Mays and Nicolson declared in *The Negro Church* (1933), "primarily because the available church money is so thinly spread over so wide an area that the effectiveness of the church program is limited, except in rare instances." They were concerned that with many churches "heavily in debt," the burden usually passed to "the faithful few."[8] In only one chapter, "The Message of the Minister," did Mays and Nicolson attempt to interpret the cultural meanings of Afro-American religious expressions. In their research they collected a "representative sample" of one hundred sermons by Afro-American ministers and concluded that the majority were "other-worldly, or concerned so predominantly with the hereafter that practical aspects of life on earth are secondary or submerged." The "dominant note" was "fear or reward, not in this life but in the world to come. . . ."[9] They also ventured an opinion on the "God Idea As Reflected in the Sermons" and concluded that these one hundred preachers emphasized too much: "God Is Love, Merciful, and Forgiving," "God Is Revengeful," "Trusting God a Panacea for All Ills," and prayers to the "God of Special Favors."[10]

Benjamin Mays pursued this issue of the meaning of God in Afro-American cultural expressions and statements in a subsequent volume, *The Negro's God as Reflected in His Literature* (1938). After examining both "classical Negro literature"—slave narratives, biographies, autobiographies, addresses, novels, poetry, and the writings of social scientists—and "mass Negro literature"—Sunday School productions, prayers, sermons, and the Negro spirituals—Mays concluded that "the ideas of God adhere strictly to traditional compensatory patterns. They are traditional in the sense that they are mainly those of orthodox Christianity as set forth in the Bible, with primary emphasis upon the magical, spectacular, powerful, revengeful, and anthropomorphic nature of God as revealed in the Old Testament; the New Testament ideas of a just, impartial God; and those ideas of God that are being rapidly discarded in an age of science." That is, those religious ideas that "encourage one to believe that God is in his heaven and all is right with the world, and finally, those that tend to produce negative goodness in the individual based on a fear of the wrath of God here or in the next world."[11]

One of the primary sources utilized by Benjamin Mays to demonstrate these "traditional compensatory patterns" of the Afro-American religious expressions was the Negro spirituals. "For the most part the authors of the Spirituals appropriated the ideas of God . . . found in the Old Testament." They are ideas "that enable the Negroes to endure hardship, suffer pain, and withstand maladjustment, but they do not necessarily motivate them to strive to eliminate the source of the ills they suffer." Mays studied over one hundred and twenty spirituals, and "most of them are other-worldly—that is, they lead one to repudiate this world, consider it a temporary abode, and look to Heaven for a complete realization of the needs and desires that are denied expression here." Generally considered the most significant cultural contributions of enslaved Afro-Americans to the nineteenth-century world, Mays found them to be compensatory in the extreme. "Pharoah and his host were drowned because they interfered with God's plan for the chosen Israelites. As God protected the Jews from Pharoah, the Negro masses have believed that God in his good time and in His own way would protect and deliver them. Until recently, they have never doubted that as God delivered Daniel, He would also deliver them in some magical, mysterious way, and in His own opportune time."[12]

For Benjamin Mays to suggest in 1938 that the idea of God in the Negro spirituals was "otherworldly" and "compensatory" was not a "new" interpretation; indeed, it was the prevailing viewpoint on this beautiful religious music until the 1960s. But Mays went further and asserted that compensatory religious ideas have "had a profound influence upon Negro life. In the midst of the most stifling circumstances, this belief in God has given the Negro masses emotional poise and balance; has enabled them to cling on to life though poor, miserable, and dying, looking to God and expecting Him, through miraculous and spectacular means, to deliver them from their plight." According to Mays, there was little "self-determination" in the religious expressions of the Afro-American masses, and God, rather than their own efforts, "will bring His own out victoriously in the end."[13] But Benjamin Mays, writing in the late 1930s, was merely the latest in a long line of collectors and researchers, stretching back to the Civil War years, who emphasized the "submission," "resignation" and "compensatory nature" of Afro-American religious expressions. The northern white abolitionists who originally collected the Negro spirituals had their own particular reasons for emphasizing the "resignation" in Afro-American religious music. Unfortunately, this particular interpretation dominated the literature on the spirituals to the advent of the Civil Rights movement in the 1950s and 1960s. Martin Luther King's success in using traditional black religious meanings and themes in raising the political consciousness of the mass of Afro-Americans led to a major reexamination of the full range of meanings and "double-meanings" in the spirituals and Afro-American religious expression in general.

Interpreting the Negro Spirituals

Before the outbreak of the Civil War, northerners, especially white abolitionists, had very little first-hand contact with enslaved Afro-Americans in the South. Through the narratives of fugitive slaves, such as Frederick Douglass and William Wells Brown, northern whites were often made aware of the brutality and barbarism of the slave regime, but they remained ignorant of the cultural values and expressions that developed among the enslaved to enable them to survive the life-threatening conditions of the antebellum South. Gradually, as northerners moved into the area as teachers, missionaries, and relief workers, assisting the fleeing slaves or "contrabands" trailing behind the Union Army as it liberated parts of Virginia, South Carolina, and Georgia, reports began to find their way into northern newspapers and magazines of the "beautiful, mournful religious songs of the slaves." One of the earliest articles on "Contraband Singing" was reprinted in *Dwight's Journal of Music* on 7 September 1861.

> *Contraband Singing.* It is one of the most striking incidents of this war to listen to the singing of the groups of colored people in Fortress Monroe, who gather at their resorts after nightfall. . . . I passed around by the Fortress chapel and adjacent yard, where most of the "contraband" tents are spread. There were hundreds of men of all ages scattered around. In one tent they were singing in order, one man leading, as extemporaneous chorister, while some ten or twelve others joined in the chorus. The hymn was long and plaintive, as usual, and the air was one of the sweetest minors I ever listened to. . . . One verse ran thus:
>
> "Shout along, children! Shout along, children! Hear the dying Lamb. Oh! take your nets and follow me, For I died for you upon the tree! Shout along, children! Shout along, children! Hear the dying Lamb!"
>
> There was no confusion, no uproar, no discord—all was as tender and harmonious as the symphony of an organ. . . .[14]

Similar reports appeared in the *New York Times,* the *New York Tribune,* and the *National Anti-Slavery Standard* well before the end of 1861. This was an important discovery for many northerners because before this time the only songs associated with the black slaves were the uncompromisingly secular "Plantation Melodies" and "Coon Songs" popularized in the minstrel shows. Performed during the initial years only by white men in black-face makeup, (who claimed they were singing "genuine Negro songs in Negro dialect,") the minstrel show, in the words of historian Robert Toll, "literally swept the nation in the 1840s, from White House to the California gold fields, from New Orleans to New England, from riverboats and saloons to 2500 seat houses. For over half a century it remained the most popular entertainment form in the country."[15] The Congo Melodists, Ethiopian Serenaders, and other groups, were known to perform such exotic movements as the "African fling," "Virginia Jungle Dance" and the "Nubian Trot," along with a song, a joke, and a skit. Among composer Stephen Foster's songs that were made famous in the 1850s by the "old" Christy

Minstrels were "Old Folks at Home," "Camptown Races," and "Ole Black Joe." Predictably, the more refined classes generally frowned on the lower element's seemingly insatiable appetite for the "Darkie Ditties."[16]

Thus, when missionaries and relief workers began to report hearing these beautiful religious songs of the slaves, this came as quite a surprise to most northern readers. Rev. Lewis C. Lockwood, who had been sent in 1861 to investigate the conditions among the refugees at Fortress Monroe, near Hampton Roads, Virginia, heard this black music for the first time while there. In a letter published in the *National Anti-Slavery Standard* on 21 December 1861, Lockwood presented a transcription of what he considered a "prime deliverance melody" of the slaves. Since they maintained that they had been singing the song for "at least fifteen or twenty years," the *Standard's* editor believed that "the slaves in a considerable part of Virginia, at least, have had a superstitious faith in being freed some time in the future." This was very likely the first published version of the now-famous spiritual "Go Down, Moses."

LET MY PEOPLE GO.
A SONG OF THE "CONTRABANDS."

When Israel was in Egypt's land,
   O let my people go!
Oppressed so hard they could not stand,
   O let my people go!

CHORUS—O go down, Moses,
   Away down to Egypt's land,
And tell King Pharaoh
   To let my people go!

Thus saith the Lord bold Moses said
   O let my people go!
If not I'll smite your first born dead
   O let my people go!

No more shall they in bondage toil,
   O let my people go!
Let them come out with Egypt's spoil,
   O let my people go! . . .[17]

It would take almost another century for scholars and writers to recognize that many of the Negro spirituals were originally "Freedom Songs."

Thomas Wentworth Higginson, Harvard educated, Unitarian minister and committed abolitionist, entered the Union Army as captain of a Massachusetts unit. But when the colonelcy of the first black regiment was offered to him in November 1862, he leaped at the opportunity. For two years he served as commander of the 1st South Carolina Volunteers, and during that time he collected the "unwritten songs" of black soldiers and refugees he encountered on his tour of duty in the South.

> Often in the starlit evening I have returned from some lonely ride by the swift river, or on the plover-haunted barrens, and, entering the camp, have silently approached some glimmering fire, round which the dusky figures moved in the rhythmical barbaric dance the negroes call a "shout," chanting, often harshly, but always in the most perfect time, some monotonous refrain. Writing down in the darkness, as I best could,—perhaps with my hand in the safe covert of my pocket,—the words of the song, I have afterwards carried it to my tent, like some captured bird or insect, and then, after examination, put it by. Or, summoning one of the men at some period of leisure,—Corporal Robert Sutton, for instance, whose iron memory held all the details of a song as if it were a ford or a forest,—I have completed the new specimen by supplying the absent parts. The music I could only retain by ear, and though the more common strains were repeated often enough to fix their impression, there were others that occurred only once or twice.[18]

As a regular contributor to the then decade-old *Atlantic Monthly,* Higginson wrote about many aspects of his military service, and in 1870 these reminiscences were published in the now famous *Life in a Black Regiment.*[19] In the June 1867 issue of the *Atlantic,* Higginson published the first serious discussion and interpretation of the "Negro Spirituals." He included the words to thirty-six songs and presented his views on the origins and meaning of this "indigenous folk music." It is important to note that many of Higginson's observations would become part of the standard interpretation of Afro-American music for the next one hundred years. For example, it was Higginson who first suggested that slave songs were essentially religious in nature.

> Almost all their songs were thoroughly religious in their tone, however quaint their expression, and were in a minor key, both as to words and music. The attitude is always the same, and, as a commentary on the life of the race, is infinitely pathetic. Nothing but patience for this life,—nothing but triumph in the next. Sometimes the present predominates, sometimes the future; but the combination is always implied. In the following, for instance, we hear simply the patience.

THIS WORLD ALMOST DONE.

"Brudder, keep your lamp trimmin' and a-burnin',
Keep your lamp trimmin' and a-burnin',
Keep your lamp trimmin' and a-burnin',
      For dis world most done.
So keep your lamp, &c.
      Dis world most done."

But in the next, the final reward of patience is proclaimed as plaintively.

I WANT TO GO HOME.

"Dere's no rain to wet you.
      O, yes, I want to go home.
Dere's no sun to burn you,
      O, yes, I want to go home;
O, push along, believers,
      O, yes, &c.
Dere's no hard trials.
      O, yes, &c.
Dere's no whips a-crackin',
      O, yes, &c.
My brudder on de wayside,
O, push along, my brudder,
      O, yes, &c.
Where dere's no stormy weather,
      O, yes, & c.
Dere's no tribulation,
      O, yes, &c."[20]

Higginson may have only heard "patience" in the words, "Dere's no whips a-crackin', O, yes, I want to go home," but the slaves were very likely referring to something else.

The beautiful poetry in the lyrics made a great impression on the young infantry officer.

[O]f all the "spirituals" that which surprised me the most, I think,— perhaps because it was that in which external nature furnished the images most directly,—was this. With all my experience of their ideal ways of speech, I was startled when first I came on such a flower of poetry in that dark soil.

I KNOW MOON-RISE.

"I know moon-rise, I know star-rise,
  Lay dis body down.
I walk in de moonlight, I walk in de starlight,
  To lay dis body down.
I'll walk in de graveyard, I'll walk through de graveyard,
  To lay dis body down.
I'll lie in de grave and stretch out my arms;
  Lay dis body down
I go to de judgment in de evenin' of de day,
  When I lay dis body down;
And my soul and your soul will meet in de day
  When I lay dis body down."

"I'll lie in de grave and stretch out my arms." Never, it seems to me, since man first lived and suffered, was his infinite longing for peace uttered more plaintively than in that line.

Higginson came across three different versions of "Ship of Zion," which he believed were "modifications of an old camp-meeting melody." He also thought that three other songs, "Sweet Music," "Good News," and "The Heavenly Road," were songs popular at evangelical revival meetings, "although I cannot find them in the Methodist hymn-books." More important, Higginson was aware that many blacks and whites considered the spirituals "Freedom Songs," but he believed this could be demonstrated for only a few. Higginson was told that the spirituals had "double-meanings," but he dismissed this as "unfounded."

Some of the songs had played an historic part during the war. For singing the next, for instance, the negroes had been put in jail in Georgetown, S.C., at the outbreak of the Rebellion. "We'll soon be free." was too dangerous an assertion; and though the chant was an old one, it was no doubt sung with redoubled emphasis during the new events. "De Lord will call us home," was evidently thought to be a symbolical verse; for, as a little drummer-boy explained to me, showing all his white teeth as he sat in the moonlight by the door of my tent, "Dey tink *de Lord* mean for say *de Yankees*."

WE'LL SOON BE FREE.

"We'll soon be free,
  We'll soon be free,

> We'll soon be free,
>> When de Lord will call us home.
> My brudder, how long,
> My brudder, how long,
> My brudder, how long,
>> 'Fore we done sufferin' here?
> It won't be long *(Thrice.)*
>> 'Fore de Lord will call us home.
> We'll walk de miry road *(Thrice.)*
>> Where pleasure never dies.
> We'll walk de golden street *(Thrice.)*
>> Where pleasure never dies.
> My brudder, how long *(Thrice.)*
>> 'Fore we done sufferin' here?
> We'll soon be free *(Thrice.)*
>> When Jesus sets me free.
> We'll fight for liberty *(Thrice.)*
>> When de Lord will call us home."

The suspicion in this case was unfounded, but they had another song to which the Rebellion had actually given rise. This was composed by nobody knew whom,—though it was the most recent, doubtless, of all these "spirituals,"—and had been sung in secret to avoid detection. It is certainly plaintive enough. The peck of corn and pint of salt were slavery's rations.

MANY THOUSAND GO.

> "No more peck o' corn for me,
>> No more, no more,—
> "No more peck o' corn for me,
>> Many thousand go.
> "No more driver's lash for me, *(Twice.)*
>> No more, &c.
> "No more pint o' salt for me, *(Twice.)*
>> No more, &c.
> "No more hundred lash for me, *(Twice.)*
>> No more, &c.
> "No more mistress' call for me,
>> No more, no more,—
> "No more mistress' call for me,
>> Many thousand go."

Overall, however, Higginson was convinced that most of the songs of enslaved Africans and Afro-Americans were religious. "I never overheard in camp a profane or vulgar song. With the trifling exceptions given, all had a religious motive, while the most secular melody could not have been more exciting." He concluded:

> There is no parallel instance of an oppressed race thus sustained by the religious sentiment alone. These songs are but the vocal expression of the simplicity of their faith and the sublimity of their long resignation.[21]

The evidence that Higginson presented in his article, however, did not wholly support this conclusion. If anything, his essay suggested that with respect to the music of African and Afro-American slaves, there was little separation of the "sacred" and the "secular," and when the former slaves were singing before a white audience—especially the members of the "Army of de Lord" who were fighting for their freedom—many former slaves seemed to believe that it was downright disrespectful to sing any of those "corn-shucking tunes" unless specifically requested.

Higginson mentioned several times in the article that he was interested in tracking down the origins of the spirituals. "I had always wondered about these, whether they had always a conscious and a definite origin in some leading mind, or whether they grow by gradual accretion, in an almost unconscious way." Higginson looked for the supposed authors of the spirituals.

> [O]ne day when I was being rowed across from Beaufort to Ladies' Island, I found myself, with delight, on the actual trail of a song. One of the oarsmen, a brisk young fellow, not a soldier, on being asked for his theory of the matter, dropped out a coy confession. "Some good spirituals," he said, "are start jess out o' curiosity. I been a-raise a sing, myself, once."
>
> My dream was fulfilled, and I had traced out, not the poem alone, but the poet. I implored him to proceed. "Once we boys," he said, "went for tote some rice, and de nigger-driver, he keep a-callin' on us; and I say, O, de ole nigger-driver! 'Den anudder said 'Fust ting my mammy tole me was, noting so bad as nigger-driver.' Den I made a sing, just puttin' a word, and den anudder word."

Then he began singing, and the men, after listening a moment, joined in the chorus as if it were an old acquaintance, though they evidently had never heard it before. I saw how easily a new "sing" took root among them.

THE DRIVER.

O, de ole nigger-driver!
O, gwine away!
Fust ting my mammy tell me,
O, gwine away!
Tell me 'bout de nigger-driver,
O, gwine away!
Nigger-driver second devil,
O, gwine away!
Best ting for do he driver,
O, gwine away!
Knock he down and spoil he labor,
O, gwine away!

It will be observed that, although this song is quite secular in its character, its author yet called it a "spiritual."

Higginson also mentioned that he stumbled upon "this remarkable ditty, 'Hangman Johnny,'" but the former slaves stopped singing when they realized he was listening.

"O, dey call me Hangman Johnny!
O, ho! O, ho!
But I never hang nobody,
O, hang, boys, hang!

O, dey call me Hangman Johnny!
O, ho! O, ho!
But we'll all hang togedder,
O, hang, boys, hang!"

My presence apparently checked the performance of another verse, beginning, "De buckra 'list for money," apparently in reference to the controversy about the pay-question, then just beginning, and to the more mercenary aims they attributed to the white soldiers. But "Hangman Johnny" remained always a myth. . . ."

Higginson admitted: "I never overheard in camp a profane or vulgar song." And this is very likely the reason why " 'Hangman Johnny' remained always a myth." But on the basis of the songs that newly emancipated Afro-Americans wanted Higginson to hear (and the songs he was looking for) he concluded these were the songs of "an oppressed race . . . sustained by religious sentiment alone."[22]

Higginson's words and music were included in the first published collection of *Slave Songs in the United States* (1867), edited by William Francis Allen, Charles P. Ware, and Lucy McKim Garrison.[23] Before the war, Allen, a well-respected historian, classical scholar, and amateur musician, was the associate principal of the English and Classical School at West Newton, Massachusetts. In April 1863, however, for reasons of patriotism and support for abolitionism, Allen and his wife, Mary, went into the employ of the Education Commission of the New England Freedmen's Aid Society and arrived in November on St. Helena Island, South Carolina. They went to instruct the freedpeople, and after leaving the Sea Islands Allen also worked in Helena, Arkansas, and Charleston, South Carolina, where he served as assistant superintendent of public schools in 1865 and 1866.[24]

Allen kept a diary and recorded his impressions of the lifestyle and culture of the people he encountered on St. Helena Island. In an entry dated "Saturday, February 13, 1864," Allen recounted an incident remarkably similar to that of Thomas Higginson in which he is told that not all of the slave songs are religious.

> *Saturday, Feb. 13* . . . When I carried Mr. Harrison's boat back the other day, Paris Tony and Taffy went with me, and I got them to sing some of their boat-songs. It didn't amount to very much, because, as Paris said, "dem boy" couldn't row and sing too well; still they gave me two or three simple ones.—"Oh Michael row the boat ashore, Hallelujah Hallelujah." "My name, my name in de book ob life, Hallelujah, etc."; Paris sang the words and they the chorus. He said the boat-songs were sometimes the same as the shouting songs, and sometimes only used for rowing. One that they sang I recognized as having heard at the shout, with the chorus "Archangel open the door," Do do, mi, re, do, re,—do, do, do, do, si, si." I have only heard good boat-singing once,—in crossing the ferry to Beaufort. That crew sings finely. I haven't heard a single piece of music here that was not religious, —except the children singing "O come, come away" which I suppose they learned at church. Flora says they have songs that are not hymns, instancing "Grandmother in the graveyard"—a very jolly carol I suppose.[25]

Despite this and other evidence that he had gathered, Allen would continually maintain that most of the slave songs were sacred in nature.

Following the war, Allen, Charles P. Ware, his cousin and fellow worker on St. Helena Island, and Lucy Garrison, a trained musician who had visited the Sea Islands for only three weeks in 1862 with her father, Pennsylvania abolitionist John Miller McKim, decided that they would gather as many of the slave songs as they could from throughout the South and publish a comprehensive collection. They expressed some fear that with the changes being brought by emancipation, the songs might soon die out. *Slave Songs in the United States* was published in 1867, and the introduction, written by Allen, stated their major conclusion at the outset. "The chief part of the negro music is *civilized* in its character—partly composed under the influence of association with the whites, partly actually imitated from their music. In the main it appears to be original in the best sense of the word, and the more we examine the subject, the more genuine it appears to us to be." Allen listed several songs that he believed "may very well be purely African in origin. Indeed, it is very likely that if we had found it possible to get at more of their secular music, we should have come to another conclusion as to the proportion of the barbaric element." Here, Allen is suggesting that the "secular music" may be more "African" and therefore more "barbaric."[26]

Most of the songs they actually published were from the Sea Islands and the South Carolina mainland, though they included some from Virginia, North Carolina, Tennessee, Arkansas, and Florida. By 1867 Allen still had heard only religious tunes among the freedpeople, but he better understood the reason for the "selective presentations."

> I never fairly heard a secular song among the Port Royal freedmen, and never saw a musical instrument among them. The last violin, owned by a "worldy man," disappeared from Coffin's Point "de year gun shoot at Bay Pint." In other parts of the South, "fiddle-sings," "devil-songs," "corn-songs," "jig-tunes," and what not, are common; all the world knows the banjo, and the "Jim Crow" songs of thirty years ago. We have succeeded in obtaining only a very few songs of this character. Our intercourse with the colored people has been chiefly through the work of the Freedman's Commission, which deals with the serious and earnest side of the negro character. It is often, indeed, no easy matter to persuade them to sing their old songs, even as a curiosity, such is the sense of dignity that has come with freedom.[27]

Therefore, Allen recognized that there was a full range of slave songs, but out of a sense of what was appropriate and dignified, the freedpeople usually sang religiously inspired freedom songs when they knew the whites were listening.

"We had hoped to obtain enough secular songs to make a division by themselves," Allen alerted the reader. "There are, however, so few of these that it has been decided to intersperse them with the spirituals under their respective states." This organization would of course add to the confusion of determining whether and how many of the slave songs were actually "spirituals." The nonsacred origin of a particular "spiritual" went unconfirmed by Allen, Ware, and Garrison (unlike Higginson who had stumbled upon a real "poet"), but they reprinted a statement by Lucy's father, Rev. J. Miller McKim, in which an account of the origin of a slave song is given.

> "Address delivered by J. Miller McKim, in Sansom Hall, Philadelphia, July 9, 1862."

> I asked one of these blacks—one of the most intelligent of them [Prince Rivers, Sergeant 1st Reg. S. C. V.]—where they got these songs. 'Dey make 'em, sah.' 'How do they make them?' After a pause, evidently casting about for an explanation, he said: 'I'll tell you it's dis way. My master call me up, and order me a short peck of corn and a hundred lash. My friends see it, and is sorry for me. When dey come to de praise-meeting dat night dey sing about it. Some's very good singers and know how; and dey work it in—work it in, you know, till they get it right; and dat's de way'. A very satisfactory explanation; at least so it seemed to me."[28]

When Thomas Higginson asked his boatman to make up a "spiritual," it had a secular thrust in a secular context; the "spiritual" that was created at "de praise meeting dat night" was very likely religious in content. In both instances, the Afro-Americans created and sang songs that were appropriate to the occasions.

Although Allen was more reserved in his judgment than Higginson, both men emphasized the centrality of the "religious sentiment" in the music and songs of the newly emancipated Africans and Afro-Americans, and for good reasons. As "radical abolitionists" and among the major supporters of an immediate end to slavery in the United States, they were concerned about the proslavery assertions about the innately "barbarous and uncivilized" nature of African people. Certainly a people capable of creating such beautiful music should not be considered completely "barbaric," fit only to be the slaves of whites. As antislavery spokesman, Theodore Tilton argued in an essay published in 1863: "Two centuries of slavery must needs have molded the character of slave. . . . The faults of a slave come from training, rather than natural endowment."[29] William Allen and his collaborators were thus suggesting that the existence of this "civilized music" among the slaves demonstrated their educability and capacity for civilization.

> The greater number of the songs which have come into our posses-

sion seem to be the natural and original production of a race of remarkable musical capacity and very teachable, which has been long enough associated with the more cultivated race to have become imbued with the mode and spirit of European music—often, nevertheless, retaining a distinct tinge of their native Africa.[30]

There was more than "a distinct tinge of their native Africa" in the music and cultural expressions of Afro-Americans, but some researchers, most notably E. Franklin Frazier, would continue to deny African influences on Afro-American cultural forms and practices even into the 1950s, mainly because of a desire to demonstrate that blacks had "imbued the spirit and the mode" of European civilization.[31]

W. E. B. Du Bois depended heavily on Thomas Higginson and William Francis Allen for the songs printed at the beginning of each chapter of *The Souls of Black Folk* and for the information included in what is generally considered the most beautiful of the essays, "Of the Sorrow Songs." Du Bois viewed the spirituals developmentally, as passing through three phases. "The first is African music, the second Afro-American, while the third is a blending of the Negro music with the music heard in the foster land. The result is still distinctively Negro and the method of blending original, but the elements are both Negro and Caucasian.

One might go further and find a fourth step in this development, where the songs of white America have been distinctively influenced by the slave songs or have incorporated whole phrases of Negro melody, as "Swanee River" and "Old Black Joe." Side by side, too, with the growth has gone the debasements and imitations—the Negro "minstrel" songs, many of the "gospel" hymns, and some of the contemporary "coon" songs,—a mass of music in which the novice may easily lose himself and never find the real Negro melodies.

Du Bois was not merely interested in typology, he was also concerned about "meanings" in the Sorrow Songs.

What are these songs, and what do they mean? I know little of music and can say nothing in technical phrase, but I know something of men, and knowing them, I know that these songs are the articulate message of the slave to the world. They tell us in these eager days that life was joyous to the black slave, careless and happy. I can easily believe this of some, of many. But not all the past South, though it rose from the dead, can gainsay the heart-touching witness of these songs. They are the music of an unhappy people, of the children of disappointment;

they tell of death and suffering and unvoiced longing toward a truer world, of misty wanderings and hidden ways.[32]

In 1938 when Benjamin Mays suggested in *The Negro's God* that "Negro mass literature," especially the spirituals, was "otherworldly" and exhibited "traditional compensatory patterns," this was not far removed from the "unhappy people" whose "music is distinctly sorrowful," which tells "in word and music of trouble and exile, of strife and hiding," described by Du Bois in *The Souls of Black Folk* in 1903. Mays's conclusions were framed in terms of the predominant ideological positions about the nature and significance of Afro-American religion in the first half of the twentieth century. Progressive radicals and Communists of the 1920s, such as A. Philip Randolph and Cyril Briggs, could not get the Negro church leaders to support their socialist-inspired campaigns for social change, therefore Negro religion must be conservative. Communist-influenced social scientists of the 1930s also characterized the Negro religion as conservative and otherworldly ("An opiate of the people"), when the institutional Negro church failed to support openly Communist-led schemes and projects "for the race." Individual black ministers may have supported "radical causes," but the Negro church watched from the sidelines. White liberals, such as Howard Odum and Robert Park, merely viewed the religion of the black masses as "primitive" and inadequate for complete assimilation into the larger (white) society.[33]

Each of these groups, as well as progressive and outspoken ministers within the Negro church, characterized Afro-American religion as "conservative" and "otherworldly" for their own particular reasons. There was little attempt made to separate the political position assumed by Afro-American religious institutions and the belief-system within Afro-American Christianity. As late as 1953 sociologist E. Franklin Frazier in his widely read monograph, *The Negro Church in America,* not only echoed the prevailing views about the "predominantly otherworldly outlook in the Negro's religion," but went so far as to deny that "distinct tinge of their native Africa" in Afro-American religious beliefs and practices. For example, Frazier disputed Du Bois's claim that there was religious continuity between the African and North American situations. "[I]n one of his studies of Negro life, he [Du Bois] makes the assertion that the Negro Church was 'the only social institution among the Negroes which started in the African forest and survived slavery' and that 'under the leadership of the priest and medicine man' the church preserved the remnants of African tribal life." Frazier completely rejected Du Bois's position. "From the available evidence, including what we know of the manner in which the slaves were Christianized and the character of their churches, it is impossible to establish any continuity between African religious practices and the Negro church in the United States."[34]

As events and research would soon demonstrate, Frazier was as wrong about the "predominantly otherworldly" nature of Afro-American religion as he was about the lack of African continuities in Afro-American religious beliefs and practices.[35] With the coming of the Civil Rights Movement, Martin Luther King, Jr., demonstrated the capacity for traditional black religious values and beliefs to sustain ideologically a mass movement among Afro-Americans for increased self-determination. King utilized the religious themes emphasizing resistance, protest against injustice, and God's support for his Chosen People to raise the political consciousness of thousands of southern blacks who implicitly understood his message.[36]

When confronted by the contemporary reality of the Civil Rights movement and the revolutionary implications of traditional black religious beliefs, several leading theologians and scholars began to reexamine and reinterpret the meaning of the Afro-American religious experience. In *Black Theology and Black Power* (1969) and *A Black Theology of Liberation* (1972), theologian James Cone argued that "Christian theology" in general should be understood as "a theology of liberation."

> It is *a rational study of the being of God in the world in light of the existential situation of an oppressed community, relating the forces of liberation to the essence of the gospel, which is Jesus Christ.* This means that its sole reason for existence is to put into ordered speech the meaning of God's activity in the world, so that the community of the oppressed will recognize that their inner thrust for liberation is not only consistent with the gospel but is the gospel of Jesus Christ.[37]

"White American theology," however, has historically been "a theology of the white oppressor, giving religious sanction to the genocide of Indians and the enslavement of black people." Cone argued, "From the very beginning to the present day, American white theological thought has been 'patriotic,' either by defining the theological task independently of black suffering (the liberal northern approach) or by defining Christianity as compatible with white racism (the conservative southern approach). In both cases theology becomes a servant of the state, and that can only mean death to black people." In other words, Cone believed that American religious hegemony had "white supremacist" values at its core.[38]

A distinctive "Black Theology" developed among Afro-Americans because of the failure of white religionists to relate the gospel of Jesus Christ to the oppression of Afro-Americans.

It arises from the need of black people to liberate themselves from white oppressors. Black Theology is a theology of liberation because it is a theology which arises from an identification with the oppressed blacks of America, seeking to interpret the gospel of Christ in the light of the black condition. It believes that the liberation of black people *is* God's liberation.

For Cone, Gayraud Wilmore, C. Eric Lincoln, and others, "the task of Black Theology then is to analyse the nature of the gospel of Jesus Christ in the light of oppressed black people. . . ." They considered it the most appropriate theology for the black community, "seeking to interpret the religious dimensions of the forces of liberation in that community."

What is important about this reinterpretation of the meaning of Afro-American Christianity is the explicit identification of the self-determinist values that underpin black religious beliefs. Cone and others of his School believe that "Black Theology seeks to articulate the theological self-determination of black people, providing some ethical and religious categories for black revolution in America. It says that all acts which participate in the destruction of white racism are Christian, the liberating deeds of God. All acts which impede the struggle of black self-determination—Black Power—are anti-Christian, the work of Satan. . . . The role of Black Theology is to tell black people to focus on their own self-determination as a community preparing to do anything which the community believes to be necessary for its existence."[39]

Some chapters and verses of the Bible are more important than others with regard to the development of Black Theology, which seeks "to create a theological norm which is in harmony with the black condition and biblical revelation." Afro-American history and culture become important as sources of information on the black condition. "Black Theology focuses on black history as a source for its theological interpretation of God's work in the world because divine activity is inseparable from the history of black people. There can be no comprehensive Black Theology without realizing that its existence comes from the community which looks back on its unique past, visualizes the reality of the future, and then makes decisions about possibilities in the present."[40]

In subsequent work scholars within the school of Black Theology analyzed the history of the Afro-American religious experience with these theological assumptions in mind. In *Black Religion and Black Radicalism* (1973), theologian Gayraud Wilmore argued that Afro-American Christianity was intrinsically "radical" because of its preoccupation with human liberation from oppression.

> Black religion has always concerned itself with the fascination of an incorrigibly religious people with the mystery of God, but it has been equally concerned with the yearning of a despised and subjugated people with the freedom of man—freedom from the religious, economic, social and political domination which white men have exercised over Black men since the beginning of the African slave trade. It is this radical thrust of Black people for human liberation expressed in theological terms and religious institutions which is the defining characteristic of Black Christianity and of Black religion in the United States. . . .[41]

Presenting a materialist account of the origins of black religion, Wilmore believes that there was little likelihood that the religion of blacks and whites in the United States would be the same. "The religious beliefs and rituals of any people are inevitably and inseparably bound up with the material and psychological realities of their daily existence. Certainly those realities for the slaves were vastly different from those experienced by the slavemasters. . . .

> The religion of Black people in the United States today, and in parts of the West Indies, Central and South America, is unquestionably predisposed to the beliefs and practices associated with the Judeo-Christian tradition. But the Christianity which had been developing for more than four hundred years among the descendants of the first slaves brought to this part of the world is a different version of the religion that is professed by the descendants of the slavemasters.[42]

Wilmore acknowledged the threads of otherworldliness that ran through Afro-American religious beliefs, but concluded that "notwithstanding the well-known elements of evangelical conservatism in the mainstream of Black Christianity in the country, there was, from the beginning, a fusion between a highly developed and pervasive feeling about the hierophantic nature of historical experience, flowing from the African religious past, and a radical and programmatic secularity, related to the experience of slavery and oppression, which constituted the essential and most significant characteristic of Black religion." Thus despite the "deliberate distortion of Christian doctrine and stringent restrictions upon religious activity, . . . a distinctive

African-American form of Christianity—actually the new religion of an oppressed people—slowly took root in the Black community." Wilmore also concluded that "it was the slave's African past that did the most to influence his style of religion, his rejection of the spiritual and political despotism of the white man, and made the most important contributions to his coming struggle for freedom."[43] When theologians began to document the distinctive character of the Afro-American Christianity that developed in the United States, they initiated the much-needed reinterpretation of the "cultural meanings" embedded in the Negro spirituals and other religious beliefs and practices of enslaved and free Afro-Americans.

Slave Theology and Morality

Despite the myriad statements and conjectures of scholars and theologians, it is not likely that *all* of the enslaved Afro-Americans believed in God or were religious. Sentiments that were generally considered "anti-religious" were found in songs and rhymes, and were quite popular among slaves and free blacks.

> I don't want to ride no golden chariot;
> I don't want no golden crown;
> I want to stay down here and be
> Just as I am without one plea.[44]

Poet Sterling Brown also reported having heard this parody of the Lord's Prayer.

> Our father, who is in heaven,
> White man owe me eleven and pay me seven,
> Thy kingdom come, thy will be done,
> And if I hadn't took that, I wouldn't had none.[45]

Some slaves could not reconcile black suffering in this world with a belief in an almighty and all-merciful God in the next. Daniel Payne, later bishop in the African Methodist Episcopal Church, believed that the slaves' disgust at the hypocrisy of "slaveholding Christianity" often spilled over into their attitude toward religion in general.

> The slaves are sensible of the oppression exercised by their masters; and they see these masters on the Lord's day worshipping in his holy Sanctuary. They hear their masters professing Christianity; they see them preaching the gospel; they hear these masters praying in their families,

and they know that oppression and slavery are inconsistent with the Christian religion; therefore they scoff at religion itself—mock their masters, and distrust both the goodness and justice of God. Yes, I have known them even to question his existence. I speak not of what others have told me, but of what *I have both seen and heard from the slaves themselves.* I have heard the mistress ring the bell for family prayer, and I have seen the servants immediately begin to sneer and laugh; and have heard them declare they would not go in to prayers; adding if I go in she will not only just read, "Servants obey your master;" but she will not read "break every yoke, and let the oppressed go free." I have seen colored men at the church door, scoffing *at the ministers,* while they were preaching and saying, you had better go home, and set your slaves free. A few nights ago . . . a runaway slave came to the house where I live for safety and succor. I asked him if he were a Christian; "no sir," said he, "white men treat us so bad in Mississippi that we can't be Christians."[46]

Among those Afro-Americans who believed they could, indeed, call themselves "Christians," there developed a theological and ethical system based on their perception of what was right and wrong in the world around them. The ultimate truth of these teachings, which they considered "Christian," was often a matter of faith. This deep religious faith did not merely rest on what a preacher or exhorter had told them was God's Word, but oftentimes it was sustained by the individual's encounters with the spiritual world. Their God was a "miracle worker," and it was often these little miracles (that seemed to happen all the time at the right time) that reinforced the religious beliefs and faith of the slaves.

Slave religion and the Holy Bible taught that the Almighty was a God of the oppressed; and just as the Children of Israel were liberated from unjust enslavement in Egypt, the enslaved Afro-Americans, who were also one of God's Chosen People, will someday be freed from bondage and allowed to reach Canaan-land. James Cone, in his theological exegesis of *The Spirituals and the Blues* (1972), argued that "the divine liberation of the oppressed from slavery is the central theological concept in the black spirituals. . . . The basic idea . . . is that slavery contradicts God; it is a denial of his will." Therefore, far from being otherworldly and compensatory, "the spirituals are black freedom songs which emphasize black liberation as consistent with divine revelation."[47] Thus Cone again confirmed in 1972 what Thomas Higginson had dismissed as "unfounded" in 1867.

But what about slave religion in general? Did it teach that "black liberation" was "consistent with divine revelation"? If so, what was sin? What was good and evil—God and the Devil? What was the nature of God?

How did one obtain salvation? There is a great deal of evidence in slave sources—narratives and autobiographies, the interview-narratives with former slaves conducted by the Federal Writers Project—which suggests that the Afro-American masses did indeed believe that black liberation and self-determination were part of God's will moving through the world and Afro-American history.

Afro-American Christians generally understood sin to be "willful disobedience of the Word of God," and since slavery was against God's will (according to the slaves' reading of the Bible), those who held their fellow-man in bondage were sinful. Whereas this was a central tenet of Afro-American Christianity, it was, of course, completely rejected by slaveholders. Aaron, a fugitive slave, provided an excellent summary of the slave's ideas on the sinfulness of slavery in *The Light and Truth of Slavery* (1843):

> We believe slavery to be a sin—always, everywhere, and only sin. Sin in itself apart, from the occasional rigors incidental to its administration, and from all those perils, liabilities, and positive inflictions to which its victims are continually exposed. Sin is the nature of the act which created it, and in the elements which constitute it. Sin, because it converts persons into things; men into property; God's image into merchandise. Because it forbids men from using themselves for the advancement of their own well being, and turns them into mere instruments to be used by others solely for the benefit of the users. Because it constitutes one man the owner of the body and spirit of other men: gives him power and permission to make his pecuniary profit the very end of their being, thus striking them out of existence as beings, possessing rights and susceptibilities of happiness, and forcing them to exist merely as appendages of his own existence, in other words, because slavery holds and uses men as mere means for which to accomplish ends, of which end, their own interests are not a part. Thus annihilating the sacred and eternal distinction between a person and a thing; a distinction proclaimed an axiom of all human consciousness; a distinction created by God. . . .[48]

Stephen Butterfield, in *Black Autobiography in America* (1974), found that most of the slave narratives made it clear that "slavery, itself is the most enormous sin, both because it is an intrinsic evil and because it forces a whole range of other sins on the people caught in its coils."[49] There was great reluctance on the part of the slaveholders to allow the evangelization of the slaves. The plantation missionaries had to convince the owners that the

Christianity that they taught would make good slaves. But when the missionaries came preaching: "Don't Steal from your master," "Don't Lie to your master," "Do everything your master says," it was completely rejected by most enslaved Afro-Americans.[50] Frederick Douglass wrote that virtually all his fellow bondsmen were "quite clear from slaveholding priestcraft."

> It was in vain that we had been taught from the pulpit at St. Michaels the duty of obedience to our masters—to recognize God as the author of enslavement—to regard running away as an offense, alike against God and man—to deem our enslavement a merciful and beneficial arrangement—to esteem our condition in this country a paradise to that from which we have been snatched in Africa—to consider our hard hands and dark color as God's displeasure, and as pointing us out as the proper subjects of slavery—that the relation of master and slave was one of reciprocal benefits and that our work was not more serviceable to our masters than our master's thinking was to us. I say it was in vain that the pulpit of St. Michaels had constantly inculcated these plausible doctrines. Nature laughed them to scorn.[51]

J. W. Lindsey, a fugitive slave, was interviewed in Canada by the American Freedman's Inquiry Commission, which had been set up by the U.S. Congress in 1863 to collect reports on runaway slaves and free blacks and to make recommendations. Lindsey told the commission officials that in Tennessee, where he had been enslaved, the white clergymen's "biggest text is 'servants, obey your masters'; and 'he that knoweth his master's will and doeth it not, shall be beaten with many stripes.'" George Moss, also interviewed by the commission in 1863, said that in Maryland, where he had been enslaved, "the religious feeling is used to induce the slaves to feel that they owe a duty to their masters and mistresses, more than to their Great Maker above. Certain parts of the Scriptures, about obeying masters and mistresses they quote very much, but not in the right light."[52]

Ex-slaves who were born in various parts of the South and interviewed in the 1930s remembered hearing these same sermons, quite often. Lucretia Alexander, who was interviewed in 1938 at the age of eighty-nine by the Federal Writers Project, had been enslaved in Virginia. She recalled that "the niggers didn't go to the church building. The preacher came and preached to them in their quarters. He'd just say, 'Serve your masters. Don't steal your master's turkey. Don't steal your master's chickens. Don't steal your master's hogs. Don't steal your master's meat. Do whatsoever your master tells you to do!' Same old thing all de time." Alice Sewell, ex-slave from Alabama, was interviewed in St. Louis, Missouri, in 1937 at the age of eighty-six and reported similar responses to white preaching:

> Dey did allow us to go to church on Sunday about two miles down de public road, and dey hired a white preacher to preach to us. He never did tell us nothing but "Be good servants, pick up old marse and old misses' things about de place, don't steal no chickens or pigs, and don't lie about nothing." Den dey baptize you and call dat you got religion. Never did say nothing about a slave dying and going to Heaven. When we die, dey bury us next day and you is just like any of the other cattle dying on de place. Dat's all 'tis to it and all 'tis of you. You is just dead, dat's all.[53]

But for many slaves the most appalling aspect of the "slaveholding piety" was its "base hypocrisy." White missionaries and ministers enjoined them: "Don't steal from your master," and the slaveholders were the biggest thieves and robbers around. In a letter of 7 October 1852, Henry Bibb, who had escaped slavery and gone to Canada and organized the black Canadian resistance against American Fugitive Slave Laws, castigated his former owner, Albert G. Silbey, about his "Christianity."

> You profess to be a christian—a leader in the M. E. Church, and the representative of the Lord Jesus Christ, and yet you sold my mother from her little children, and sent them away to a distant land—you sold my brother George from his wife and dear little ones while he was a worthy member, and Clergyman, of the same church, to which *you belong*. In early life you also compelled me to cheat, lie, and steal from your neighbours. You have often made me drive up sheep and hogs which you knew to be the property of your neighbour [illegible line] and the use of your own table.
>
> The language of Holy writ is that "thou shalt not steal" "let every man have his own wife, and every woman her own husband" and parents are strictly required to train up their children in the fear and admonition of the Lord. Every one of these Holy injunctions you have wickedly and willingly broken. Oh! what hypocrisy is this! A Methodist class leader, separating husbands and wives—a Methodist class leader, stealing and slaughtering his neighbours sheep and hogs. Vain is your religion—base is your hypocrisy.

Bibb ended on a collective note: "We have no confidence in your sheep stealing and man robbing religion."[54]

In *The Narrative of His Life* (1845) Frederick Douglass talked about white American churches so badly that he felt obliged to add an appendix on "true Christianity" for fear that readers would get the impression he was against religion.

> What I have said respecting and against religion, I mean strictly to apply to the *slaveholding religion* of this land, and with no possible reference to Christianity proper; for, between the Christianity of this land, and the Christianity of Christ, I recognize the widest possible difference—so wide, that to receive the one as good, pure, and holy, is of necessity to reject the other as bad, corrupt, and wicked. To be the friend of the one, is of necessity to be the enemy of the other. I love the pure, peaceable, and impartial Christianity of Christ: I therefore hate the corrupt, slaveholding, women-whipping, cradle-plundering, partial and hypocritical Christianity of this land.

Douglass could find no reason, "but the most deceitful one," for calling the United States a Christian nation. "Never was there a clearer case of 'stealing the livery of the court of heaven to serve the devil in.' " As far as white preaching was concerned: "We see the thief preaching against theft, and the adulterer against adultery. We have men sold to build churches, women sold to support the gospel, and babes sold to purchase Bibles for the *poor heathen! all for the glory of God and the good of souls!*"[55]

Robert Falls complained to the Knoxville interviewer from the Federal Writers Project that the slaveholders "learned us to steal." He and his family had been enslaved on the Goforth Plantation in North Carolina, and at the age of ninety-seven Falls was still bitter. The master and mistress were often ready with the whip, and "didn't half feed us either. They fed the animals better. . . .

> Learned us to steal, that's what they done. Why, we would take anything we could lay our hands on, when we was hungry. Then they'd whip us for lying when we say we don't know nothing about it. But it was easier to stand when the stomach was full.[56]

Henry Johnson, who was born in Patrick County, Virginia, and raised "all over the state," remembered incidents similar to those mentioned by Henry Bibb in 1852. Every Sunday, while the white people rode in buggies, the slaves from the Johnson Plantation were forced to walk the entire distance.

> When we got dat four or five miles we had to sit on a log in de broiling sun, while a white man preached to us. All dey ever would say would be: "Niggers, obey your masters and mistress and don't steal from 'em."

And, lo and behold, de masters would make us slaves steal from each of the slave owners. Our master would make us surround a herd of his neighbor's cattle, round dem up at night, and make us slaves stay up all night long and kill and skin every one of dem critters, salt the skins down in layers in de master's cellar, and put de cattle piled ceilin' high in de smokehouse so nobody could identify skinned cattle.

Den when de sheriff would come around lookin' for all dem stolen critters, our boss would say, "Sheriff, just go right on down to dem niggers' cabins and search dem good. I know my niggers don't steal." 'Course de sheriff come to our cabins and search. Sure we didn't have nothin' didn't belong to us, but de boss had plenty. After de sheriff's search, we had to salt and smoke all dat stolen meat and hang it in Old Marse's smokehouse for him. Den dey tell us, don't steal.[57]

When a black preacher, who spouted the same "slaveholding piety" as the whites, asked John White "to join up with the Lord," he refused. The preacher was officially sanctioned by the owners of the Davenport plantation, located in northern Texas, near Linden. "I never join because he don't talk about the Lord. Just about the master and mistress. How the slaves must obey around the plantation—how white folks know what is good for slaves. Nothing about obeying the Lord and working for him [sic]. I reckon the old preacher was worrying more about the bullwhip than the Bible. . . ."[58] Even Charles Colcock Jones, the leading white spokesman for the evangelization of the slaves, confirmed in 1833 the response of many Afro-Americans to his "slaveholding priestcraft."

I was preaching to a large congregation on the Epistle of Philemon: and when I insisted upon fidelity and obedience as Christian virtues in servants and upon the authority of Paul, condemned the practice of running away, one half of my audience deliberately rose up and walked off with themselves, and those that remained looked any thing but satisfied, either with the preacher or his doctrine. After dismission, there was no small stir among them; some solemnly declared "that there was no such an Epistle in the Bible"; others, "that they did not care if they ever heard me preach again!" . . . There were some too, who had strong objections against me as a Preacher, because I was a master, and said, "his people have to work as well as we."[59]

Most slaves who could not read suspected that there were more command-ments in the Bible than the two or three featured in the sermons of the plantation missionaries. Once they learned to read, their suspicions were confirmed. James Curry, who later escaped and fled to Canada, learned to read while still in bondage; and as a youth in Pierson County, North Carolina, in the 1820s, he studied the Scriptures.

> When my master's family were all gone away on the Sabbath, I used to go into the house and get down the great Bible, and lie down in the piazza, and read, taking care, however, to put it back before they returned. There I learned that it was contrary to the revealed will of God, that one man should hold another as a slave. I had always heard it talked among the slaves, that we ought not to be held as slaves; that our forefathers and mothers were stolen from Africa where they were free men and free women. But in the Bible I learned that "God hath made of one blood all nations of men to dwell on the face of the earth."[60]

The slaves also suspected that the ministers themselves did not believe the doctrines they were preaching. John Brown has been described as "an obscure common man, an unpretentious refugee" who had a story to tell. In *Slave Life in Georgia: A Narrative of the Life, Sufferings, and Escape of John Brown, A Fugitive Slave* (1855), Brown recalled that he was "often asked how we slaves, being so ignorant, come to know that holding a human creature as a slave is wrong and wicked.

> I say that, putting the cruelties of the system out of the question, we cannot be made to understand how any man can hold another man as a slave, and do right. A slave is not a human being in the eye of the law, and the slaveholder looks upon him just as what the law makes him; nothing more, and perhaps even something less. But God made every man to stand upright before him, and if the slave law throws that man down . . . then the law unmakes God's work; the slaveholder lends himself to it, and not all the reasoning or arguments that can be strung together, on a text or on none, can make the thing right. I have heard long preachments from ministers of the Gospel to try and show that slavery is not a wrong system; but somehow they could not fix it right to my mind, and they always seemed to me to have a hard matter to bring it square to their own.[61]

If the slaveholders knew that the enslavement of one's fellowman was wrong (and the slaves suspected just that), but continued the practice; then they were guilty of sin and would be subject to the judgment of God. Theologian James Cone in his study of the spirituals argued that "despite the clear implication that the white system of slavery is generally Satanic, there is a surprising absence of references to white people as a special object of hate and scorn. One would expect indirect expressions of resentment, if not direct references. But aside from 'Everybody talking about heaven, ain't going there' and 'When I get to Heaven, goin' to sing and shout, there will be nobody there to turn me out'; the spirituals are strangely silent on the ethical behavior of white masters."[62] As we have seen, because of a sense of dignity and what was appropriate for a white audience, Afro-Americans sang primarily religious freedom songs for the collectors of the spirituals. These songs contained few references to whites. But slave letters, narratives, and interviews are filled with statements about God's justice v. the evil slaveholder. When Henry Bibb got no response from his former owner to his correspondence of 7 October 1852, he sent a follow-up letter on 4 November 1852. Bibb detailed the brutal separations of mother and children that the slaveholder, Albert Silbey, had forced upon Bibb's family.

> And now remember—that for all of these things "God will bring you into judgement." You have not only lived up on the unrequited toil of your fellow men, from your cradle up to the present time: but you have wilfully destroyed their social happiness, by forcibly making orphans and widows of those for whom Christ suffered and died on the cross— by withholding from them the word of Eternal Life, by enforcing adultery and concubinage among the enslaved and by inflicting stripes, chains, imprisonment and unutterable suffering upon the children of God. . . . Be not deceived by the long practice of your church; you have an awful account to render to the great Judge of the Universe, slave holding religion is of the devil, and your only chance for salvation lies in repentance before God and "faith in our Lord Jesus Christ."[63]

Henry Atkinson, another refugee who fled to Canada following the passage of the Fugitive Slave Law of 1850, made clear his belief that the slaveholders will be made to pay in the next world for the viciousness and cruelty associated with slavery. "I think slavery is the worst and meanest thing to be thought of. It appears to me that God cannot receive into the kingdom of heaven those who deal in slaves." Atkinson went on to stress that "God made all men, He is no respecter of persons—and it is impossible that He should, on account of color, intend that I should be a slave of a man because he is of a brighter skin than I am."[64] James Curry recalled "many instances of cruelty practiced on the plantations" in Pierson County, North Carolina, in the 1830s. And if a white person asked him if he wanted to be free, "I should have answered, 'No Sir.' Of course, no slave would dare say in the presence of a white man, that he wished his freedom. But among themselves, it is a constant theme. No slaves think that they were made to be slaves. Let them keep them ever so ignorant, it is impossible to beat it into them that they were made to be slaves. I have heard the most ignorant I ever saw, say, 'It will not always be so, God *will* bring them to an account.' "[65] And fugitive slave William Craft, after describing the brutality of slave-holders, found that "there is, however, great consolation in knowing that God is just, and will not let the oppressor of the weak, and the spoiler of the virtuous, escape unpunished here and hereafter. I believe a similar retribution to that which destroyed Sodom is hanging over the slaveholders."[66]

Former slaves interviewed in the 1930s often clung to the same views about slaveholders expressed by the fugitive slaves in the 1840s and 1850s. Robert Falls remembered that Robert Goforth, his owner, had four sisters, all of whom had slaves, but "they wasn't mean to them like our old Master and Old Mistress. . . . But they never dispute none with their brother about how mean he treat his slaves. And him claiming to be such a Christian! Well, I reckon he's found out something about slave driving now. The Good Lord has to get his work in sometime. And he'll take care of them low down patterollers and slave speculators and mean marsters and mistresses."[67] Sarah Fitzpatrick, an ex-slave interviewed in Alabama in 1938, merely pointed out: "De lawd's got a han' in workin' dis thing out, 'cause ya know it says in de Bible, 'Dat de bottom rail will become de top one fo' de end uv times.' "[68] And Jane Simpson, interviewed in St. Louis at the age of ninety, said, "I used to hear old slaves pray and ask God when would de bottom rail be de top rail, and I wondered what on earth dey talkin' about. Dey was talkin' about when dey goin' to get from under bondage."[69]

The God of the Negro spirituals and the enslaved Afro-Americans was a just God who would sit in judgment over all humanity, the high and the low, the good and the evil.

> Just as you live,
> Just so you die,
> And after death,
> Judgment will find you so.
>
> O, brethren, brethren
> Watch and pray,
> Judgment will find you so.
> For Satan's round
> You every day,
> Judgment will find you so. . . .
>
> Oh! Hallelujah to the Lamb

> Judgment will find you so,
> The Lord is on the giving hand
> Judgment will find you so. . . .[70]

Faith in God's will and living according to his commandments saved the Children of Israel, and faith would save the enslaved Afro-Americans, God's Chosen People in America. One of the major functions of slave religion and the spirituals was to help sustain that faith.

> Come along, Moses, don't get lost,
> Don't get lost, don't get lost,
> Come along Moses, don't get lost
> We are the People of God.
>
> We have a just God to plead our cause,
> Plead our cause, Plead our cause,
> We have a just God to plead our cause,
> We are the People of God.
>
> He sits in the Heaven and he answers prayer
> Answers prayer, answers prayer;
> He sits in the Heaven and he answers prayer,
> We are the people of God.[71]

Slavery was against the will of God, and thus God would eventually bring about freedom for the enslaved. As James Cone pointed out, "That is why the spirituals focus on biblical passages that stress God's involvement in the liberation of oppressed people."

> Black people sang about Joshua and the battle of Jericho, Moses leading the Israelites from bondage, Daniel in the lions' den, and the Hebrew children in the fiery furnace. Here the emphasis was on God's liberation of the weak from the oppression of the strong, the lowly and downtrodden from the proud and mighty. And blacks reasoned that if God could lock the lion's jaw for Daniel and could cool the fire for the Hebrew children, then he could certainly deliver black people from slavery.

> My Lord delivered Daniel,
> My Lord delivered Daniel,
> My Lord delivered Daniel,
> Why can't He deliver me?[72]

As long as the slaves remained faithful to God's will, they would be saved. But this was far from easy, especially in situations where the slaveholders would not allow regular religious services among the slaves. In those instances, the slaves would have to sneak off to their "prayer grounds" and "brush arbors" to praise God and pray for their deliverance.

> O brothers, don't get weary,
> O brothers, don't get weary,
> O brothers, don't get weary,
> We're waiting for the Lord!
>
> We'll land on Canaan's shore,
> We'll land on Canaan's shore,
> When we land on Canaan's shore
> We'll meet forever more.[73]

In teaching the enslaved Afro-Americans to ignore or disobey the rules of the slaveholders and praise God among themselves, slave religion fostered self-determinist values among Afro-Americans. Some slaveholders aided the development of these self-determinist values by letting the slaves hold their own religious services. But on those farms and plantations where religious meetings were restricted or forbidden, Afro-American slaves often risked brutal persecution for spreading the Word of God or sneaking off into the woods to pray. Fugitive slave Moses Roper sent a letter to Rev. Thomas Price in response to the suggestion that he had not witnessed "the burning alive of a slave in the United States." Roper had earlier mentioned the incident in an autobiography he dictated to Mr. Price, editor of *Slavery in America,* but several persons had raised "questions of accuracy." Dated 27 June 1836, London, Roper described in gruesome detail the "horrid spectacle." A black preacher had been told by his master, "if he continued his preaching to his fellow-slaves, he would for the next offense give him 500 lashes." George, the slave preacher, continued to hold services, was threatened by his master, and fled to the woods, where he was pursued and captured after beating two members of the posse. George was taken to jail in Greenville, South Carolina.

> The facts having transpired, through the newspapers, his master came to Greenville to claim him as his property, but consented, upon being required to do so, to receive 550 dollars as his value, with which he returned home. Shortly after this, George was burnt alive within one mile of the court-house at Greenville, in the presence of an immense assemblage of slaves, which had been gathered together to witness the horrid spectacle from a district of twenty miles in extent.

Roper did not feel a need to provide further corroboration for his story. "When I was last there, which was about two years before I left America for England, not only was the stump of the tree to which the slave George had been fastened, to be seen, but some of his burnt bones."[74]

To avoid George's fate, or at least a whipping, the slaves did not assemble openly, but off in the canebreaks and fields in the evening and at night. And they tried to restrain themselves, or at least muffle the sound when the spirit hit them. John B. Cade, a historian in the Extension Department of Southern University, in Baton Rouge, Louisiana, requested the students in his history class in 1929 to interview as many former slaves in the area as possible. "Every member of the class entered enthusiastically into the project, and thirty-six reported interviews totaling eighty-two." In these interviews, the former slaves over and over again mentioned the secret religious meetings and services where no whites were present.

"If dey had prayer meeting dey would turn a wash pot down to ketch de sound to keep de marsters from hearing um. Didn't have no church; sometimes a white man would go around through the quarters preaching to de slaves telling dem to obey dey marsters and missus and dey would be good to dem."

"Slaves were not allowed to have church, but they would have prayer meetings secretly. They would place pots in the door to keep the sound in the house to prevent their masters from hearing them."

"On this plantation, there were about one hundred and fifty slaves. Of this number, only about ten were Christians. We can easily account for this, for religious services among slaves were strictly forbidden. But the slaves would steal away into the woods at night and hold services. They would form a circle on their knees around the speaker who would also be on his knees. He would bend forward and speak into or over a vessel of water to drown the sound. If anyone became animated and cried out, the others would quickly stop the noise by placing their hands over the offender's mouth."

"On Sunday they [the slaves] would have services after the white people had had theirs. Most times, however, the slaves held their meetings in the woods under [brush] arbors made by them. The preacher came from some other plantation; he preached about heaven and hell. There they were not allowed to pray for freedom, but sometimes the slaves would steal away at night and go into the cane thickets and pray for deliverance; they always prayed in a prostrate position with the face close to the ground so that no sound could escape to warn the master or the overseer."

"The slaves did not have churches as we have now. They made arbors of small pine trees. Some of them didn't have arbors. When they wanted to sing and pray, they would steal off into the woods. During that time, most of the masters were cruel. If they would hear them [slaves] singing, they would get their whips and whip them all the way home. Whipping did not stop them from having meetings. When one place was located they would find another one. They didn't have many preachers. Everyone was so anxious to have a word to say that a preacher did not have a chance. All of them would sing and pray."[75]

Cade also reported the story of Kalvin Woods, a slave preacher who at the time was "about ninety-five or a hundred years old."

When he was a slave, he always would try to preach to the other slaves and would slip about from plantation to plantation preaching. However, the women slaves would take old quilts and rags and wet them thoroughly; then hang them up in the form of a little room and the slaves who were interested about it would huddle up behind these quilts to do their praying, preaching and singing. These wet rags and quilts were used to keep the sound of their voices from penetrating the air. They didn't want their masters to hear them, for they knew it meant a punishment for them. Mr. Woods says many a happy meeting was carried on behind these quilts and rags.[76]

Alice Sewell, who was interviewed by the Federal Writers Project in 1937, vividly described similar events that took place regularly near Montgomery, Alabama.

"We used to slip off in de woods in de old slave days on Sunday evening way down in de swamps to sing and pray to our own liking. We prayed for dis day of freedom. We come from four and five miles to pray together to God dat if we don't live to see it, to please let our chillen live to see a better day and be free, so dat dey can give honest and fair service to de Lord and all mankind everywhere. And we'd sing "Our little meetin's about to break, chillen, and we must part. We got to part in body, but hope not in mind. Our little meetin's bound to break." Den we used to sing "We walk about then shake hands, fare you well my sisters, I am going home."

Ms. Sewell firmly believed that "God planned dem slave prayers to free us like he did de Israelites, and dey did."[77]

Tom Robinson was born and raised in Catawba County, North Carolina and remembered how his mother "used to take us children and kneel down in front of the fireplace and pray.

> She'd pray that the time would come when everybody could worship the Lord under their own vine and fig tree—all of them free. It's come to me lots of times since. There she was a-praying, and on other plantations women was a-praying. All over the country the same prayer was being prayed. Guess the Lord done heard the prayer and answered it.

And Andrew Moss recalled that "down in Georgia where I was born—dat way back in 1852—us colored folks had prayer grounds. My mammy's was an old twisted thick-rooted muscadine bush. She'd go in dere and pray for deliverance of de slaves. Some colored folks cleaned out kneespots in de canebrakes. Cane, you know, grows high and thick, and colored folks could hide themselves and nobody could see and pester them."[78]

There was often great risk in going off into the woods to pray or conduct a "praise session." W. L. Bost remembered that in North Carolina, where he was enslaved, "us niggers never had a chance to go to Sunday school and church. The white folks feared for niggers to get any religion and education, but I reckon somethin' inside just told us about God and that there was a better place hereafter. We would sneak off and have prayer meetin'. Sometimes the patterollers catch us and beat us good but that didn't keep us from tryin'." Mingo White, who was enslaved in Alabama, recalled an even more dreadful occurrence. At the end of the day, "de slaves would be found locked in deir cabins prayin' for de Lord to free dem like he did de chillen of Israel. Iffen dey didn't lock up, de marsa or de driver would of heard 'em and whipped 'em. De slaves had a way of puttin' a wash pot in de door of de cabin to keep de sound in de house.

> I 'member once old Ned White was caught prayin'. De drivers took him de next day and carried him to de pegs, what was four stakes drove in de ground. Ned was made to pull off everything but his pants and lay on his stomach between de pegs whilst somebody strapped his legs and arms to de pegs. Den dey whipped him till de blood run from him like he was a hog. Dey made all of de hands come and see it, and dey said us'd get de same thing if us was cotched. Dey don't allow a man to whip a horse like dey whipped us in dem days.

White noted that after the beating old Ned "slipped off and went to de North to join the Union Army."[79]

"The slaves would pray for to get out of bondage," mused John White, ex-slave from Texas. "Some of them say the Lord told them to run away. Get to the North. Across the Red River. Over there would be folks to guide them to the free state—Kansas. The Lord never tell me to run away. I never tried it, maybe, because mostly they was caught by patrollers and fetched back for a flogging—and I had whippings enough already!"[80] Slave testimony was filled with accounts of slaves and slave preachers being cruelly persecuted for practicing their religion openly, so the slave church became an underground institution that prepared the oppressed spiritually for that ultimate triumph over physical bondage. The slave preacher could not openly discuss the gospel according to the oppressed Africans and Afro-Americans. That message of freedom and deliverance in this world and the next was subversive to the power and control over life and death exercised by the slaveholders and the entire slave regime.

In *Roll, Jordan, Roll* (1974), Eugene Genovese argued that the planter-dominated "cultural hegemony" of the antebellum South extended into "the world the slaves made." Genovese suggested that the antebellum southern plantation witnessed the development of a "paternalistic ethos" that defined the nature of relations between the slavers and the enslaved, and was integral to the value-system and cultural superstructure of the South. "Southern paternalism, like every other paternalism, had little to do with old Massa's ostensible benevolence, kindness, and good cheer. It grew out of the necessity to discipline and morally justify a system of exploitation." While few historians have questioned the evidence demonstrating that southern slaveholders paid a great deal of lip service to paternalism, Genovese provides very little evidence that the slaves generally viewed the masters as "paternalistic father figures." From the perspective of enslaved Afro-Americans, slavery was sinful because their enslavement was illegitimate; it was the slaveholders (and Genovese) who "defined the involuntary labor of the slaves as a legitimate return to their masters for protection and direction."[81]

The religious teachings of the slaveholders and plantation missionaries were almost completely rejected by the masses of enslaved Afro-Americans. Far from looking to the slavers for "protection and direction," Afro-Americans created their own version of Christianity, which spoke to their particular needs and only on a more superficial level resembled the religion of white southerners. Historian Paul Escott examined the hundreds of Federal Writers Project interviews and concluded that "southern plantations encompassed two worlds, one white and one black, one the master's and one the slaves'."[82] Within these separate worlds were separate gospels, distinct perspectives on Christianity, that guided the lives and behavior of blacks and whites. The gospel of the oppressor taught obedience and submission, and it was rejected by the enslaved. The gospel of the oppressed spoke of freedom, the ultimate justice of God, and His support for His chosen people.

When we examine slave testimony to determine how these Afro-American religious values functioned in the daily lives of individual slaves, we find a close and explicit relationship between religion and resistance. Afro-American Christianity taught that slavery was sinful, and so to resist the brutality and degradation of the slavers was "good" and in keeping with God's will. Whereas the religious teachings of the plantation missionaries endorsed accommodation and resignation to the powers of this world, the religion of the slaves sanctioned all forms of mental and physical resistance against the brutal and dehumanizing forces of evil inherent in the antebellum slave regime.

THREE

Let Your Motto Be Resistance!

If hereditary bondsmen would be free, they must themselves strike the blow.

HENRY HIGHLAND GARNET, 1843

> Run, nigger, run;
> de patter-roller catch you;
> Run, nigger, run,
> it's almost day.
>
> Run, nigger, run;
> de patter-roller catch you;
> Run, nigger, run,
> and try to get away.
>
> Afro-American folk song

FANNIE MOORE WAS BORN A SLAVE on the Moore Plantation in Moore, South Carolina, on 1 September 1849. "De Moores had owned de same plantation and de same niggers and dey children for years back." One of twelve children, her mother worked in the fields all day, and "granny she cook for us chillens while our mammy away in the field." Fannie Moore told the white interviewer from the Federal Writers Project, Marjorie Jones, that "nowadays [1937] when I hear folks a-growlin' and a-grumblin' about not having' this and that I just think what would they done if they be brought up on de Moore Plantation." She pulled up her right sleeve and showed scars to Ms. Jones, who may have been skeptical. When Fannie's mother came home from the fields, she had to "piece and quilt all night." Her mother made quilts for the family and "for de white folks, too." Fannie and her brother, George, often stayed up with their mother, each one taking turns holding the "rich pine branches," which was "all de light we ever had. My brother was a holdin' de pine so's I can help mammy tack the quilt and he go to sleep and let it drop." Fannie wore the scars to her grave.

Fannie Moore also remembered that her mother often suffered from "trouble in de heart" over the way she and her family were treated on the Moore Plantation after so many years, and "every night she pray for de Lord to get her and her chillen out of de place." One of the main reasons why conditions were so horrible, according to Ms. Moore, was because "de old overseer he hate my mammy." There were very likely many reasons for their mutual animosity, but one major bone of contention was the fact that Fannie's mother continually resisted any brutal treatment of her children. The white overseer, Hill, hated her " 'cause she fight him for beaten her chillen. Why she get more whippin' for dat den anythin' else." These beatings continued even though Fannie's father was a skilled worker and the plantation blacksmith. "He shoe all de horses on de plantation. He work so hard he have no time to go to the fields."[1]

In a recent essay, "The Legacy of Slavery: Standards for a New Womanhood," Angela Davis examined the peculiar problems faced by the black female slave in the antebellum South. These women were expected to work in the fields, same as the men, but were victimized and oppressed *more* than men. "It is important to remember," wrote Ms. Davis, "that the

ent inflicted on women exceeded in intensity the punishment suf-
their men, for women were not only whipped and mutilated, they
... also *raped*." She also noted that "women, it was generally assumed, were
full hands—unless they had been expressly assigned to be 'breeders' or 'suck-
lers' in which case they sometimes ranked less than full hands."[2] But according to Fanny Moore, some slaveholders in South Carolina viewed "de breed
woman" as more valuable than male slaves. It was, of course, a rather
dubious distinction.

> De "breed woman" always bring more money den de rest, even de men.
> When dey put her on de block dey put all her chillen around her to
> show folks how fast she can have chillen. When she sold, her family
> never seen her again. She never know how many chillen she have.
> Sometime she have colored chillen and sometimes white. 'Taint no use
> to say anything, 'cause if she do she just get whipped.[3]

Despite the sometimes brutal treatment, Stephen Moore and his family
managed to survive these conditions with their individual and collective
dignity intact through resisting the dehumanizing practices of "old Marse
Jim Moore." For example, when Marse Jim would not let them attend the
white church with any degree of regularity, "de niggers slip off and pray and
hold prayer-meetin' in de woods, den dey turn the big wash pot and prop it
up with a stick to drown out de sound of de singin'." Old Granny Moore,
Marse Jim's mother (whom Fannie dubbed the "rip-jack": "She say niggers
didn't need nothin' to eat. Dey just like animals, not like other folks."),
vehemently opposed the instruction of even the most trusted servants, but
"my daddy slip and get a Webster book and den he take it out in de field and
he learn to read. De white folks afraid to let de chillen learn anythin'. They
afraid dey get too smart and be harder to manage."

Some may argue that Fannie Moore and her family were merely surviv-
ing an oppressive situation by accommodating to, rather than resisting, the
brutalizing treatment they received. This is, of course, very much open to
debate.[4] However, Fannie Moore did mention two incidents which suggest
that when the choice was between survival or loss of dignity—accommodation versus loss of self-worth—the Afro-Americans enslaved on the Moore
Plantation in the 1850s resisted unjustified brutality even to death. Ms.
Moore recalled that one day her mother was "plowin' in de cotton field. All
sudden like she let out a big yell. Den she start singin' and a shoutin' and a
whoopin' and a hollerin'. Den it seems she plow all de harder.

> When she come home, Marse Jim's mammy say: "What all dat goin' on
> in de field? You think we send you out there just to whoop and yell? No

siree, we put you out there to work and you sure better work, else we get de overseer to cowhide you old black back."

My mammy just grin all over her black wrinkled face and say: "I'se saved. De Lord done tell me I'se saved. Now I know de Lord will show me de way, I ain't gwine to grieve no more. No matter how much you all done beat me and my chillen de Lord will show me de way. And some day we never be slaves." Old Granny Moore grab de cowhide and slash Mammy cross de back but Mammy never yell. She just go back to de field a singin'.[5]

Fannie's mother had evidently undergone a "conversion experience" while she was working in the field. She believed this spiritual experience had changed her relationship to God. Sociologist Charles S. Johnson, in his introduction to *God Struck Me Dead* (1969), which contained numerous first-hand accounts of these incidents, claimed that "a conversion experience—whether it be religious or other form—is marked by a sudden and a striking 'change of heart' with an abrupt change in the orientation of attitudes and beliefs. It is accompanied by what can be described as an emotional regeneration, typically sudden in its advent and consummation." Conversion radically affected one's outlook toward life and one's conception of "self." Fundamentally, it means a new beginning, for one was reborn—"born again"—and worldly concerns and masters became secondary to one's new birth in Jesus Christ. Since for Fannie Moore's mother this change meant that she would work harder, there was no reason (other than spite and pure viciousness) why old Granny Moore should have been concerned about the event. Fannie's mother believed that she had witnessed the truth, and she spoke it, and for that reason she was slashed across the back.[6]

Fannie Moore related another incident of unorganized resistance, but this one was in the form of violence, rather than nonviolence (Fannie's mother, of course, could have responded violently and snatched the cowhide from Granny Moore and hacked her across the face and back)—and the result was (or may have been) death.

I remember one time dey was a dance at one of de houses in de quarters. All de niggers was a-laughin and a-pattin' dey feet and a-singin', but dey was a few dat didn't. De patterollers shove de door open and start grabbin' us. Uncle Joe's son he decide dey was one time to die and he start to fight. He say he tired standin' so many beatin's, he just can't stand no more. De patterrollers start beatin' him and he start fightin'. Oh lordy, it was terrible. Dey whip him with a cowhide for a long time, den one of dem take a stick and hit him over de head, and just bust his head wide open. De poor boy fell on de floor just a-moanin' and a-groanin. De patterrollers just whip about half dozen other niggers and send 'em home and leave us with de dead boy.[7]

Slave testimony is replete with similar incidents of Afro-Americans resisting the brutalization of slavery nonviolently for religious reasons, or resisting through violence for the sake of dignity. In these instances the act of resistance was an act of self-definition and self-respect. Perhaps the most famous rendition of this act of unorganized violent resistance is found in Frederick Douglass's *Narrative* when he mentions how he resisted the unprovoked attack of Mr. Edward Covey, the notorious "nigger-breaker." One Monday morning Douglass was working in the horses' stable and Mr. Covey came in with a long rope and "he caught hold of my legs." Douglass was thrown to the ground. "Mr. Covey seemed now to think that he had me, and could do what he pleased; but at this moment—from whence came the spirit I don't know—I resolved to fight; and suiting my action to the resolution, I seized Covey hard by the throat; and as I did so, I rose." The two men battled for nearly two hours; Covey receiving no assistance from other hired slaves. "Covey at length let me go . . . saying that if I had not resisted, he would not have whipped me half so much. The truth was, that he had not whipped me at all. . . . The whole six months afterwards, that I spent with Mr. Covey, he never laid the weight of his finger upon me in anger." Douglass then related the "personal meaning" he attached to this act of violent resistance.

> This battle with Mr. Covey was the turning-point in my career as a slave. It rekindled the few expiring embers of freedom, and revived within me a sense of my own manhood. It recalled the departed self-confidence, and inspired me again with a determination to be free. The gratification afforded by the triumph was a full compensation for whatever else might follow, even death itself. He only can understand the deep satisfaction which I experienced, who has himself repelled by force the bloody arm of slavery. I felt as I never felt before. It was a glorious resurrection, from the tomb of slavery, to the heaven of freedom. My long-crushed spirit rose, cowardice departed, bold defiance took its place; and I now resolved that, however long I might remain a slave in form, the day had passed forever when I could be a slave in fact.[8]

Similar incidents that elicited similar responses were found in the narratives of William Wells Brown, John Thompson, Solomon Northrup, Moses Grandy, Samuel Ringgold Ward, and others, as well as in the narrative-interviews with ex-slaves conducted by the Federal Writers Project.[9] The heightened level of awareness that resulted from these individual acts of resistance usually had a profound influence on the personal identity of the individual resister and oftentimes on the self-perception of the entire slave community. Frederick Douglass later recalled that "the doctrine that submission to violence is the best cure for violence did not hold good as between slaves and overseers. He was whipped oftener who was whipped easiest."

> That slave who had the courage to stand up for himself against the overseer, although he might have many hard stripes at first, became while legally a slave virtually a free man. "You can shoot me," said a slave to Rigby Hopkins, "but you can't whip me," and the result was he was neither whipped nor shot. [10]

These individual acts of resistance had a profound meaning in the evolution of slave culture. Through violent opposition to brutality, the enslaved Afro-Americans were able to define the limits and power of "the bloody arm of slavery." Through individual acts of resistance the slave was often able to determine his or her personal destiny; and through collective acts of resistance the entire community was involved in the creation of one of the "core values" of the Afro-American cultural system developing in the United States.

Run, Nigger, Run—A Song of Resistance

Within the slave community, freedom and self-determination were not tied to some abstract, bourgeois notion of "individualism," but were defined in terms of the amount of personal control that an individual had over his or her destiny and that of the immediate family. Thus despite the indiscriminate acts of violence, the long working hours, and the lack of adequate food, clothes, and other necessities, Fannie Moore viewed old Marse Jim as "a good master." "De year before the Civil War started," she recalled, "Marse Jim died. He was out in the pasture pickin' up cow loads, a throwin' 'em in de garden. And he just drop over. I hate to see Marse Jim go, he not such a bad man." And in contrast to the violent, vindictive old Granny Moore, Marse Jim's wife, Mary Anderson Moore, was "the sweetest women I ever saw. She was always good to every nigger on de plantation. . . . All de little niggers like to work for her. She never talk mean. Just smile dat sweet smile and talk in de softest tone." Thus there were positive and negative aspects of the interactions between the black and white Moores on that South Carolina plantation, and only one of the two major characteristics that defined a "mean master"—unjustified and unnecessary brutality and a willingness to sell members of the immediate family—was present. Since the black Moores themselves did not believe they were the victims of extreme brutality, they were able to live and survive with dignity.[11]

"It was a terrible sight to see de speculators come to the plantation," proclaimed Fannie Moore. "Dey would go through the fields and buy de slaves dey wanted." The tyranny that was exercised by slaveholders over the enslaved was never more clearly visible than when they broke up Afro-American families through participation in the domestic slave trade. "When de speculator come all de slaves start a-shakin'. No one know who is a-goin'." There was always the possibility that they would not merely be taken to a situation that was worse than the one they were leaving, but also that they would never see members of their family again. Slave trading provided a primary justification for a major form of resistance employed by the en-slaved—running away. Fannie Moore considered Marse Jim Moore a good master because "he never sell Pappy or Mammy or any of dey chillen. He always like Pappy."[12] This may account for the fact that in a narrative that was otherwise filled with details that typified the experiences of thousands of enslaved Afro-Americans, there was no mention made by Fannie Moore of runaways or attempts at flight.

Herbert Aptheker, in his study, *American Negro Slave Revolts* (1943), examined "individual acts of resistance" as well as organized rebellions. "Sabotage, shamming illness, stealing, suicide and self-mutilation, and strikes were other devices which plagued slaveholders," wrote Aptheker. "The carelessness and deliberate destructiveness of the slaves, resulting in broken fences, spoiled tools, and neglected animals were common phenomena." But Aptheker also concluded that "flight was a major factor in the battle against bondage.

> Slaves fled wherever havens of liberation appeared, to the Spaniards, Mexicans, Dutch, Canadians, French; to the armies of Britain and France; and, of course, to the army of Lincoln; to mountains, forests, and swamps in the South (often establishing camps therein); and, along the routes of the Underground Railroad. The figures here again must be only guesses, but it is probable that hundreds of thousands in the course of slavery *succeeded* in gaining liberty by flight.[13]

Leslie Howard Owens presented a lengthy discussion of the "logic of resistance" in *This Species of Property: Slave Life and Culture in the Old South* (1976). Owens made a comprehensive survey of the records of the slave-holders and found that "manuscript information especially indicates that slave disturbances were widespread. . . . Many involved no more than one slave, but the response of slaveholders to even limited disruptions was never gentle." Owens focused on "slave resistant behavior" which was "intended to force masters and overseers to make some considerable adjustment in their relationships with slaves." He was able to document arson and other forms of sabotage, self-mutilation, suicide, and flight as examples of acts of resistance, common throughout the South, "that challenged an uneven system of authoritarian control." Owens believed that "at the core of such behavior was the slave's lack of accommodation to much that confronted him in bondage. Bondage continually worked against the bondsmen, though he never left its functioning untampered with."[14]

More recently, in *There Is a River: The Black Struggle for Freedom in America* (1981), Vincent Harding has argued that these individual acts of resistance—"the subterranean acts of individual defiance, resistance, creative rebellion, sabotage and flight"—fed into the larger stream and movement for black freedom in this country.

> It rose out of the broad base of all the men, women, and children who offered their personal, rudimentary challenges to the system. One time it was manifested in the decision of a solitary person to kill his master on a dark road as they traveled home at night. Another time it came when a group of black men determined that white patrolmen had broken up their social gatherings once too often and chose to resist to the death.[15]

As a result, the resistance movement among enslaved Afro-Americans was a collective struggle, and the "act of resistance" became a cultural symbol and event whose meaning was understood by all who shared in the experience.

> Engaged in day-to-day survival to maintain integrity, identity, and life, the vast majority who formed the mainstream were constantly in touch with the runaways, outlyers, and arsonists, and with those men and women who sneaked back into their cabins before dawn after attending secret planning meetings. In addition, the fugitive, exciting word from white political sources, telling of arguments and debates over the operation of the institution of slavery, continued to seep into the life of the Southern black community, hinting, suggesting, revealing the basic tensions which lurked deep in the larger white society. Always, too, there was word from farther away (and nearer), from San Domingo and other parts of the African diaspora in the Caribbean— word of struggle and victory, even of emancipation. Then, beyond and above all these, was the word from the Lord, word from the Word, word of delivering Daniel, word that "Jesus do most anything / Oh, no

man can hinder me." There were words not only to hear, but to eat and drink, words to ponder, words to surrender to.[16]

When we examine the cultural beliefs and practices that developed among enslaved Afro-Americans we find that this value of "resistance against oppression" was pervasive. This cultural value was found in the secular "songs of resistance" that most of the slaves knew and sang among themselves. Through these songs and folktales the enslaved Afro-Americans taught their children and themselves that through wit, quickness, guile, and courage they could outmaneuver even the strongest overseer, outsmart the meanest master, and elude the most relentless patrollers.[17] Thus if "Roll, Jordan, Roll" was one of the most popular songs sung by the slaves for white listeners, "Run, Nigger, Run" appears to have been the most popular song of resistance that the slaves sang among themselves.

> Run, nigger, run
> De Patteroll get you!
> Run, nigger, run,
> De Patteroll come.
> Watch, nigger, watch,
> De Patteroll trick you,
> Watch, nigger, watch,
> He got a big gun!

Anthony Dawson, who was born in slavery near Greenville, North Carolina, in 1832, remembered that this was one of the tunes "de children down on de twenty acres used to sing when dey playing in de moonlight round de cabins in de quarters."[18] It is very likely that the earliest published version of "Run, Nigger, Run" is found in the collection of *Slave Songs in the United States* edited by Allen, Ware, and Garrison in 1867. This version had been transcribed by E. J. Snow of Pine Bluff, Arkansas.

> O, some tell me,
> That a nigger won't steal
> But I've seen a nigger,
> in the cornfield.
> O, run, nigger, run
> for the patrol will catch you
> O, run, nigger, run
> for 'tis almost day.[19]

Dora Franks was born in Choctaw County, Mississippi, around 1840 and recalled singing "Run, Nigger, Run," but she associated the song with her Uncle Alf, who was a runaway and maroon.

> Lots o' niggers would slip off from one plantation to de other to see some other niggers. Dey would always manage to get back before daybreak. De worst thing I ever heard about dat was once when my Uncle Alf run off to "jump de broom." Dat was what dey called goin' to see a woman. He didn't come back by daylight, so dey put de nigger hounds after him. Dey smelled his trail down in de swamp and found where he was hidin'.
>
> Now, he was one o' de biggest niggers on de place and a powerful fast worker. But dey took and give him one hundred lashes with de cat-o'-ninety-nine-tails. His back was somethin'awful, but dey put him in de field to work while de blood was still a-runnin'. He work right hard till dey left. Den, when he got up to de end o' de row next to de swamp, he lit out again.

Ms. Franks went on to note that "dey never found him dat time." Her uncle lived in a cave and "at nights he would come out on de place and steal enough t' eat and cook it in his little dugout. When de War was over and de slaves was freed, he come out."[20]

Running away was not merely an individualistic response to a personal affront or grievance, but a collective act of resistance in which the runaways were assisted by other slaves. Julia Brown, an ex-slave who was born in Commerce, Georgia, in 1853, recalled that despite the "patty rollers, . . . sometimes the slaves would run away.

> Their masters was mean to them that caused them to run away. Sometimes they would live in caves. They got along all right—what with other people slippin' things into 'em. And, too, they'd steal hogs, chickens, and anything else they could get their hands on. Some white people would help, too, for there was some white people who didn't believe in slavery.
>
> They would always try to find them slaves that run away, and if they was found they'd be beat or sold to somebody else.

Women ran away as well as men, and they were also assisted by the slave community. Julia Brown mentioned that "my grandmother run away from her master. She stayed in the woods and she washed her clothes in the branches. She used sand for soap."[21] Elizabeth Sparks, an ex-slave from Virginia, declared that her first master, "Shep Miller, was terrible. . . . He beat women as well as men.

Beat women just like men. Beat women naked and wash 'em down in brine. Sometimes they beat 'em so bad they just couldn't stand it and they run away to the woods. If you get in the woods, they couldn't get you. You could hide and people slip you somethin' to eat. Then he call you every day. After while he tell one of colored foreman tell you come on back. He ain't a-goin' beat you anymore. They had colored foreman but they always have a white overseer. Foreman get you to come back and then he beat you to death again.[22]

Benjamin Johnson, who did not know how old he was when he was interviewed in Georgia in 1937, recalled that his old mistress, Betsy Johnson, wife of Judge Luke Johnson, "would come along and she would be mad with some of de women and she would want to go to whippin' on 'em. Sometimes de women wouldn't take it and would run away and hide in de woods. Sometimes de would come back after a short stay and den again de would have to put de hounds on deir trail to bring 'em back home."[23]

Thomas Monroe Campbell was one of the first black farm demonstration agents for the U.S. Department of Agriculture, and as he traveled throughout the South in the late 1930s he collected stenographic reports of the former slaves' life stories. Campbell interviewed Sarah Fitzgerald at age ninety in Alabama, where she had spent most of her life. She mentioned the patrollers who "went round at night and caught 'Niggers' when dey went off de place an' if dey didn't have no pass dey'd beat 'em an' run 'em back home. Dats where dat song come f'om 'bout 'Run, Nigger, Run, de Pattero's Ketch 'ya.' Ef dey caught a 'Nigger' 'way f'om home an' he couldn't sho' no pass, he jes' had'ta take a beatin' or outrun 'em." Campbell also interviewed Henry Baker in Alabama at the age of eighty-three, and he also stated, "De niggers made up a song 'bout de 'patrollers.'"

Run, Nigger, Run—De Patarolls Ketch Yuh Jes' fo' Day

> Please Ol' Marster
> Don' whup me
> Whup Dat Nigger
> Behin' dat tree.
>
> I run I run,
> I run mah bes'
> I run putty clos'
> Tuh er hornets nes'.
>
> De Pataroes run
> Dey run dere bes'

Dey run right in,
De hornets nes'.[24]

"Run, Nigger, Run" was obviously *not* one of the tunes the slaves would harmonize in the fields in front of a white audience. Elijah Green, an ex-slave who was born in Charleston, South Carolina, in 1853 remembered the words to a song "I used to sing to the slaves when master went away, but I wouldn't be so fool as to let him hear me."

Master gone away
But darkies stay at home
The year of jubilee is come
And freedom will begun.[25]

And Harriet Robinson recalled a tune that the "nigger fiddlers" would play at slave gatherings.

I fooled Old Marster seven years
Fooled the overseer three;
Hand me down my banjo
And I'll tickle your bel-lee.[26]

Once the Civil War began, the enslaved Afro-Americans continued to make up songs about "their white folks" and this was in keeping with the African penchant for satire and the Afro-American value of resistance. Folklorist William D. Pierson examined some of the African wit and satire that was transferred to the various parts of the New World. He found that "in their songs the slaves were able to voice subtle grievances before their masters or openly vent their frustration and disdain. . . . We have long known that slaves adept at dissembling behavior relished 'puttin' on Ole Massa' as it was known, but there was more to African wit than the clever lie, and in the satire of song and pantomime, slaves not only put ole Massa on, they put him down as well."[27]

When General William T. Sherman's army came marching through South Carolina, Lorenzo Ezell recalled that his master, Ned Libscomb, "run off and stay in de woods a whole week," and the slaves made up a song about it.

White folks, have you seed old massa
Up de road, with he mustache on?
He pick up he hat and he leave real sudden
And I believe he's up and gone.

Old massa run away

And us darkies stay at home.
It must be now dat Kingdom's comin'
And de year of Jubilee.

He look up de river and he seed dat smoke,
Where de Lincoln gunboats lay.
He big 'nough and he old 'nough and he orter know better
But he gone and run away.

Now dat overseer want to give trouble
And trot us 'round a spell.
But we lock him up in de smokehouse cellar,
With de key done throwed in de well.[28]

The mixture of satire and resistance in the creation of slave songs was vividly described by Susan Snow, who was born in Wilcox County, Alabama, in 1850. When the war broke out, "de white chillen was singin' dis song":

Jeff Davis, long and slim,
Whipped old Abe with a hickory limb.

Jeff Davis is a wise man,
Lincoln is a fool,
Jeff Davis rides a gray,
And Lincoln rides a mule.

Susan Snow became angry, "so I hopped up and sung dis one":

Old Gen'l Pope had a shot gun,
Filled it full o' gum,
Killed 'em as dey come.

Called a Union band,
Make de Rebels understand
To leave de land
Submit to Abraham.

Unfortunately for Susan Snow, "Old Missus was a standin' right behind me. She grabbed up de broom an laid it on me." Ms. Snow later mentioned that she had heard the other slaves singing that song, but "I didn't know dey was a-singin' in dey sleeves."[29]

Individual acts of resistance did not merely have meaning in the lives of the slaves who were engaged in the act, they had meaning within the larger cultural context of the slave community. Whether it was as significant as organized aggression in the form of a conspiracy or running away, or as minor as singing a dangerous tune, enslaved Afro-Americans learned that the only way they were going to survive the degrading conditions of slavery with their manhood and womenhood intact was to resist the forces of evil and oppression around them. Faith in God not only helped to sustain His children in the land of bondage, but also supported their attempts to resist the brutality and injustice of the slave regime. And since brutality, injustice, and discrimination against Afro-Americans did not stop at the Mason-Dixon line, there was great continuity in the values supporting resistance between the slave and the free black communities in antebellum America.

The Free Black Resistance Movement

When an enslaved Afro-American decided to take control of his or her personal destiny in the hostile environment of the slave South and flee, both the state and federal government considered this individual a "fugitive from justice." The statutes and ordinances passed by planter-dominated state legislatures to discourage assistance of runaways were further bolstered by federal law. In effect, the two worked hand in hand to trip up those Africans and Afro-Americans who made that dash toward freedom. From the perspective of the slaveholder and the entire American legal establishment the slave was bound in service for life, and any attempt to change that relationship would have to be carried out with the written approval of the masters. Most runaways did not have this written approval, and thus were fugitives from the law.[30]

From early in the nineteenth century, however, an entire network of committees and individuals, white and black, arose to help the fugitives in their bids for real self-determination, and the high degree of success of the organized resistance movement associated with the "Underground Railroad" threatened the smooth functioning of the southern slave economy. Whereas running away to the woods for a few days or weeks to "cool out" after some explosive encounter might at times have been tolerated by some of the more calculating slave managers, the flight to the free states and Canada of up to two thousand slaves each year soon began to have an effect on the overall efficiency and profits of the southern economic system—a system already under serious political attack.[31]

The existence of this "network of resistance" was viewed as a threat to the system by the slaveholders, but as a godsend by the enslaved. Thus when a runaway was successful and managed to elude the bloodhounds, patrollers, and slave catchers, was able to reach a safer ground, more likely in a community usually surrounded by relatives, friends, fellow fugitives, and free blacks; he or she did not forget his brothers and sisters in bondage and, indeed, sometimes returned to free them. Henry Bibb, Frederick Douglass, and Harriet Tubman were three of the most noted examples of fugitive slaves who joined, and in these cases led, the resistance movement against the legalized oppression of southern slavery. For in both the literal and figurative sense these so-called "free" blacks were still "Bound with Them in Chains."[32]

What must be kept in mind is that for fugitive slaves who came into a new territory to make a fresh start and recently manumitted Afro-Americans or those who had been "free" for two or more generations, "freedom" and manumission did not confer the right of American citizenship. Although legally free blacks could *not* expect to be treated like white citizens (or even white aliens), there was some recognition by the state and local governments of the need to extend to them "legal protection." Leon Litwack, in *North of Slavery: The Negro in the Free States, 1790–1860* (1961), emphasized that "most northern whites would maintain a careful distinction between granting Negroes legal protection—a theoretical right to life, liberty, and property—and political and social equality."

> No statute or court decision could immediately erase from the public mind, North or South, that long and firmly held conviction that the African race was inferior and therefore incapable of being assimilated politically, socially, and most certainly physically with the dominant and superior white society. Despite the absence of slavery in the North, one observer remarked, "chains of a stronger kind still manacled their limbs, from which no legislative act could free them; a mental and moral subordination and inferiority, to which tyrant custom has here subjected all the sons and daughters of Africa."[33]

Alexis de Tocqueville, the French traveler and social commentator who made an extensive tour of the United States in 1831, was somewhat surprised to find that "the prejudice of race appears stronger in the states that have abolished slavery than in those where it still exists; and nowhere is it so intolerant as in those states where servitude has never been known."[34] Restrictions on Afro-Americans' right to vote, work at certain occupations, to trial by jury, or to redress of grievances by the courts were sanctioned by white "public opinion" in virtually all of the so-called free states. Therefore, the free black resistance movement was as concerned with the organized attempts to deprive Afro-Americans of the rights of citizenship in the North as it was with the protection of fugitives and the campaigns to end slavery altogether in the South.

Although many northern states had provided for the immediate or gradual demise of slavery before 1804, and thus contained large free black populations by the 1830s and 1840s, white settlers in Ohio, Indiana, Illinois, and other parts of the old northwestern frontier did not wish to compete for land, status, and power with Africans and Afro-Americans. Eventually, the state and territorial governments passed laws restricting the migration of free blacks into these territories. As a result, many fugitive slaves fled the United States altogether and became refugees in Canada and Mexico. It has been estimated that by 1860, there were over 20,000 Afro-American refugees living in western Canada alone (where they were also the victims of discriminatory treatment). Given these formidable restrictions on the rights of free blacks in the North (and South), some researchers have been tempted to characterize this group as "Slaves Without Masters." But there were profound and fundamental differences between the conditions of slaves and those of the free black population.[35] Leon Litwack for example, admitted that "the northern Negro . . . faced political, economic, and social restrictions. Nevertheless, he spoke out freely against his condition; he organized, agitated, penned editorials and pamphlets, and petitioned state and federal bodies to improve his condition."[36] The black resistance activities in the North were generally organized on a community by community basis, where free blacks were taught the values of mutual cooperation and self-determination as well as resistance to oppression.

The earliest social organizations among free blacks were for purposes of mutual aid and assistance, rather than resistance and protest. The African Union Society of Newport, Rhode Island, was organized in 1780 primarily for the "moral improvement" of the free Africans; it provided assistance for widows and children, preserved records of birth, death, marriage, and manumission, and served as a forum for debating and acting on issues of importance to the community.[37] Similar "free African societies" were formed among Africans and Afro-Americans living in Providence, Boston, and Philadelphia in the 1780s, and in their initial years, none of these organizations was involved in specifically "religious" activities. Richard Allen and Absalom Jones, who were instrumental in the founding of the Free African Society of Philadelphia in April 1787, reported that initially they attempted to form an organization around common religious beliefs, "but there being too few to be found of like concern, and those who were, differed in their religious sentiments, with these circumstances they labored till it was proposed . . . that a society should be formed without regard to religious tenets."[38]

As part of the early emphasis on resisting oppression in this country, the free African societies often worked for increased black self-determination through a return to Africa. From as early as 1773 four Africans living in Boston petitioned the Massachusetts General Assembly for assistance in a plan of emigration and pledged their willingness to "submit to such regulations as may be made relative to us, until we leave the province which we determine to do as soon as we can from our joynt labours procure money to transport ourselves to some part of the coast of Africa, where we propose settlement."[39] With the formation of the African Union Society in 1780, free blacks moved beyond petitions to organized efforts to achieve this end. As one of the major seaports on the eastern coast, Newport contained a high concentration of Africans who wanted to return home and establish an independent black settlement. While Prince Hall and seventy-five other Boston blacks were petitioning the Masachusetts Assembly in 1787 for assistance in a "return to Africa, our native country . . . where we shall live among our equals and be more comfortable and happy, than we can be in our present situation, and at the same time may have a prospect of usefulness to our brother;" Newport blacks were making plans for emigration to Africa among themselves and gathering support for the scheme among blacks in other cities.[40] Free black Philadelphians were mostly native-born and there was less support for emigration, but in Providence, free blacks welcomed the overtures of the Newport group and eventually helped to finance the voyage of James McKenzie to Freetown, Sierra Leone, in 1796, where British officials agreed to accept twelve black families from Rhode Island. Unfortunately, there were strings attached, and these families were required to get a statement of "good character" from white ministers and the Rhode Island Abolition Society. When one of the ministers, Samuel Hopkins, refused to endorse the Providence group, the emigration plans fell through.[41]

Although there was no mass emigration or repatriation of free Africans and Afro-Americans to Africa in the eighteenth century, the African dream of increased black self-determination through emigration would continue to fill the minds and hearts of Africa's oppressed children in the United States, well into the twentieth century. The constant influx into the slave and free black communities of Africans with news of the homeland helped to keep the dream alive, especially when the likelihood of black freedom and equal treatment in this country appeared more and more an "impossible dream." Black self-determination through participation in a larger African nationality was considered a viable alternative to remaining on the fringes of white American society as a despised and exploited group. As the petitions sent to state and federal legislatures in the 1770s and 1780s made clear, the new United States of America viewed itself as a "white, Christian nation," and the free Africans and Afro-Americans in Boston, Newport, and Providence preferred to return to the land that they believe God had prepared for them.[42]

Free black Philadelphians understood and supported the emigrationist activities of their brothers to the North, but being less familiar with Africa and more "Afro-American," they set about the task of creating a lifestyle that would sustain them in this somewhat hostile environment. Whereas the emigrationist campaigns for black self-determination trace their origins back to the activities of free blacks in Providence and Newport, the organized campaigns for religious self-determination had their origins among free blacks in Philadelphia. The story of the walkout by black communicants of St. George Episcopal Church in 1787 and the subsequent organization of the first independent black religious denomination has been recounted by numerous scholars of the Afro-American experience. Led by Absalom Jones and Richard Allen, free blacks in Philadelphia and later other cities believed that they had to take responsibility for their own salvation and began to organize religious services and groups where they would control how and under what conditions they would "give praise to the Lord."[43]

From its inception, the black independent church movement was an important part of the larger free black resistance campaigns. Theologian Gayraud Wilmore in *Black Religion and Black Radicalism* declared that "the independent church movement among Blacks, during and immediately following the period of the Revolutionary War, must be considered, *ipso facto,* an expression of Black resistance to white oppression—the first Black Freedom movement.

> It had the advantage of being carried on under the cloak of ecclesiastical business rather than as an affair of state, and as such could pass as representing the more or less legitimate desire of Black people to have "a place of their own in which to worship." But it was, in fact, a form of Black insurrection against the most vulnerable and accessible form of institutionalized racism and oppression in the nation—the American churches themselves.[44]

From this independent religious base, free blacks moved into other areas and organized or supported resistance campaigns against the political and social oppression of Afro-Americans. The connection between the new independent black churches and the secular resistance movement was made vividly clear in the organized free black opposition to the activities of the American Colonization Society (ACS). It was formed in December 1816 in Washington, D.C., among many "distinguished Americans" for the purpose of "Colonizing the Free People of Colour in the United States" on the west coast of Africa. The first major free black protest meeting against the group was held within a month at Bethel African Methodist Episcopal Church in Philadelphia, under the leadership of Bishop Richard Allen, the pastor, and James Forten, a wealthy sailmaker and businessman. Over three thousand persons attended, "a mixture of the well-to-do and literate with the poor and unschooled." They unanimously condemned the colonization scheme "as an unmerited stigma upon the free Negro." Some black Philadelphians even went further and pledged that they "would never voluntarily separate themselves from their brethren in slavery."[45]

The supporters of the colonization movement argued that they were doing free blacks and the nation a service in founding the organization. In the first volume of the *African Repository,* the official publication of the American Colonization Society, the editors asserted that the free blacks, "introduced among us by violence, notoriously ignorant, degraded and miserable, mentally diseased, broken spirited, acted upon by no motive to honorable exertions, scarcely reached in their debasement by the heavenly light, wander unsettled and unbefriended through our land, or sit indolent, abject and sorrowful, by the streams which witness their captivity."[46] The colonizationists (and many other blacks and whites) believed that there were "insurmountable forces" that made it virtually impossible for blacks and whites to coexist in the same social system as free persons. The causes were "fixed, not only beyond the control of the friends of humanity, but of any human power. . . . This is not the fault of the coloured man, nor the white man, nor Christianity; but an ordination of Providence and no more to be changed than the laws of nature." As far as the white colonizationists were concerned, the likelihood of black advancement in American society was slim at best, and while some went so far as to recognize that a few free blacks had managed to live respectable and productive lives, "as a class," Harvard University President Edward Everett contended, "they are depressed to a low point on the social scale."[47]

Very few free blacks were fooled by the sincerity and earnest appeals of the white colonizationists. They knew the major reason they were "depressed" in the North was discrimination and injustice. Would it not have been cheaper to change the laws that specifically suppressed the citizenship rights of free blacks than to expend hundreds of thousands of dollars on "hazardous overseas projects"? The objective of the Colonization Society was the removal of the free black population, and gaining this end, many argued, would make slavery more secure at a time when many white citizens were beginning to call for its immediate abolition. Most free blacks preferred to remain in the United States and participate in the organized resistance campaigns, which seemed to grow stronger and stronger each year. As Peter Williams, pastor of St. Phillip's Episcopal Church in New York City, declared in 1819, "We are natives of this country; we only ask that we be treated as well as foreigners. Not a few of our fathers suffered and bled to purchase its independence; we ask only to be treated as well as those who fought against it."[48]

Many free blacks opposed colonization, but many of these same individuals also supported voluntary emigration to an independent black nation as a means of obtaining increased black self-determination. From as early as 1787 free blacks were demonstrating that they knew the difference between leaving the United States for a black nation and emigrating to a white-controlled "colony." When Rhode Island free blacks were inquiring about possible places to settle in west Africa, they made clear their objections to becoming "a part of any colony in which they would be subservient to white interests. . . ."[49] Richard Allen, James Forten, and Peter Williams, who were the leaders of the anti-colonization campaign, were also prominent in the movement for free black emigration to Haiti in the 1820s. From as early as 1804 the Haitian government made it clear that Afro-Americans from this country would be welcome there, and by 1824 Haitian emigration societies had been formed in New York, Baltimore, and Philadelphia. Over two thousand free blacks emigrated to Haiti that year, and hundreds continued to leave through the end of the decade. Thus during the same years Allen, Forten, Williams and many other free blacks were denouncing the establishment of the colony of Liberia by the American Colonization Society, they were actively involved in promoting emigration to Haiti. Unfortunately, severe problems arose almost immediately for the Haitian emigrants with regard to language, religious practices, and climate. Complaints of ill-treatment and deprivation began filtering back to the United States, and when Peter Williams, representing the Haitian Emigration Society of Coloured People of New York, made an inspection tour in the spring of 1825, at least fifty-six emigrants returned with him. By April 1826 it was estimated that one third of the six thousand government-sanctioned settlers had been repatriated; and the remainder, rather than settling in the countryside on government-sponsored land grants, were flocking to the larger Haitian cities.[50]

Several historians who have examined the issue of "emigration versus colonization" among free blacks in the 1820s have accused Allen, Forten, Williams, and others of "ideological inconsistency and ambivalence." They argued that these black leaders were inconsistent in supporting emigration to Haiti and opposing the ACS settlement in Liberia.[51] But these leaders, as well as the free blacks in Newport and Providence in the 1780s, knew that becoming a part of a white-controlled colony in Africa would not guarantee black self-determination. One of the major purposes served by emigration was freedom from white domination, and this would not be accomplished by emigrating to the British colony of Sierra Leone in the 1780s or to the American colony of Liberia in the 1820s. Those free blacks who left the United States and settled in Liberia in the 1820s and 1830s were seeking social advancement, but unlike Allen, Forten, and Williams, they were willing in the process to sacrifice black self-determination. But the important question that had to be addressed was, Could black advancement be guaranteed without genuine black self-determination?

In the 1830s and 1840s, many black leaders involved in the national black conventions believed that participating in the antislavery movement led by William Lloyd Garrison could lead to black advancement, while others argued that joining the radical abolitionist movement would not advance *free* blacks and could further diminish the possibility of achieving black control over black life in this country. The national black conventions held in the 1830s generally had three major objectives: first, the organizing of free black opposition to the "black laws" being passed in several northern states; second, the examination of the best strategies for advancing the free black population; and third, the discussion of the ways of bringing about an immediate end of slavery in the United States. At the national meeting held in Philadelphia in 1832 the delegates were treated to a debate between William Lloyd Garrison and Rev. R. R. Gurley, secretary of the ACS, over the merits of colonization. In the "Address to the Free Coloured Inhabitants of the United States" issued by the delegates, they noted that "we have been told in this convention, by the Secretary of the American Colonization Society, that there are causes which forbid our advancement in this country, which no humanity, no legislation, and no religion can control. Believe it not.

> Is not humanity susceptible of all the tender feelings of benevolence? Is not legislation supreme—and is not religion virtuous? Our oppressed situation arises from their opposite causes. There is an awakening spirit in our people to promote their elevation, which speaks volumes in their behalf.

The free black delegates had been convinced by William Lloyd Garrison's arguments and had vowed that in future conventions their numbers would be increased and American society would be confronted by "the *phenomena* of an *oppressed people,* deprived of the rights of citizenship, in the midst of an enlightened nation, devising plans and measures, for their personal and mental elevation, by *moral suasion alone.*"[52]

Unfortunately, by the end of the 1830s, it was unmistakably clear that "moral suasion alone" would not be sufficient to achieve the "elevation" that the free blacks sought. The larger abolitionist movement was in turmoil, with the older "moral suasionists" or Garrisonians in the American Anti-Slavery Society being challenged by the "political abolitionists" who supported "social reform through political action," rather than through "education and propaganda" or moral suasion alone. Lewis Tappen, James Birney, and the other members of the American and Foreign Anti-Slavery Society were among the leading members and supporters of the Liberty Party and later the Free-Soilers. The political abolitionists saw nothing wrong with alliances with nonabolitionists to stem the growth and influence of the "slave power" in the United States.[53]

Among free blacks the Garrisonian position held sway in Philadelphia and centered on the activities of the American Moral Reform Society, which was formed there following the 1834 national black convention. The new organization had four "rallying points": "Education, Temperance, Economy, and Universal Liberty."

> We hope to make our people, in theory and practice, thoroughly acquainted with these subjects, as a method of future action. Having placed our institution on the high and indisputable ground of natural laws and human rights, and being guided and actuated by the law of universal love to our fellow men, we have buried in the bosom of Christian benevolence all those national distinctions, complexional variations, geographical lines, and sectional bounds that have hitherto marked the history, character and operations of men; and now boldly plead for the Christian and moral elevation of the human race.[54]

The American Moral Reform Society was interested in the uplift or "elevation" of the entire human race, was opposed to any kinds of "complexional" distinctions, but was made up almost entirely of free people of color.[55]

Samuel Cornish, editor of *The Colored American,* a New York City newspaper, viewed as "visionary in the extreme" the attempts of the black moral reformers to bypass "complexional distinctions." Much of the literature disseminated by the society was signed, "Oppressed Americans." Cornish was flabbergasted. "Oppressed Americans! *who are they?* nonsense brethren!! You are COLORED AMERICANS."[56] Despite this criticism, the American Moral Reform Society and the entire black convention movement throughout the 1830s remained, according to Howard Bell, "completely

Garrisonian in outlook, championing equality of women, opposing 'complexional' conventions, and placing emphasis upon the plight of the slave rather than the elevation of the free."[57]

New York blacks were firmly allied with the political abolitionists and held "complexional conventions" to deal with "complexional issues," such as the need to repeal the New York State law that required only free blacks to own $250 worth of taxable property to vote. The New York State Convention meeting at Troy in August 1841 addressed this and a number of other *political* issues facing free blacks. Howard Bell believed that this New York meeting set a number of important precedents. "It was the first convention held with the chief emphasis upon the suffrage. It was probably the first state colored convention to send an appeal to the state legislature. And finally, it stands as the first of the Negro conventions on record to declare its independence of white meddling. In this respect it is the harbinger of a new age in Negro thought and action."[58]

The tone and emphasis on resistance and self-determination that began to surface at the New York State Convention in 1841 came to dominate the debates at the national black conventions in 1843, 1847, and 1848. Henry Highland Garnet, a fugitive slave, and a recently ordained Presbyterian minister in Troy, attended the 1843 national meeting, which was being held in Buffalo, New York. Garnet took the opportunity to point out that the free black conventions had been held for several years, "but we never, until this time, sent a word of consolation and advice to you." In his "Address to the Slaves of the United States of America," Garnet counseled resistance. He argued that Christian teachings opposed slavery and that the slaveholder "commits the highest crime against God and man," and thus it would be "sinful in the Extreme for you to make voluntary submission" to the slave masters. Enslaved Afro-Americans had a "moral obligation" to resist.

> The diabolical injustice by which your liberties are cloven down, NEITHER GOD, NOR ANGELS, OR JUST MEN, COMMAND YOU TO SUFFER FOR A SINGLE MOMENT. THEREFORE IT IS YOUR SOLEMN AND IMPERATIVE DUTY TO USE EVERY MEANS, BOTH MORAL, INTELLECTUAL, AND PHYSICAL, THAT PROMISES SUCCESS. If a band of heathen men should attempt to enslave a race of Christians, and to place their children under the influence of some false religion, surely, Heaven would frown upon the men who would not resist such aggression, even to death. If, on the other hand, a band of Christians should attempt to enslave a race of heathen men, and to entail slavery upon them, and to keep them in heathenism in the midst of Christianity, the God of heaven would smile

upon every effort which the injured might make to disenthral themselves.[59]

Garnet told the slaves to go to their oppressors "and tell them plainly, that
you *are determined to be free.*" If they do not respond to an appeal to their sense
of justice, "for ever after cease to toil for the heartless tyrants, who give you
no other reward but stripes and abuse. If they then commence the work of
death, they and not you, will be responsible for the consequences." Garnet
firmly believed that it would be better "to die freemen, than live to be slaves.

> Brethren, arise, arise! Strike for your lives and liberties. Now is
> the day and the hour. Let every slave throughout the land do this, and
> the days of slavery are numbered. You cannot be more oppressed than
> you have been—you cannot suffer greater cruelties than you have al-
> ready. *Rather die freemen than live to be slaves.* Remember that you are
> FOUR MILLIONS!

Garnet suggested that enslaved Africans and Afro-Americans must "so tor-
ment the God-cursed slaveholders, that they will be glad to let you go
free. . . .

> Let your motto be resistance! *resistance!* RESISTANCE! No oppressed
> people have ever secured their liberty without resistance. What kind of
> resistance you had better make, you must decide by the circumstances
> that surround you, and according to the suggestion of expediency.
> Brethren, adieu! Trust in the living God. Labor for the peace of the
> human race, and remember that you are FOUR MILLIONS.[60]

Despite its force and eloquence, Frederick Douglass objected strongly
to Garnet's declaration. The minutes to the 1843 Convention report that
Douglass complained "that there was too much physical force," in Garnet's
address and remarks. Douglass was for "trying the moral means a little
longer; that the address, could it reach the slaves, and the advice . . . be
followed, while it might not lead the slaves to rise in insurrection for liberty,
would nevertheless and necessarily be the occasion of an insurrection." Douglass believed the role of the delegates was "to avoid such a catastrophy." He
wanted "emancipation in a better way" and "he expected to have it." The
delegates were swayed by Douglass's opposition and they refused to endorse
Garnet's speech.[61]

Henry Highland Garnet attended the national black convention in
1847 in Troy, New York, and again spoke out for the violent overthrow of
slavery by the enslaved. William Wells Brown, ex-slave, friend of Douglass,
and strong Garrisonian, felt obliged to comment that "to those acquainted

with his talent and eloquence, it will be unnecessary to mention that the address produced much sensation."[62] In the 1844 state and national elections Garnet had worked strenuously for the Liberty Party, along with hundreds of other politically inclined abolitionists. James Birney, an abolitionist newspaper editor with strong religious convictions against slavery, was twice nominated for the presidency of the United States on the Liberty Party ticket. Garnet lectured at numerous Afro-American meetings and gatherings on the need for Afro-Americans to support Birney and the "party of abolition."[63]

Douglass and the black Garrisonians, however, dominated the proceedings at Troy in 1847, and despite Garnet's heated objections to the "moral suasionist tone," the concluding "Report of the Committee on Abolition" stated that the "best means of abolishing slavery is the proclamation of the truth, and the best means of destroying caste is the mental, moral, and industrial improvement of our people." They went on to proclaim "their entire disapprobation of any plan of emancipation involving a resort to bloodshed.

> With the facts of our condition before us, it is impossible for us to contemplate any appeal to the slave to take vengeance on his guilty master, but with the utmost reprobation. Your Committee regard any counsel of this sort as the perfection of folly, suicidal in the extreme, and abominably wicked. We should utterly frown down and wholly discountenance any attempt to lead our people to confide in brute force as a reformatory instrumentality. All argument put forth in favor of insurrection and bloodshed, however well intended, is either the result of an unpardonable impatience or an atheistic want of faith in the power of truth as a means of regenerating and reforming the world. Again we repeat, let us set our faces against all such absurd, unavailing, dangerous and mischievous ravings, emanating from what source they may. The voice of God and of common sense, equally point out a more excellent way, and that way is a faithful, earnest, and persevering enforcement of the great principles of justice and morality, religion and humanity. These are the only invincible and infallible means within our reach with which to overthrow this foul system of blood and ruin.

In keeping with the convention's overall concern for the establishment of a "National black press" that would be involved in "education and propaganda," the committee resolved "that, in the language of inspired wisdom, there shall be no peace to the wicked, and that this guilty nation shall have no peace, and that we will do all that we can to agitate!! agitate!! *Agitate!!*

till our rights are restored and our Brethren are redeemed from their cruel chains."[64]

And suppose this agitation led to a violent response by the dominant white society against the slave or free black population? Douglass, Alexander Crummell, Thomas Van Rensselaer, and the other delegates did not address that possibility at the conventions in 1847 or 1848. Indeed, at the meeting in Cleveland in September 1848, the entire issue of the potential for violent upheaval in the slave states was not even discussed, perhaps in part because Henry Garnet decided not to attend. Frederick Douglass, still a Garrisonian, was elected president of the meeting and there was only a half-hearted endorsement of the new Free-Soil Party, which had been formed in Buffalo earlier in the year by a coalition of northern white interest groups, only some of which were calling for the immediate end of slavery. In the resolution that finally passed, the moral suasionist thrust was quite apparent.

> RESOLVED, That while we heartily engage in recommending to our people the Free Soil movement, and the support of the Buffalo Convention, nevertheless we claim and are determined to maintain the higher standard and more liberal views which have heretofore characterized us as abolitionists.

In a statement that was later added as a preamble to the above resolution, the delegates did admit the need of *some* political activity, since "American Slavery is politically and morally an evil of which this country stands guilty, and cannot be abolished alone through the instrumentality of moral suasion. . . ."[65]

In the final "Address to the Colored People in the United States" issued by the 1848 convention, the free black leaders counseled their "brethren to occupy memberships and stations among white people, and in white institutions just so fast as our rights are secured to us." Afro-Americans "must avail themselves of *white* institutions, not because they are white, but because they afford a more convenient means of improvement." They wanted the free black masses to "dispense with finery, and the gaities which have rendered us proverbial, and save your money." In pursuit of "the equality we aim to accomplish, we should therefore press into all the trades, professions and callings into which honorable white men press." But since it was often difficult for free blacks to move into the same states with whites as settlers, it was certainly going to be difficult to enter the same trades and professions with whites. "Visionary in the extreme" was how Samuel Cornish characterized the attempts of the American Moral Reform Society to work for black advancement on a noncomplexional basis. The same charge could be hurled with some degree of accuracy at the "Address to the Colored People" issued by the 1848 national black convention.[66]

Political events in the United States in the early 1850s, were moving against them, however, and free blacks had to move beyond protest to renewed organized resistance to survive the increasing oppression they confronted in this country. As part of the famous (or infamous) Compromise of 1850, introduced by Kentucky Senator Henry Clay, a new Fugitive Slave Law was included to stem the increasing secessionist sentiments in the slave South. Many aspects of the compromise touched on the issue of slavery, such as the prohibition on Congress to interfere with the domestic slave trade, and the opposition to the abolition of slavery in the District of Columbia. The fugitive slave bill was added in hopes of bolstering the constitutional guarantees of the right of slaveholders to retrieve their slave property in states opposed to "slave catching."[67]

Article 4, Section 2, Clause 3 of the United States Constitution stated: "No person held to service or labor in one State, under the laws thereof, escaping into another shall, in consequence of any law or regulation therein, be discharged from such service or labor; but shall be delivered up on claim of the party, to whom such service or labor may be due." The United States Congress passed the Fugitive Slave Law of 1793 to spell out and clarify this clause. It provided that the owner of an escaped slave could apply to a district or circuit judge of the United States for a certificate to enable him to return the slave to the state from which he fled. According to the General Assembly of Virginia in 1849, however, the 1793 law was inadequate and impractical "because the master . . . a stranger, must go into a free state, seize his slave without form or process of law, and unaccompanied by a single civil officer, must carry that slave in the face of a fanatical and infuriated population . . . a distance of two or three hundred miles to the place where the judge may happen to reside, before he can have any legal or judicial action in his case. . . ." Since there were no provisions for assistance from federal marshals to enforce a ruling of the judge, the slaveowner had to make it back to his home territory with the slave without federal or local protection.[68]

Under the provisions of the bill introduced in Congress by Democratic Senator James M. Mason of Virginia in January 1850, slaveholders or their agents were permitted to arrest fugitives without due process and without warrants, and the enforcement of this procedure was now placed in the hands of U.S. commissioners and marshals. If satisfactory proof was given that the individual taken was indeed a fugitive who owed service to the claimant, these federal officials were required to issue a certificate that would be "sufficient warrant for taking or removing such fugitive . . . to the State or territory from which he or she had fled." This initial measure also provided that anyone attempting to harbor, conceal, or rescue a fugitive slave would be liable to a one thousand dollar fine, but in the final version, signed by President Millard Fillmore on 18 September 1850, persons assisting fugitives were liable to the fine *and* imprisonment for up to six months. The accused fugitive was not allowed a trial by jury, and if the fugitive was remanded to the claimant, the federal commissioners were to receive ten dollars, but under other circumstances (for example, if the accused was set free) the commissioner received only five dollars. To many abolitionists, this latter provision appeared to be a virtual bribe of federal officials to turn the alleged fugitive over to the claimant.[69]

The substantial disarray that plagued the abolitionist movement in the 1840s meant that the task of assisting runaway slaves, "fugitives from justice," had fallen primarily on the shoulders of the free black resistance movement. As historian Benjamin Quarles made clear, before 1850 (and afterwards), "many of the vigilance committees had totally or predominantly Negro membership." The New York Committee of Vigilance, led by David Ruggles, the New England Freedom Association in Boston, the Colored Vigilance Committee of Detroit, and the Philadelphia Vigilance Committee were made up of free blacks (and not a few ex-slaves) who took responsibility for aiding the fugitives in a variety of ways. The committees provided the runaways with lodging for a few days, "purchasing clothing and medicine for them, providing them with small sums of money, informing them as to their legal rights and giving them legal protection from kidnappers." Benjamin Quarles also noted that "a primary function of the vigilance committee was to help a slave establish himself in a new location, to furnish him with letters of introduction, to help him find a job, and to give him guidance and protection while he was thus engaged in getting started."[70]

With the passage of the Fugitive Slave Law of 1850, however, many former slaves who had become "established" in northern communities now felt threatened and fled to Canada. Every northern city with even a small free black population was touched by this new "black exodus," although "outright defiance" of the law was advocated at mass meetings held within months in Pittsburgh, Boston, and Philadelphia.[71] Larry Gara in his study of the underground railroad pointed out that the 1850 law "stimulated some new activity on the part of northern blacks.

In Chicago they organized a police organization to protect themselves against "being brought back to bondage." The organization of seven divisions of six men each was to patrol the city in turns and "keep an eye out for interlopers." A New York meeting of Negroes, mostly women, passed resolutions condemning the Fugitive Slave Law and counseled armed resistance to it. The chairman appointed a secret committee to assist any fugitives whose liberty might be endangered.[72]

Following the return to slavery of the first fugitive under the terms of the new law—James Hamlet in New York in the fall of 1850—the worst fears of many free blacks and ex-slaves were confirmed, and thousands left Pittsburgh, Cleveland, and Boston for Canada. At a meeting held on 14 October 1850 at Faneuil Hall in Boston, Frederick Douglass, flanked by Charles Remond and William and Ellen Craft, counseled black Bostonians to die rather than return their brothers and sisters to slavery. "We must be prepared should this law be put into operation to see the streets of Boston running with blood." It should be recalled that two years before, Douglass was opposing violence and supporting "moral suasion" as the best means for dealing with the legalized oppression of Afro-Americans.[73]

In the July 1853 call for a national black convention in Rochester, the signatories mentioned several of the reasons for this national meeting.

> The Fugitive Slave Act, the most cruel, unconstitutional and scandalous outrage of modern times—the proscriptive legislation of several States with a view to drive our people from their borders—the exclusion of our children from schools supported by our money—the prohibition of the exercise of the franchise—the exclusion of colored citizens from the jury box—the social barriers erected against our learning trades— the wily and vigorous efforts of the American Colonization Society to employ the arm of government to expel us from our native land—and withal the propitious awakening to the fact of our condition at home and abroad, which has followed the publication of "Uncle Tom's Cabin"—call trumpet-tongued for our union, cooperation and action in the premises.[74]

There was no mention in this 1853 statement of an interest in considering emigration outside the United States as a way of dealing with the problems facing free blacks. But for the previous six years, the black *state* conventions were debating emigration as an alternative strategy for the advancement of Afro-Americans toward greater freedom and self-determination. Henry Highland Garnet was joined by Martin Delany and Samuel Ringgold Ward in open support for Afro-American emigration to Canada, the Caribbean, or Africa. At the Ohio state convention in 1849, two moral suasionists, David Jenkins and John Mercer Langston, declared that they looked forward "to see the emigration of the colored people and the establishment of a Negro nation."[75] Despite the pleas of Langston and others, the Ohio conventions of 1849 and 1852 narrowly defeated a resolution endorsing the emigrationist position. But the Maryland state convention held in Baltimore in late July 1852 passed resolutions supporting emigration, with a slight preference for Liberia over Canada as a place of settlement (to the delight of the American Colonization Society). In September 1852, however, at a meeting of black refugees in Toronto, Canada, led by Henry Bibb, then editor of *The Voice of the Fugitive,* a resolution was passed inviting the entire free black population of the United States to come to Canada. This invitation was once again extended at a meeting held in Amhurstburgh, Canada, in June 1853.[76]

When the national black convention opened in Rochester, New York, in August 1853, it was dominated by the more conservative black leaders, including Frederick Douglass, J. W. C. Pennington, James McCure Smith, and Charles Ray; and there was no serious discussion of the need to endorse "emigration" as a worthwhile form of resistance against free black oppression resulting from the enforcement of fugitive slave laws. Howard Bell has argued that "national organization on the home front from food supply to propaganda, and from education to semi-judicial decisions, was the proposed answer then of the conservatives to the challenge of the emigrationists for leadership of Negro thought in America." Disappointed with what they considered were the inadequacies of "the Colored National Convention," the emigrationists, led by Martin Delany and J. Theodore Holly, issued a "Call for a National Emigration Convention" only six weeks after the meeting in Rochester.[77]

In October 1853, a full-fledged debate took place in the columns of *Frederick Douglass' Paper* between James H. Whitfield, a young black poet, and William Watkins, Douglass's associate editor, over the merits of the emigrationist schemes. Letters flew back and forth for several issues between supporters and opponents of emigration and colonization, and usually the only pro-emigrationist statements published were those of Whitfield. Frederick Douglass did not participate in the debate, but his newspaper was otherwise filled with editorials and resolutions condemning the emigrationist position.[78]

Floyd Miller, in *The Search for a Black Nationality: Black Colonization and Emigration, 1787–1863* (1975), presented a detailed, though somewhat misleading, account of this debate among Afro-American leaders. When the conservative leaders met in Rochester in 1853, they passed a resolution calling for the formation of a "National Council of the Colored People" for the purpose of "improving the character, developing the intelligence, maintaining the rights, and organizing a Union of the Colored People of the free states."[79] Floyd Miller argued that the creation of the National Council demonstrated that Douglass, James McCure Smith, William Watkins, William Whipper, Charles Ray, and the other conservatives had accepted "the basic premise that blacks could, through unity, operate outside the structure of white society while remaining within the United States." Miller also asserted that these leaders "also recognized that blacks were a separate caste within the larger society, united by the oppression which they faced in common, and they sought to capitalize on this sense of group identity by forging a network of separate institutions—under the aegis of a National Council—for the advancement of the race."[80] But as we have seen, separate or "complexional" institutions were exactly what Frederick Douglass, William Whipper, William Watkins, and the other black Garrisonians, who dominated the national black convention movement, had been *opposing* for years. In supporting the formation of a National Council, the delegates to the 1853 convention were actually dodging the issue of emigration that was pressing upon the free black community at the time. The temporary support that they gave to a "complexional" National Council was really an attempt to avoid having seriously to deal with the emigrationist challenge.

Miller and several other historians who have examined this period did not fully comprehend the relationship between the political alternatives being offered the free black masses in the 1840s and 1850s, and emerging Afro-American cultural values. When Henry Highland Garnet, Martin Delany, J. Theodore Holly, or Henry Bibb suggested that for the "colored people of the United States" to elevate themselves and control their own destiny, they must consider mass emigration to more hospitable environments; these more militant emigrationist leaders were appealing to the notions of "peoplehood," resistance, and self-determination that were becoming part of Afro-American culture during the antebellum period. At the same time, when Douglass, Whipper, Purvis, Watkins, and the conservatives suggested that Afro-Americans not have "complexional institutions," or perhaps have them temporarily, or when they objected to the word "African" in the name of predominantly black organizations and endorsed "assimilation" or "integration" into white institutions, they were appealing to values prominent among some white Americans (the radical abolitionists), but these values and positions were basically alien to the antebellum Afro-American experience, both slave and free.

Frederick Douglass and the other supporters of assimilation were caught up in "the Promise of American Democracy"—liberty, equality, the pursuit of the dollar—and firmly believed that this promise had also been extended to Afro-Americans. But the experience of Afro-Americans living in antebellum America provided very little support for the acceptance of a value system emphasizing individualism, liberty, and advancement through capitalistic exploitation of the laboring classes. Floyd Miller in *The Search for a Black Nationality,* Leonard Sweet in *Black Images of America, 1784–1870* (1976), and Wilson Moses in *The Golden Age of Black Nationalism, 1850–1925* (1977), all spend a great deal of time examining the "ideological inconsistency and ambivalence" of antebellum black leaders who at one point were supporting integration into the larger white society, and at other points supported separate or "complexional institutions" and emigration as the more important means for advancing the race. But when we examine these leaders within the larger cultural as well as the social and political context of Afro-America, we find that their shifting from support of one position or strategy to another was often dictated by the social and political exigencies of the moment. However, it was only when these leaders supported strategies guaranteeing survival with dignity, resistance against oppression, self-determination, and social advancement that they enunciated political positions complementary to the system of values and beliefs developing among the Afro-American masses. Since Miller, Sweet, Moses, and others did not place their discussions of the strategies advocated by Afro-American leaders within this larger Afro-American cultural context, they provide us with no explanation of why certain leaders and strategies for advancement were popular among the black masses, or why certain other leaders and positions had very little mass support during the same period.[81]

Frederick Douglass supported integrationist strategies for black advancement, and at times counseled "violent resistance against unjust oppression." Henry Highland Garnet also advocated resistance, but by the 1850s he despaired of the possibility that Afro-Americans would be treated fairly in this country. Along with Martin Delany, J. Theodore Holly, and others, Garnet actively worked for the emigration of free blacks to an independent settlement in Africa. This latter group of leaders supported freedom, resistance, *and* self-determination.

The material conditions of enslaved and free Afro-Americans provided the experiential bases for the development of the cultural values of freedom, resistance, and black control over black life and destiny in antebellum America. The possibility of integration into American society as equal citizens appeared remote at best. Emigration, on the other hand, was a viable alternative, given the enforcement of the Fugitive Slave Law, and had great potential for bringing about freedom from oppression and self-determination. As full-fledged citizens in a black-controlled nation in the Caribbean or a black-controlled settlement in West Africa, Africans and

Afro-Americans hoped to be free of the domination of whites and in positions of authority to determine their own destiny. While there were numerous strategies suggested as to how free and enslaved blacks could improve their social and economic status, the emigrationists appealed to both the emerging Afro-American cultural value system and the individual and collective interests of many free blacks before the coming of the Civil War.

FOUR

Keep Your Mind on Freedom

I's free, I's free, I's free at las'!
Thank God A'mighty, I's free at las'!

Once was a moaner, jus' like you,
Thank God A'mighty, I's free at las'!

I fasted an' I prayed till I came thew,
Thank God A'mighty, I's free at las'!

Afro-American freedom song

When de war wuz ovuh, de govn'ment jes let de slaves drop. Den
ye had tuh, 'root like a pig er die. . . . Some white folks kep'
slaves wukin aftuh de war. Way back in de woods dey made ye
wuk an' give ye nuffin fur it. Po' slaves! Dey didn't know no
bettuh. Dey doin' it now down Souf. Dem sharecropper is jes like
slaves. Dey don' know slavery is ovuh.

ARCHIE BOOKER, ex-slave, 1937

THE MEANING OF FREEDOM changed for the masses of Afro-Americans after the Civil War. Afro-Americans had been praying unceasingly for their deliverance from bondage, and once that "Day of Jubilee" came and went, many initially suffered from feelings of profound disappointment. Freedom had been considered the ultimate goal of their individual and collective struggles under slavery and had become one of the predominant values that defined the Afro-American experience in the United States. The conditions that the freedpeople faced in the South following emancipation meant that freedom continued to be valued, not primarily as an objective, but as a means or strategy for obtaining more elusive and substantial goals, such as self-determination and social advancement. Although many Afro-Americans were disappointed by the severe limitations placed upon their newly acquired freedom, most were not as cynical in their judgment as Patsy Mitchner, a former slave interviewed in the 1930s, who compared slavery and freedom to two snakes, both of them "full of pisen" [poison]. Slavery was a "bad thing," but freedom "of de kin' we got wid nothin' to live on was bad [too]. . . . Both bit de nigger, an' dey was both bad."[1]

The former slaves interviewed in the 1930s were questioned about the responses to emancipation of their families, friends, and communities. Their testimony provides important insights into "what freedom meant" to the masses of newly emancipated Afro-Americans.[2] Wylie Nealy, for example, recollected that "liberty and freedom was all I ever heard any colored folks say dey expected to get out of de War, and mighty proud of dat." Among those Afro-Americans enslaved in Gordon County, South Carolina, "nobody knowed they was goin' to have a war till it was done broke out and they was fightin' about it." Nealy was literally swooped up by Sherman's invading army and eventually he joined "a colored regiment nine months." Nealy remained with the Union Army camp in Georgia for a while before being mustered out in August 1865. "Everybody was proud to be free. They shouted and sung." And initially food rations and cabins were provided for the liberated Afro-Americans by Union forces.

They all did pretty well till the War was about to end, then they was told to scatter and nowheres to go. Cabins all tore down or burned.

No work to do. There was no money to pay. I got hungry lots of times.
No plantations was divided and the masters didn't have no more than
the slaves had when the War was done. I never went back or seen any
more of Old Master or Missus. Everybody left and a heap of the colored
folks went where rations could be issued to them and some followed on
in the armies.[3]

Charles Grandy, who was enslaved in Virginia, believed that everybody
was happy when the war came.

When de gun was turned on Sumter, many a nigger's heart was set at
ease. . . . Slaves was some kind o' glad when dey 'mancipated, all dey
sing was:

> Slavery chain is broke at las'
> Broke at las', broke at las'
> Slavery chain is broke at las'
> Praise God 'till I die.
>
> Come along valiant souls
> Git yo' words all ready
> Ma'ch wid General thoo de fiel'
> Dis ole chatterin' groun'
> Oh! Slavery chain is, etc.

Some o' de slaves didn' hardly b'lieve dey was free. After de war
was over, de army had to stay in de Souf twelve months fo' dey could
make de niggers know dey was free. An' dey jes' kept a wukin' fer de
white man fer nuttin'.[4]

Many former slaves, especially those residing in Virginia during the
war, described the initial euphoria and celebrations of freedom. "De news
come on a Thursday," recalled Charlotte Brown, a former slave from Woods
Crossing, Virginia, "An' all de slaves been shoutin' an' carrin' on till ev'ry-
body was all tired out." What was even more memorable was "de fust Sunday
of freedom."

We was all sittin' roun' restin' an' tryin' to think what freedom meant
an' ev'ybody was quiet an' peaceful. All at once ole Sister Carrie who
was near 'bout a hundred started in to talkin':

> Tain't no mo' sellin' today.
> Tain't no mo' hirin' today,
> Tain't no pullin' off shirts today,

> Its stomp down freedom today.
> Stomp it down!

An' when she says, "Stomp it down," all de slaves commence to shoutin' wid her:

> Stomp down Freedom today—
> Stomp it down!
> Stomp down Freedom today.

Wasn't no mo' peace dat Sunday. Ev'ybody started in to sing an' shout once mo'. Fust thing you know dey done made up music to Sister Carrie's stomp song an' sang an' shouted dat song all de res' de day. Chile, dat was one glorious time![5]

Annie Harris, also from Virginia, remembered when freedom came.

We was dancin' an' prancin' and yellin' wid a big barn fire [bonfire] jus' ablazin' an' de white folks not darin' to come outside de big house. . . . [E]verybody fo' miles around was singin freedom songs. One went like dis:

> I's free, I's free, I's free at las'!
> Thank God A'mighty, I's free at las'!
>
> Once was a moaner jus' like you.
> Thank God A'mighty, I's free at las'!
>
> I fasted an' I prayed till I came thew,
> Thank God A'mighty, I's free at las'![6]

After the celebrations the former slaves had to deal with the ambiguous reality of freedom, and their responses reflected the dark shadows lingering over their precarious future. "Free at las' de Mancipation Proclamation done set us free!" Marrinda Jane Singleton still recalled this cry of the slaves, "as well as 'de slavery chain done broke and gone!'

Slaves were runned from the plantation 'dout nothin' but us han's, no house to shelter us, and no food. We jes' had to make hit de best dat we could. Dis, you see, caused mo' crime 'specially stealin' 'mong us slaves. Dis caused a heavy leavin' of slaves after freedom from de country to flockin' to dem large cities and towns lookin' fer wurk in order to git a livin'. Many hired dem selves to po' white farmers fer little or no wages to wurk on de farm as a wash woman and whatever she could do. Some found wurk in cities 'round docks, on boats as cooks, waiters, etc.

As a rule dar was very few slaves what didn't know how to cook and do dat house wurk.[7]

Fannie Berry, another Virginian, was unimpressed by the Yankee gift of "temporary" freedom.

> When de Yankees come dey sot de niggers free an' de niggers went on wukin' jus' like dey did befo' only now whut dey make is dere'n an' dey don't have tuh take et an' put et away in de master's barn. An' de whites couldn't say nothin' 'cause dey was po' as de niggers an' besides de Yankees was dere to watch 'em.
>
> But after while de Yankees went on back up North, an' den de "po'hickories" got tuh actin' up. Dey would put on de ole uniforms de Yankees done lef' behin' an' go ridin' all over de lan' at night in bands jus' ah shootin' up all de niggers dey saw. Dey would shoot 'em daid an' ride on. An' some one finally sent word up No'th to de Yankees an' de Yankees come aridin' back an' dem ole whites was jus' as nice an' pleasant fo' a while as could be. Long as de Yankees was aroun'. But soon's de Yankees leave dey start in again. An' don't you know, Yankees had tuh come back tuh Appamattox three times fo' de whites leave us po' niggers alone?[8]

Many Afro-Americans enslaved in the lower South—Alabama, Texas, Mississippi, Louisiana—only learned of their freedom with the coming of Union troops. Susan Merritt believed that "lots of niggers was kilt after freedom." She had been enslaved in Rusk County, Texas, and "the slaves in Harrison County turn loose right at freedom and them in Rusk County wasn't.

> But they hears about it and runs away to freedom in Harrison County and they owners have 'em bushwacked, that shot down. You could see lots of niggers hangin' to trees in Sabine bottom right after freedom, 'cause they catch 'em swimmin' 'cross Sabine River and shoot 'em. They sure am goin' be lots of soul cry against 'em in Judgment.[9]

John White, who was enslaved in Georgia, claimed that even after the war ended, "I stay on the plantation till a soldier tells me about freedom. The master never tells us—Negroes working just like before the War. That's when I leave the fust time."[10]

Given the conditions surrounding emancipation and freedom, especially for the "contrabands" or refugees who followed the Union Army, James Lucas believed that "some of 'em was worse 'n slaves after the War." Lucas was enslaved in Mississippi and "was a grown-up man with a wife and two chillen when de War broke out.

> Slaves didn't know what to 'spect from freedom, but a lot of dem hoped dey would be fed and kept by de government. Dey all had different ways o' thinkin' about it. Mostly, though, dey was just like me, dey didn't know just 'zackly what it meant. It was just somethin' dat de white folks and slaves all de time talk about. Dat's all. Folks dat ain't never been free don't rightly know de *feel* of bein' free.

When the Union troops came through his area, Lucas joined up and fought in several major battles in Mississippi, Pennsylvania, and Virginia. "I was on hand when General Lee handed his sword to General Grant." As a recruit, he visited many camps opened for the contrabands and recalled the desperate straits in which the ex-slaves found themselves.

> After de War was over de slaves was worse off dan when dey had marsters. Some of 'em was put in stockades at Angola, Louisiana, and some in de terrible corral at Natchez. Dey weren't used to de stuff de Yankees fed 'em. Dey fed 'em wasp-nest bread, 'stead o' corn pone and hoecake, and all such like. Dey caught diseases and died by de hundreds, just like flies. Dey had been fooled into thinkin' it would be good times, but it was de worst times dey ever seen. 'Tweren't no place for 'em to go, no bed to sleep on, and no roof over dey heads. Dem what could get back home set out with dey minds made up to stay on de land. Most of dey marsters took 'em back so dey worked de land again. I means dem what lived to get back to dey folks was more'n glad to work! Dey done had a sad lesson.[11]

The "sad lesson" of freedom was only beginning for thousands of freedpeople with the conditions they faced in Union camps and forts around Washington, D.C., Alexandria, Fortress Monroe, Hampton Roads, Norfolk, and Portsmouth, Virginia.[12] When the news arrived in many rural sections, the newly emancipated Afro-Americans began to drift toward the larger urban areas in hopes of finding friends, family, and subsistence, or as Marrinda Jane Singleton put it, the freedpeople were "flockin' to dem large cities and towns lookin' fer wurk in order to git a livin'." But in both rural and urban areas the former slaves, who were merely testing the waters of freedom, found themselves inundated by a tidal wave of white opposition, contempt, violence, and terror. Whereas during the war "black freedom" was considered a military strategy by the Union leadership, immediately after the war it became part of a political strategy for maintaining Republican strength and power in the reconstruction of the South.

Black Freedom versus White Terrorism

When twenty local black ministers and church officials visited the headquarters of Major General William Sherman at Savannah, Georgia, in January 1865, they made it clear that they knew the primary and secondary objectives of the war. As 67 year-old Reverend Garrison Frazier put it:

> The object of the war was not, at first, to give the slaves their freedom, but the sole object of the war was, at first, to bring the rebellious States back into the Union, and their loyalty to the laws of the United States. Afterwards, knowing the value that was set on the slaves by the rebels, the President thought that his Proclamation would stimulate them to lay down their arms, reduce them to obedience, and help to bring back the rebel States; and their not doing so has now made the freedom of the slaves a part of the war.

The spokesmen for the black ministers, however, also made it clear that despite the secondary consideration given black freedom, "there is not a [black] man in this city that could be started to help the rebels one inch, for that would be suicide."[13]

After the surrender of the Confederate Army, the use of black troops as part of the occupying forces, and the attempt of the Republican Party to use the freedpeople to establish a political base in many parts of the South, served as the major justifications for violence and terrorism by the vanquished white southerners. When the war ended, there were nearly 125,000 black troops in the Union Army, out of a total of 1,052,038. But too many war-weary white soldiers were mustered out too quickly, so that by the fall of 1865 there were 226,611, most of them troops stationed in the former Confederacy, with a disproportionately high number of black soldiers (83,079), many of whom had nowhere else to go.[14]

Most white southerners objected to the occupying troops, and it was doubly offensive when the Union soldiers were black. Many of the early incidents of violence following the surrender were sparked by clashes between white civilians and black soldiers. The "mass slaughters" of Afro-Americans in Memphis in April and May 1866 and in July in New Orleans had as precipitating events the conflicts arising from the stationing of black troops in these cities. As Herbert Aptheker has pointed out, "In the Memphis outbreak, forty-six Negroes (most of them Union veterans) and two white radicals were slaughtered, about seventy-five more were wounded, five Negro women were ravished, ninety homes, twelve schools and four churches were burned, and several radical whites, especially teachers, were driven out of the city. . . .

> In the New Orleans affair, the official casualties totaled thirty-five Negroes dead, three whites dead, one hundred and twenty-seven Negroes wounded, and nineteen whites (including ten policemen) wounded. The Army Surgeon at the scene expressed the belief, in his official report, that about ten more Negroes were killed and another twenty wounded, whose identities he never learned.

In many other instances of violence and rioting in southern cities and towns in the decade following the war, black soldiers and veterans were the objects of organized violence and mayhem by white vigilantes.[15]

The political organizing carried out by the "Union Leagues" or "Loyal Leagues" of the Republican Party was considered another major provocation to white terrorism. During the same years the Union Leagues were organizing black Republicans (1865–67), former Confederates were beginning to reassume power in southern state legislatures.[16] Under the terms of Presidential Reconstruction, many of the same persons who had led the Confederate governments were returned to office in the elections of 1865 and 1866. These legislators saw as one of their major tasks the restoration of the mechanisms for maintaining black forced labor following the end of slavery. The Mississippi Constitutional Convention in 1865, for example, outlined the problem in this fashion: "The institution of slavery having been destroyed . . . the legislature at its next session . . . shall provide by law for the protection and security of the person and property of the freedmen of the state, and guard them and the State against any evil that may arise from their sudden emancipation."[17]

The notorious "Black Codes" would be one of the responses of the southern white legislators elected under the terms of Presidential Reconstruction to the passage of the Thirteenth Amendment, which outlawed "involuntary servitude." Passed in 1865 and 1866 in all of the Confederate states, the Black Codes took a wide variety of forms, but as a group they most resembled the old Southern slave codes and fugitive slave laws, and had as one of their prime objectives the re-establishment of white control over black labor. Historian John Hope Franklin has provided a concise summary of the thrust of these laws.

> Several of them undertook to limit the areas in which Negroes could purchase or rent property. Vagrancy laws imposed heavy penalties that

were designed to force all Negroes to work whether they wanted to or not. The control of blacks by white employers was about as great as that which slaveholders had exercised. If a Negro quit his job, he could be arrested and imprisoned for breach of contract. Negroes were not allowed to testify in court except in cases involving their race. Numerous fines were imposed for seditious speeches, insulting gestures or acts, absence from work, violating curfew, and the possession of firearms. There was, of course, no enfranchisement of blacks and no indication that in the future they could look forward to full citizenship and participation in a democracy.[18]

This white supremacist legislation, the widespread violence and terrorism, the rejection by these southern legislatures of the Fourteenth Amendment to the Constitution, which guaranteed citizenship and "due process" to former slaves, outraged northern public opinion and led to the overthrow of Presidential Reconstruction and the assumption of control over the unrepentent South by the so-called Radical Republicans in the U.S. Congress.[19] With the passage of a series of reconstruction acts between March 1867 and March 1868, over the vetoes of President Andrew Johnson, the Confederacy was divided into five military districts in which martial law would prevail. Each state was to draw up a new constitution at a convention to which delegates were elected on the basis of universal manhood suffrage. No state was to be readmitted to the Union until the state constitution was approved by Congress and the Fourteenth Amendment had been ratified. The acts also barred former Confederate officials from participating in the new governments unless they submitted to an "iron-clad oath of allegiance" to the Union.[20]

The elimination of thousands of ex-Confederates from participation in the new Reconstruction governments and the enfranchisement of the freedmen further infuriated southern whites and ushered in a new era of terror and violence led by the Ku Klux Klan. Allen Trelease, in his study, *White Terror: The Ku Klux Klan Conspiracy and Southern Reconstruction* (1971), made it clear that "the overriding purpose of the Ku Klux movement . . . was the maintenance or restoration of white supremacy in every walk of life. In the minds of many [white] men, the most urgent reason for resorting to vigilante activity was to check any incipient Negro rising." The newly emancipated Afro-Americans were to be kept "in their place" through threats, intimidation, and violence more ferocious in nature than anything carried out during the antebellum years.[21]

The prototypes for the postbellum vigilantes or "regulators" were the antebellum slave patrols and local "white militias." In most southern communities before the Civil War, serving on the slave patrols was considered part of a white landowner's "civic duty." In other areas hired patrollers were compensated by the local slaveholders. Theoretically, the duties of the patrollers were to break up unlawful slave assemblies, to seize any slaves away from their plantation without a pass, and to search for runaways and any stolen goods in the slave quarters. In Mississippi and several other states the patrollers were given permission by law to administer at least fifteen lashes to slaves they encountered without proper passes.[22]

The former slaves themselves, however, provide a somewhat different perspective on the historical reality of the slave patrols. Robert Falls, who was enslaved on the Goforth Plantation in Chatham County, North Carolina, offered this personal account of how the patrollers operated.

> Marster Goforth counted himself a good old Baptist Christian. The one good deed he did, I will never forget, he made us all go to church every Sunday. That was the onliest place off the farm we ever went. Every time a slave went off the place, he had to have a pass, except we didn't for church. Everybody in that county knowed that the Goforth niggers didn't have to have a pass to go to church. But that didn't make no difference to the patterrollers. They'd hide in the bushes, or wait alongside of the road, and when the niggers come from meeting, the patterrollers say, "Where's your pass?" Us Goforth niggers used to start running soon as we was out of church. We never got caught. That is why I tell you I can't use my legs like I used to. If you was caught without a pass the patterrollers give you five licks. They was licks! You take a bunch of five to seven patterrollers each giving five licks and the blood flows.[23]

John B. Cade, who collected over eighty interviews with former slaves in Louisiana, concluded that for the patrollers and others, "Negro hunting, Negro catching, Negro watching, and Negro whipping constituted the favorite sport of many youthful whites."[24]

The "ghostly garb" and "satanic equipment" associated with the Klan evidently originated with the "paddle-rollers." Marshall Butler, an ex-slave interviewed by the Federal Writers Project, recalled that "de white folks were the 'Paddle-Rollers' and had masks on dere faces. They looked like niggers wid de devil in dere eyes." In these disguises the patrollers would attempt to frighten unsuspecting slaves, but as ex-slave Leonard Franklin recalled, sometimes this practice backfired.

> A paterole come in one night before freedom and asked for a drink of water. He said he was thirsty. He had a rubber thing on and drank two or three buckets of water. His rubber bag swelled up and made his

head or the thing that looked like his head under the hood grow taller. Instead of gettin' 'fraid, mother threw a shovelful of hot ashes on him and I'll tell you he lit out from there and never did come back no more.[25]

Folklorist Gladys-Marie Fry, in her *Night Riders in Black Folk History* (1975), examined both plantation records and slave sources and found that for a variety of reasons the slave patrols were generally ineffective. Through a communication system developed by the slaves, they were usually able to circumvent the techniques of surveillance utilized by the patrols. Not only did the slaves put their ears to the ground to detect approaching horses, but according to Mamie Ardella Robinson, the slaves also made use of the "first telephone . . . in existence."

I know they used to break up their meetings and that they had the first telephone that was in existence. They . . . tied a rope running it up across the mountain, or through the valley, and somebody up there to watch the road while the rest of them was down there having service. Well, when he saw someone coming and knew that they were in danger, he would just pull this. They might be a mile away but they'd know to scatter. They used a rope, across a woodland, maybe across a field. It had to be something there to support the rope, so it had to be up off the ground in order to make a sound over where it was supposed to be. . . . And then they would have their meeting around there and that tree began to shake, they'd know that there was a danger and they would run.[26]

West Turner, who was born in 1842 in Virginia, also made it vividly clear that "there was ways of beating the patterollers.

De best way to head 'em off. I 'member once when we was gonna have a meetin' down in de woods near de river. Well, dey made me de lookout boy, an' when de paddyrollers come down de lane past de church—you see dey was 'spectin' dat de niggers gonna hold a meetin' dat night— well, sir, dey tell me to step out f'm de woods an' let 'em see me. Well, I does, an' de paddyrollers dat was on horse back come a chasin' arter me, jus' a-gallopin' down de lane to beat de band. Well I was jus' ahead of 'em, an' when they got almost up wid me I jus' ducked into de woods. Course de paddyrollers couldn't stop so quick an' kep' on 'roun' de ben', an' den dere came a-screamin' an' cryin' dat make you think dat hell done bust loose. Dem ole paddyrollers done rid plumb into a great line of grape vines dat de slaves had stretched 'cross de path. An' dese vines tripped up de horses an' throwed de ole paddyrollers off in de bushes. An' some done landed mighty hard, cause dey was a-limpin' roun' an' cussin' an' callin' fo' de slaves to come an' help dem, but dem slaves got plenty o' sense. Dey lay in de bushes an' hole dere sides a-laughin', but ain't none o' 'em gonna risk bein' seen.[27]

This trick of stringing grapevines across the roads often caused great injury to the patrollers. Former slave, Mandy Cooper, remembered an incident in which several patrollers were killed.

> Paddy-Rollers were a constant dread to the Negroes. They would whip the poor darkeys unmercifully without any cause. One night while the Negroes were gathering for a big party and dance they got wind of the approaching Paddy-Rollers in large numbers on horseback. The Negro men did not know what to do for protection, they became desperate and decided to gather a quantity of grapevines and tied them fast at a dark place in the road. When the Paddy-Rollers came thundering down the road bent on deviltry and unaware of the trap set for them, they plunged head-on into these strong grapevines and three of their number were killed and a score was badly injured. Several horses had to be shot following injuries.

> When the news of this happening spread it was many months before the Paddy-Rollers were again heard of.[28]

The effectiveness of using passes to allow slaves to move about from plantation to plantation was undercut when one of the slaves learned how to forge them. This system of passes served as a powerful incentive among enslaved Afro-Americans to learn to read and write. Former slave Joseph Holmes of Pritchard, Alabama, recollected that "Ol' Miss taught de niggers how to read and write, an' some ob dem got to be too 'ficient wid de writin', 'cause dey larn how tuh write too many passes so de pattyrollers wudn't get dem. Dat was de onliest time I ebber knowed Ol' Missus tuh hab de slaves punished."[29] Moreover, we know that the patrols were often made up of lower class whites who were quite illiterate. Therefore, if this account of the patrollers in Georgia recited by Floyd Warlaw Crawford's grandfather, a former slave, is accurate, there was little or no need to worry about forging passes.

> Now I've heard that not only was it true that the patrollers couldn't read, but most of the policemen in the little towns couldn't read, and consequently, sometimes, the Negroes would take a pass a year old and put it in his pocket and when he met a policeman or met a patroller,

hand it to him. And the policeman or the patroller did not want the Negro to know that he couldn't read, so he would pass him on. . . . The Negroes were smart enough themselves to know that most of the police and most of the patrollers couldn't read, and they knew the ones who couldn't read. But the patrollers and the police didn't know the Negroes knew they couldn't read. So the Negroes could hand him a pass a year old, and he would pass him right on. Yes, that many times did happen.[30]

The largest complaint by the slaveholders regarding the ineffectiveness of the slave patrol system was the fact that from fifteen hundred to two thousand slaves each year managed to elude the patrollers and escape to the free states and Canada.[31] But there were other complaints as well. The patrollers beat and abused their slave property, and set a bad example by their drinking and carousing while on duty. Some farmers did not allow patrollers on their land for fear that they might engage in destructive activities. From the perspective of the slaves and the slaveowners, the patrol system and the patrollers left a great deal to be desired.[32]

Although there were a great many similarities between the antebellum slave patrols and the postbellum vigilante groups such as the Ku Klux Klan, the differences between the two are even more striking and important to understand. Since the slaves were considered "valuable property," there were limitations to the amount of brutality tolerated from the patrollers. As one former slave put it, "The rule was not to whip you on your master's plantation, or they would have to pay for it." Thus the pattern of black resistance was based on "beating the patroller back home."[33] On the other hand, the purpose of the Klan and similar groups was to control the social, political, and economic behavior of Afro-Americans to insure that Yankee-imposed "black freedom" did not in any way threaten "white supremacy." The limitations on brutality practiced by the patrollers were not imposed on the white regulators, and these vigilantes often resorted to torture, mutilation, and sadistic sexual "outrages" to demonstrate white power and superiority.[34]

Black freedom was almost immediately confronted by white terrorism after the Civil War. There was a struggle for political and economic control in each of the ex-Confederate states and black freedom became a political pawn in a deadly game of "reconstructing the South." Between 1865 and 1880 sometimes violent confrontations occurred in southern statehouses between black and white Democrats and Republicans. The masses of newly emancipated Afro-Americans, however, were not altogether sure they could afford the high stakes involved in maintaining even a tenuous grip on black freedom. They were competing against the demoralized, though still powerful southern aristocracy—planters, white merchants, fledging industrial capitalists—and the lower-class whites, who were particularly bitter after being beaten by the Yankees. Both considered themselves victimized ("oppressed" even!) by the vengeful Radical Republicans in power in Washington. White Republicans (or "Scalawags") at the state and local levels had a vested interest in black freedom, out of which they hoped to create a powerful political base. The new black Republican politicians quickly found out that they were a particularly vulnerable target, and they could not guarantee the preservation of black freedom even in areas where Afro-Americans were the great majority. Wealthy free blacks and upwardly mobile former slaves throughout the South were anxious to organize the black communities, and state conventions, similar to those held before the war in the North, were organized beginning in 1865 to outline black interests in the new southern social order. Many leaders of these state black conventions became Republican politicians who recognized the opportunities presented for themselves and their people in black freedom.[35]

The white Democrats included the former slaveholders, and for that reason alone many former slaves spurned that political party. At the same time, some Democratic politicians openly flaunted their ties to the Ku Klux Klan and other white terrorist groups in hopes of intimidating black voters. Allen Trelease found that in many areas "the Klan became in effect a terrorist arm of the Democratic party, whether the party leaders as a whole liked it or not." Its membership included all strata within the white community, and was not confined to what the ex-slaves considered "low white trash." "The Ku Klux Klan was a mass movement of many sides, but nearly all of them slanted toward white supremacy."[36]

The amount of violence perpetrated against black families and communities by "Night Riders" was awesome. But blacks were not the only victims of white vigilantism. White unionists, Republicans, government officials, Yankees, Carpetbaggers and "nigger-lovers" were also regularly shot, beaten, "bulldozed," and "outraged" by white terrorist groups in the half-decade following the war. On 23 March 1871 President Ulysses S. Grant sent an urgent message to Congress in which he made the following points:

> A condition of affairs now exists in some of the States of the Union rendering life and property insecure, and the carrying of the mails and the collection of the revenue dangerous. The proof that such a condition of affairs exists in some localities is now before the Senate. That the power to correct these evils is beyond the control of State authorities, I do not doubt. That the power of the Executive of the United States,

acting within the limits of existing laws, is sufficient for present emergencies, is not clear.

A joint congressional committee was appointed consisting of seven senators and fourteen representatives "whose duty it shall be to inquire into the condition of the late insurrectionary states, so far as regards the execution of the laws and safety of the lives and property of the citizens of the United States. . . ." Under the chairmanship of Republican Senator John Scott of Pennsylvania, who had headed an earlier investigation into "political outrages" in North Carolina, the committee held extensive hearings in Alabama, Mississippi, South Carolina, North Carolina, Georgia, Florida, Tennessee, and the District of Columbia.[37] The committee's report and testimony filled thirteen volumes and is considered by many scholars "perhaps the richest single source of Southern history for this period." The volumes contain thousands of pages of testimony by ex-slaves and poor black southerners about whippings, shootings, torture, and "outrages" committed against blacks and whites in (and out of) the Republican party.[38]

Black tenant farmer, James Hicks, for example, testified before the committee on 14 November 1871 in Columbus, Mississippi.[39] He had been living in Caledonia, but was forced to leave "on account of the Ku Klux."

> *Question.* What did they do to you?
> *Answer.* Well, they came to my house, and, as it happened, I got out of the way that night, and they went in where my wife was; they never whipped her; they threatened to pull her out of the bed, but they did not do much to her that night, and then I moved from there.

Hicks and his wife fled to Columbus, but they were followed there. "I reckon it was three months or four months before they came down here; they followed me down here and whipped me." Hicks and his wife were attacked by a group of forty night riders and were whipped by two of the men.

> *Question.* How many times were you struck?
> *Answer.* I reckon they gave me one hundred and fifty lashes; maybe more; maybe two hundred.
> *Question.* What did they whip you with?
> *Answer.* They whipped me with a strap.
> *Question.* Did they tell you what they were whipping you for?
> *Answer.* They said that they understood I had talked some talk concerning some white woman that was not nice, they thought, but I have witnesses that night that they tried to make me own, and I said that I didn't say it; it was only got up, that chat was, and they wanted

to run me off, the man I lived with did, on account of my crop and that was why they got the Ku-Klux to get after me, and that night they tried to make me own it, and I told them I didn't say it; and at last one of them said he reckoned I didn't say it, and there was no use to try to beat me to make me own what I didn't say, and Edmund Gray [another black tenant farmer] was present there and heard them say that.

In both Caledonia and Columbus, Hicks was "run off" the land he was renting by the Ku Klux Klan at the request of the white landowners. In the second instance when he was whipped, Hicks was forced to leave his home furnishings as well as a portion of the crop.

>*Question.* You moved off and left your crop?
>
>*Answer.* I left a portion of it; but they broke me teetotally up. I left my things and they would not allow me to go back there, and I had to slip back and get my wife and children the best I could. They took everything I had, and all my wife had, and broke us teetotally up. I had to come away with nothing. I am not able to say that I have got anything yet. I made a very good crop this year, and will be able to come out right smart, but I have lost all my house furniture; every bit of it.

The Klan thus worked hand in hand with white landowners to steal the crop and belongings of a black tenant farmer who had "a good year."

A similar situation occurred for Edward Carter, a black tenant farmer in Tuscaloosa, Alabama, who rented a piece of land from James W. Mayfield. Carter testified[40] before the congressional investigators that he "was run away" from Tuscaloosa by a large group of white men in disguises.

>*Question.* How were they disguised?
>
>*Answer.* They had handkerchiefs on their faces; the one that came that I saw had his jaws bound. He came to the gate and hailed, like he had business, and had the gate open, and ordered me to come out and march up the hill; I objected. He held a pistol in his hand. I backed down and run to the house, about thirty steps, and when I run off he fired the pistol at me; it missed me as I ran, and it went through the entry, and struck the table in the entry; the bullet struck it, and went to the back yard, and hit the fence. I ran off two or three hundred yards, and stopped, to go back. They fired a pistol again, and I went off to the man I rented of, J. W. Mayfield, to get some protection—about a mile off. He told me to stay away that night, and I staid an hour or two, and went back again, and they knocked around right smart, and cut up, and

at the time they cut up, my daughter was in the lot, milking the cows, and my little boy, nine years old next December; she had a light in the lot and was milking, and two of them came in there, before she knew anybody was in the lot, and in scuffling their hats fell off, and one was John Cook, that used to be in Mississippi, here, and the other Diller Suddith. He was raised about two miles and a half from me. She went to holler, and John Cook put a leather girth on her neck, to prevent her hollering, and they carried her about a quarter or a half a mile from the house, and they ravished her.

Question. These two men did?

Answer. Yes, sir.

A few days after the incident Carter "went down to the landlord's house I rented land from to see what I could learn from him, and talked to him. Two of these men came with a double-barreled gun, and I got mighty uneasy; I didn't know what they meant by it. They told him [the landlord] they wanted to go driving the next day; he said he didn't know what they meant." The landowner's wife also mentioned to Carter that John Cook had come to their house and said with regard to "this rape case, he acknowledged he had done that, and that he intended to do it again, and would do as he pleased with all of them. . . ." James Mayfield told Carter "he didn't consider me safe then there at night, and it was best to stay out of the way a while until things got quiet. . . ." The chairman of the committee, John Scott, asked Carter why he was attacked. "There was no charge against me. I never could learn, and I have inquired of the neighbors what report they made, and I learned they run me off to get what I had. . . ."

> *Question.* Did you ever prosecute either Cook or Diller Suddith?
>
> *Answer.* No, sir.
>
> *Question.* Why?
>
> *Answer.* I had no protection there at all; they threatened to kill me, because I told in the neighborhood what they had done; we had no friends. Since I have left, they have taken everything I had, and sold it, and I have nothing to go upon—crop and all.
>
> *Question.* Did you bring your family here?
>
> *Answer.* I have two children here, and two up there now with their grandfather.

Lewis Perkins, a black farmer, and his wife lived outside of Columbus, Mississippi, down the road from where James Hicks had been living. According to the official congressional report,[41] it appears that the same night, after giving a whipping to Hicks and his wife, the Klan came to Perkins's home to threaten a northern white teacher, Mr. Farmer, who was living with the Perkins and keeping a school for black children.

Question. What, if anything, do you know about his being driven away and his school broken up?

Answer. Well, sir, I was taken very suddenly by, as well as I could state the amount, of forty men arriving to my house, asking at the door, "Where is that damned schoolteacher?" My wife reported as being a little scared—I don't know—and immediately she spoke to them, and says she, "Come out, Mr. Farmer, and answer for yourself." He walked to the door. "How are you, gentlemen?" And says he, "I understand, sir, you are here teaching niggers and boarding with a nigger." Says he, "I am boarding with old man Lewis Perkins, which, you all know, is a nice, quiet old gentleman." Says he, "I haven't been long in this country; I don't know old man Perkins; but," says he, "are you from Chicago, sir?" Well, I can't say, but I think he said, "I am from New York, sir." Says he, "All ways you are boarding with a nigger; why don't you board with your own color?" "Gentlemen," says he, "I endeavored to do so, and I had not the opportunity to do so." Says he, "How can you prove that?" Says he, "I can go over to Mr. Whiteside's"—about a half a mile from that place—"I went there and tried to take board with them." After that his reply was, says he, "Why is the reason that they didn't board you?" Says he, "Gentlemen, I don't know." "Who authorized you to come here to teach niggers?" Says he, "Mr. Bishop and Mr. Simons and other authorities." "Well, Mr. Bishop"—that was remarked to my wife—"he is as black inside as that old nigger woman is outside. . . ."

Question. You mean he said that Mr. Bishop was as black inside as your wife outside?

Answer. Yes, sir. Then the remarks was, "Come here, captain." Two gentlemen rode around the house, and one says, "We'll hang him, anyhow." "No," he says; "lieutenant, come here." They rode around the house, and says he, "Sir, I give you ten days to get away from here, and if you don't be away from here in ten days I wouldn't give you anything for your head nor body." Well, gentlemen, I think, as far as the United States oath is, I have delivered all I know with truth.

Perkins offered to build a house for Mr. Farmer "outside of the African tribe," but the white teacher got the Klan's message and decided to leave the area.

The complex motives behind the attacks of the Ku Klux Klan against the masses of average or drylongso (as opposed to politically active) black southerners is well illustrated in the congressional committee's investigation of the "outrages" committed against Mary and Joseph Brown and their family in White County, Georgia.[42] Mary Brown was on her way home one evening in May 1871, and she encountered two white men, their faces blackened and hair tangled in an attempt to appear "colored." As she passed they spoke to her and she recognized one to be Bailey Smith, a former employer and "moonshiner," and the other was Frank Hancock. When she reached home, she heard some shots and the next day she learned that Mr. Cason, the white revenue collector down the road, had been killed. The following morning the Browns were visited by the Kluxers. Mary Brown described what happened.

They came to my house on Sunday morning, the 21st of May; it was between two and a half and three hours before day that they came. They came to the house with a dreadful noise; for a few minutes I hardly knew how I did feel. After they broke the doors open and came in I got over my scare, for I said to myself "I have not done anything; I have not stolen anything, or murdered anybody; so I will not be scared." They took my mother out first, and asked her where I was; she told them I was in the house. They said: "Make up a light; we are going to kill her." She asked them "What for?" I did not get a chance to speak to her and tell her to hush for I wanted to hear what it was for. They took Joe out of the house (he is my husband) and stripped him naked and whipped him terribly; they beat him with very large cane-poles, as large as any of these chair-rounds here. There were a couple of new hoes sitting in the yard, and they broke one handle over his head. Then they put a chain around his neck. I was the last one they took out of the house. They just dragged me out in my night-clothes. They said: "What is that you are going down to Atlanta to swear about? Tell us all about it; what men are those you saw?" I said, "Hold on; I cannot talk to about forty of you; give me time, and I will talk." They said, "We are not going to hold on at all; we are going to kill you." I said, "I hope you will not kill me; spare my life." He said, "I do not know whether we will or not." They threw me down on my face, stripped my clothes up over my head, and gave me about twenty-five licks before they let me up. They then jerked me up, and said, "Now tell us who are those you are going to swear against." I said, "I will tell you; I did not know I was going to swear to any one." They said, "We heard you was." I said, "You can't prove it." They said, "We can prove it." Said I, "Prove it; that is all you have got to do." They said, "We can prove it." Said I, "I would like to see you." There was one fellow there, a close neighbor to us, of the name of Coleman Alley; he ran up and struck me on the head with a pistol, and said, "Don't dispute my word; a white woman told me all about your going to swear." I said, "She told you more than I know, then." Two fellows, Isaac Oakes and Dick Palmer, come up and said, "Now, Mary, just tell us what you know, and you shall not be hurt."

Mary Brown went on to relate what she had seen, and they whipped her again. "After they got done with me Oakes and two boys . . . come up with a rope. They had a chain around my neck, and they drew on it until it choked me so I fainted."

Joseph Brown also testified that he and his wife were stripped, beaten, and hanged. "They took the chain fetched it around our necks, and swung us up from the ground. They first called for a rope and said they were going to hang us." The night riders then sexually assaulted the three other women, Rachel Arnold, Mary's sister; Mary Neal, a friend; and Caroline Benson, Mary's mother. They also assaulted the children. "They made all the women show their nakedness; they made them lie down and they jabbed them with sticks, and made them show their nakednesses; and they made their little children show their nakedness."

Question. Did they do any mischief to the children?

Answer. They jabbed them with a stick, and went to playing with their backsides with a piece of fishing-pole.

Question. How old are those children?

Answer. I do not exactly know; I cannot exactly tell, point-blank how old these were, but I should say that Augustus would be going on eight or nine or ten years old; Alfred is a good big plow-boy; has been plowing now for two summers.

The witnesses were asked why they had been "outraged." Joe Brown believed that these men were afraid his wife would testify against Bailey Smith and Frank Hancock in the killing of Mr. Cason. "They said they had heard we had talked about it, and they wanted to run us out of the State to keep us from being witnesses." This was likely the immediately precipitating event, but other possible reasons were also mentioned. Mary Brown, for example, suggested that they had whipped her husband "because they could not make him vote the democratic ticket. I suppose that is all they had against him." But that was evidently *not* all they had against Joe Brown. Mrs. Caroline Benson provided another, more plausible reason for the attack. She recalled Joe Brown saying, " 'I ain't done anything, gentlemen; what are you abusing me for?' They said, 'We will kill you, God damn you; you shall not live here a bit.' He said, 'I have bought my land, and got my warrantee title to it, why should I be abused in this way?' They said, 'We will give you ten days to leave, and then, God damn you, we will burn your house down over you if you don't leave. . . ."

> *Question.* Did they give any reason why they wanted your son-in-law to go away?
>
> *Answer.* They just said he should not live there.
>
> *Question.* Why?
>
> *Answer.* I could not find out exactly. I think it was just this: When he bought this plantation there was a white man wanted it; but Joe paid the money to a widow woman who only wanted the money, and Joe had it, and the other man did not.
>
> *Question.* How much did he pay for it?
>
> *Answer.* He paid $120 for his part; two of them went in together—he and another black man named Jim Dover; they two went in together and bought the land.

The Browns were outraged and driven off their land, but Joe Brown returned in several weeks, when "the troops came for me and fetched me home." His wife and family "stayed away from home all summer, afeared to go home."

Each of the reasons suggested by the Brown family for the outrages committed against them by the Klan were considered, from their perspective, sufficient justification for the white terrorist attack. It could be argued that these reasons could provide sufficient justification for attacks on virtually *all* of the newly emancipated Afro-Americans in Georgia or throughout the South in 1871. Mary Brown had very likely heard that Afro-Americans who refused to vote for the Democratic Party—the party of white supremacy—were subject to outrages, and believed this is why they attacked her husband. Joe Brown was not involved in Republican politics, but his refusal to vote for Democrats was sufficient reason to be "Ku Kluxed."

Despite the fact that Mary Brown had seen Smith and Hancock before the shooting of Mr. Cason, the economic motive appeared to be the underlying reason for the attack. Caroline Benson knew that some white people wanted her son-in-law's land, and believed that her daughter's encounter with Smith and Hancock was merely a pretext for the outrage. Joe Brown provided corroboration for this explanation when he mentioned that the Klansmen had come looking for him several weeks before his wife saw Smith and Hancock in the woods.

Question. How long had you been looking for the Ku-Klux to come there?

Answer. Well, they came on the children when they were by themselves. They thought they would catch me and my wife there, but we were not there.

Question. How long before was that?

Answer. I cannot exactly tell, point-blank, the time, but, I allow it was pretty well on to three weeks, or almost a month, as near as I can remember it, before they came on us any more.[43]

White resentment at black advancement and competition—politically, educationally, and economically—served as sufficient justification for the outrages committed in the 1860s and 1870s by white terrorists.

It has been recently suggested that the strong desire on the part of the freedpeople to acquire land following the general emancipation should be considered one of the more important "cultural values" within the emerging Afro-American nation. In west African villages from which they were stolen, land was owned by the extended families that made up the village communities. Individuals and families also worked on larger agricultural units to produce subsistence in times of hardship, and surplus in times of prosperity. Within the free black communities of the antebellum North and South, there was a noticeable preoccupation with the acquisition of property, for it was through ownership of land that one demonstrated one's fitness for participation in the "body politic."[44] In the statements and activities of the freedpeople, it was clear that they knew that in order to make their newly acquired freedom useful to their advancement, they would have to acquire land. Bayley Wyat, a Virginia freedman, spoke for thousands of his brothers and sisters in 1866 when he declared: "I may state to all our friends and to our enemies, that we has a right to the land where we are located. For why? I tell you. Our wives, our children, our husbands has been sold over and over again to purchase the lands we now locates upon; for that reason we have a divine right to the land."[45]

When land was not redistributed, the freedpeople pooled their resources and purchased a piece of property, as in the case of the Brown family in Georgia; or they rented a piece of land, made a crop, and saved their money to try to purchase land in the future, as did Edward Carter in Alabama and James Hicks in Mississippi. But by 1880 comparatively little progress had been made and the proportion of black landowners in the South remained extremely low. Edward Magdol, in *A Right to the Land* (1977), examined "the connection between land and the making of the freedmen's community." Magdol documented the newly emancipated Afro-Americans' strong desire "to acquire land in order to realize the American nineteenth-century dream: an independent homestead in their own version of the happy 'republican township.'" Magdol revealed an Afro-American "ethos of mutuality" that developed within the slave and free black communities, and between free blacks and slaves. This cultural value developed out of the Afro-American experience and persisted because it served important functions within the emerging Afro-American nation. "The ethos of mutuality, based ultimately on bonds of real and fictive kinship, shaped the process of making and remaking the community in the Reconstruction." Even more important, this cooperative ethos was evoked not only when Afro-Americans were pooling their resources to purchase land, but also when arrangements had to be made to flee persecution and white oppression.[46]

The failure of large numbers of Afro-Americans to acquire land in the South before 1880 cannot be traced to a lack of effort and desire on the part of the South's "wandering darker children." In the competition for ownership of land, Afro-Americans had many obstacles and disadvantages to overcome, not the least of which was organized white opposition. In many instances this simply meant that white landowners refused to sell land to Afro-Americans. But even when blacks managed to acquire a piece of land, as in the case of the Brown family, there were no guarantees that they could keep it. Thus by 1880 in state after southern state, the statistics on black landownership were depressing—100,000 acres in South Carolina, less than that in Virginia, Arkansas, and North Carolina. Vernon Wharton estimated that not one in a hundred black families in the seventeen black-belt counties of Mississippi in 1880 owned the land on which they worked.[47]

While the Afro-Americans' desire for land was strong following the general emancipation, their instinct for survival, as well as the cultural goals of black advancement and self-determination, were even stronger. The Civil War had brought "one kind of freedom," but unfortunately it was not the kind that allowed the acquisition of land in many parts of the South. Black freedom, however, did provide the means for acquiring land and other objectives by allowing Afro-Americans to flee the oppressive conditions created in the wake of the widespread white supremacist campaigns. Through the "act of migration," Afro-American individuals, families, and entire communities moved to control their own destinies and to give greater meaning and substance to the cultural value of black freedom.

The Fiat to Go Forth Is Irresistible

W. E. B. Du Bois presented an eloquent account and assessment of the newly emancipated Afro-American's sullen discontentment over freedom in

The Souls of Black Folk. "A way back in the days of bondage they thought to see in one divine event the end of all doubt and disappointment; few men ever worshipped Freedom with half such unquestioning faith as did the American Negro for two centuries." Once the emancipation was accomplished, however, black freedom still remained a cultural value.

> The first decade was merely a prolongation of the vain search for freedom, the boon that seemed ever barely to elude their grasp,—like a tantalizing will-o'-the-wisp, maddening and misleading the headless host. The holocaust of war, the terrors of the Ku-Klux Klan, the lies of carpet-baggers, the disorganization of industry, and the contradictory advice of friends and foes, left the bewildered serf with no new watchword beyond the old cry for freedom.

Du Bois believed that this situation obtained well into the first decade of the new century. Writing in 1903, he suggested that the "nation has not yet found peace from its sins; the freedman has not yet found in freedom his promised land. Whatever good may have come in these years of change, the shadow of a deep disappointment rests upon the Negro people,—a disappointment all the more bitter because the unattained ideal was unbounded save by simple ignorance of a lowly people."[48]

Since the migration of thousands of poor and oppressed Afro-Americans from the rural to the urban South, and from the urban South to the urban North, was a gradual movement until 1900, Du Bois did not recognize it as another example of self-determinist activity among the black masses. While it is undeniable that the acquisition of land and the use of the ballot were considered important by Afro-Americans to give real meaning to their freedom, black landownership and political participation were viewed by white southerners as threats to white supremacy. In the face of organized white opposition and terrorism, migration out of the rural South was seen by thousands of Afro-Americans as the only way to achieve individual or collective advancement and self-determination.

The voluntary (and involuntary) movement of masses of poor blacks out of the former Confederacy to the North and West did not become a "national issue" until 1879, but the plans for the exodus had been made four or five years earlier. Although most Democratic leaders believed the migration was a "political strategy" to increase Republican voting strength in western and northern states, it is more accurate to understand the exodus as a "mass movement" assisted by "grass roots organizers" rather than "colored politicians." Henry Adams, for example, was born in slavery in Newton County, Georgia in 1843, but was taken to Louisiana in 1850. He was hired out by his mistress, Nancy Emily Adams, and managed to acquire some personal property, "three horses, and a fine buggy, and a good deal of money both gold and silver." After the Civil War, Adams remained with his latest employer and tried to work for part of the crop, but was given "not a cent" for his labor. So he left De Soto Parish and headed for Shreveport. Henry Adams's contemporary account of the conditions for Afro-Americans immediately after emancipation corresponded very closely to the recollections of former slaves recorded in the 1930s.

> I ran away, as also did most of the rest, and the white people did not sympathize with us; they would take all the money that we made on their places when we went to leave; they killed many hundreds of my race when they were running away to get freedom. After they told us we were free—even then they would not let us live as man and wife together. And when we would run away to be free from slavery, the white people would not let us come on their places to see our mothers, wives, sisters, or fathers. We was made to leave the place, or made to go back and live as slaves. To my own knowledge there was over two thousand colored people killed trying to get away, after the white people told us we were free, which was in 1865. Many of the colored people were killed, but the white people pretended to know little about it. I seen some shot dead because they left with a white woman. This was after they told us we were free, in the year 1865; this was between Shreveport and Logansport.[49]

In September 1866 Adams enlisted in the United States Army, and while stationed at Fort Jackson, Louisiana, he learned to read and write. Upon discharge in September 1869 he returned to Caddo Parish (Shreveport), but "the whites would not rent houses," so he stayed with a black preacher. When the black veterans arrived, "the white people began saying they were going to kill us; to kill all the discharged negro soldiers," because they believed "these discharged men were going to spoil all the other negroes, so that the whites could do nothing with them. . . ." Adams and other Union veterans helped many illiterate formers slaves with their labor contracts, their accounts, and business dealings with whites. As a result, they were continually harassed and threatened by "white regulators," and thus in 1870 Adams and several other black Civil War veterans formed "the Committee," whose purpose was to collect information on Afro-American social, economic, and political conditions and "to look into affairs and see the true conditions of our race, to see whether it was possible we could stay under a people who had held us under bondage or not."[50]

The original founders did not consider it a "political organization," and they allowed no black Republican politicians to join. But Adams often did present his views on "political issues" when asked by his people. The increasing prosperity and organization among blacks in Caddo Parish led to the formation of numerous "White Leagues" in 1874, and as part of the overall campaign for "white solidarity," many blacks were fired from their jobs, including Henry Adams, who at the time managed a mill and plantation. "I think a heap of you as a man, I know you are a true man," Adams's white employer confessed, "but under this order I cannot employ you. . . . You are a good old Republican, and I cannot employ you because you are a Republican." The increased terrorism in Caddo Parish following the organization of the white leagues led Republican Governor William Pitt Kellogg to request federal troops in 1874, and thereafter the violence subsided for a while. Adams worked as an "undercover agent" for the Seventh Calvary during this period, gathering and disseminating information for and about his people.[51]

In December 1875 a national black convention was held in New Orleans, and Henry Adams attended it. There he learned that the conditions Afro-Americans faced in Caddo Parish existed throughout the South and that the delegates advocated migration to the North and West, or emigration to Liberia, as a way of dealing with the conditions. When one delegate asked, "Do you think we will do better if we were to ourselves and out of the South?" another made this reply:

> Yes; for we will get what we make, our crops or their value; if we get in jail, we will have a chance to get bond and a chance to prove our innocence, and not be taken out by a mob and hung or shot before they know whether we are guilty or not; and may not have to work on the railroad or levees in chain-gangs when we are not guilty of any crime, and not to be whipped as if we were dumb brutes; not hated because we are black.[52]

The delegates decided to gather more information and collect the names of Afro-Americans interested in leaving. Following the increase in "outrages" during the election of 1876, the Committee, which now referred to itself as the "Colonization Council," held a series of mass meetings to assess the situation. According to Adams:

> We found ourselves in such condition that we looked around and we seed that there was no way on earth, it seemed, that we could better our condition [in Louisiana], and we discussed that thoroughly in our organization along in May 1877. We said that the whole South—every State in the South—had got into the hands of the very men that held us

slaves—from one thing to another—and we thought that the men that held us slaves was holding the reins of government over our heads in every respect almost, even the constable up to the governor. We felt we had almost as well be slaves under these men. In regard to the whole matter that was discussed, it came up in every council. Then we said there was no hope for us and we had better go.

By August 1877 the Colonization Council had "enrolled 69,000 men and women who wished to be colonized in Liberia or some other country."[53]

After 1876 Louisiana was "redeemed" by white Democrats and the elections of 1878 were considered the most fraudulent and corrupt to date. Henry Adams wrote the United States Attorney General, Charles Devens, in late November 1878 describing the violence and fraud that took place in Caddo Parish during the election.

[I]f we put our tickets in the Ward box they counted nothing only for the Ward and the Parish & Congressional boxes they counted them for one Side or the others, and part of the Col[ored] people tore their tickets into [three parts] and put them in all three of the boxes—and the democrats found out that we were beating them, and so they hunted and swore that they could not find our names on the list of Registration. . . .

[A]t about ten or eleven o'clock in the day we all found out that they aimed for the Col[ored] man's vote to count nothing and so there were orders given for them all to stop voting and so we did so and in the other parts of the parish where they did not stop they were driven from the polls with Sticks and guns. In the Campobella Ward which is Called the 8th the white league have killed or wounded and ran off 200 Col[ored] people—out of that Ward—and even killed three Col[ored] women and children about their husbands. . . .

Some of the Democrats tells me just so long as we Colored people fools with politics, and try to vote here in the South, So long as the white man of the South are going to kill us and from what I can see it seem so—and they have threatened about a hundred of our lives now and many are scared to stay in their houses at night and the White League have made some of them leave the State and my life is threatened . . . I trust God that the United States will give us some Territory to our selves—and let us leave these Slave holders to work their own land, for they are killing our race by the hundreds every day and night. . . .[54]

On 17 December 1878 the United States Senate passed a resolution forming a select committee of nine senators to inquire and report on "whether in recent elections the constitutional rights of American citizens were violated in any of the States of the Union. . . ." The committee was to determine whether the "right of suffrage" was abridged "by action of the election officers of any State . . . in refusing to receive their votes, in failing to count them, or in receiving and counting fraudulent ballots in pursuance of a conspiracy to make lawful votes of such citizens of more effect; and whether such citizens were prevented from exercising the elective franchise, or forced to use it against their wishes, by violence or threats, or hostile organizations, or by any other unlawful means or practices. The committee shall also inquire whether any citizen of any State has been dismissed or threatened with dismissal from employment or deprivation of any right or privilege by reason of his vote or intention to vote at the recent elections, or has been interefered with."[55]

Since this was exactly what had occurred in Caddo Parrish, at the congressional hearings held in January 1879 in New Orleans, the Senate committee was told of the "band of armed men who took possession of the ballot box, and broke it up, and destroyed the ballots. . . ." Other conspiracies and illegalities were investigated. In the final report submitted by Senator Henry M. Teller (R., Colorado), chairman of the committee, it was noted that, because of extreme time limitations, the investigation had to be "partial and incomplete." However, "the testimony that was taken [in South Carolina and Louisiana] was amply sufficient to show conclusively that in several districts in each State not only the elections of the Congressmen, but for the State and County officers as well, were neither fair nor free; that by violence and fraud the honest expression of the will of those entitled to vote was prevented, and thousands of citizens of those states were deprived of the elective franchise. In Louisiana, both violence and fraud was extensively used; in South Carolina, while violence was not rare, fraud was more largely relied upon." The report recommended that "Congress should exercise the power it clearly possesses of providing by law for fair and free elections of members of Congress." The national government could not depend on the states "for the punishment of offenses against its own laws upon laws of the several States. This statement of such a claim is sufficient to show its absurdity."[56]

The violence, intimidation, fraud, and terrorism continued in Louisiana and Mississippi, and by April 1879 the Colonization Council had over 98,000 names of blacks willing to migrate to the North or West or to emigrate to Liberia. When Benjamin "Pap" Singleton and others began to promote migration to Kansas in the late 1870s, the council and other groups were instrumental in providing information to those willing to leave. In North Carolina, the Baltimore and Ohio Railroad competed with other rail lines to be the exclusive carrier of black migrants to Indiana. And it was estimated that during the spring and summer of 1879 and 1880 nearly 60,000 blacks left Northern Louisiana, North Carolina, Texas, Mississippi, and Alabama for Kansas and Indiana to take advantage of the federal government's offer of land for homesteading.[57]

Following the movement of thousands of Afro-Americans from Louisiana to Kansas and from North Carolina to Indiana, Senator Donald W. Voorhees (D., Indiana) introduced a resolution into the United States Senate on 18 December 1879 noting that "it is currently alleged that they are induced to do so by the unjust and cruel conduct of their white fellow citizens toward them in the South; therefore:

> *Be it Resolved,* That a committee of five members of this body be appointed by its presiding officer, whose duty it shall be to investigate the causes which have led to the aforesaid migration, and to report the same to the Senate; and said committee shall have power to send for persons and papers, compelling the defense of witnesses, and to sit at any time.[58]

Senator Voorhees was made chairman of the Senate committee and it began hearing testimony on 19 January 1880. One hundred fifty-three black and white witnesses were examined from North Carolina, Georgia, Alabama, Mississippi, Louisiana, Texas, Missouri, Kansas, and Indiana. Two separate reports, majority and minority, were issued by the committee, and their conclusions and recommendations were completely different. In the majority report, Democratic Senators Voorhees, Zebulon Vance of North Carolina, and George Pendleton of Ohio argued "that it was clear from the testimony of both whites and blacks, Republicans and Democrats, that the causes of discontent among these people could not have arisen from any deprivation of their political rights or any hardship in their condition." With regard to wages in North Carolina, for example, "the general average of compensation for labor in that State [was] quite equal to, if not better than, in any Northern State to which these people were going, to say nothing of the climate of North Carolina, which was infinitely better adapted to them." The majority also under "the closest scrutiny could detect no outrage or violence inflicted upon their political rights in North Carolina for many years past." Blacks could vote, their votes were counted fairly, they could purchase real estate, and they "were enjoying the privileges of education for their children precisely that whites were enjoying."

The majority report dismissed all this loose talk about "political outrages."

> With regard to political outrages which have formed the staple of complaint for many years against the people of the South, your committee diligently inquired, and have to report that they found nothing or almost nothing new. Many old stories were revived and dwelt upon by zealous witnesses, but very few indeed ventured to say that any considerable violence or outrage had been exhibited toward the colored people of the South within the last few years, and still fewer of all those who testified upon this subject, and who were evidently anxious to make the most of it, testified to anything as within their own knowledge. It was all hearsay, and nothing but hearsay, with rare exceptions.[59]

According to these Democratic Senators, the exodus was inspired by "outside agitators" bent on "political colonization" to the North and West. The "aid societies" that had sprung up and were supposed to be assisting the migrants once they arrived in Kansas and Indiana, actually "operated to cause the exodus originally. . . ." These societies "stimulated it directly by publishing and distributing among the colored men circulars artfully designed and calculated to stir up discontent. Every single member, agent, friend, or sympathizer with these societies and their purposes were ascertained to belong to the Republican party, and generally to be active members thereof."

The majority ultimately concluded that this exodus benefitted no group or interests, not even those of the Afro-American masses.

> On the whole, your committee express the positive opinion that the condition of the colored people of the South is not only as good as could have been reasonably expected, but is better than if large communities were transferred to a colder and more inhospitable climate, thrust into competition with a different system of labor, among strangers who are not accustomed to them, their ways, habits of thought and action, their idiosyncrasies, and their feelings. While a gradual migration, such as circumstances dictate among the white races, might benefit the individual black man and his family as it does those of the whites, we cannot but regard this wholesale attempt to transfer a people without means and without intelligence, from the homes of their nativity in this manner, as injurious to the people of the South, injurious to

the people and the labor-system of the State where they go, and, more than all, injurious to the last degree to the black people themselves.[60]

Republican Senators Henry Blair of New Hampshire and William Windom of Minnesota completely disagreed with their Democratic colleagues. In the minority report, they first exposed the absurdity of the "political colonization" argument in accounting for the exodus. If the Republican party "proposed to import negroes into Indiana for political purposes, why take them from North Carolina?

> Why import them from a State where the Republicans hope and expect to carry the election, when there were thousands upon thousands ready and anxious to come from States certainly Democratic. Why transport them by rail at heavy expense half way across the continent when they could have taken them from Kentucky without any expense, or brought them up the Mississippi River by steamers at merely nominal cost? Why send twenty-five thousand to Kansas to swell her 40,000 Republican majority, and only seven or eight hundred to Indiana? These considerations brand with falsehood and folly the charge that the exodus was a political movement induced by Northern partisan leaders.

The migrant aid societies, Blair and Windom said, were made up mostly of Afro-Americans in the North and West who wanted to help their destitute and desperate brothers and sisters in the South. "Their piteous tales of outrage, suffering and wrong, touched the hearts of more fortunate members of their race. . . . That they were organized to induce migration for political purposes, or to aid or encourage these people to leave their homes for any purpose or that they contributed one dollar to that end is utterly untrue, and there is absolutely nothing in the testimony to sustain such a charge. Their purposes and objects were purely charitable."[61]

The Senators quoted from the testimony of Henry Adams of Caddo Parish about the grass-roots support that existed for migration.[62] For example, Adams had been asked about the participation of politicians in the activities of the Committee or "Colonization Council."

> *Question.* Now, let us understand more distinctly, before we go any further, the kind of people who composed that association. The committee, as I understand you, was composed entirely of laboring people?
> *Answer.* Yes, sir.
> *Question.* Did it include any politicians of either color, white or black?
> *Answer.* No politicianers didn't belong to it, because we didn't

allow them to know nothing about it, because we was afraid that if we allowed the colored politicianer to belong to it he would tell it to the Republican politicianers, and from that the men that was doing all this to us would get hold of it too, and then get after us.

Adams also made it clear that the Colonization Council did not give up on the possibility of remaining in the South until 1877 when "we looked around and seed that there was no way on earth, it seemed, that we could better our condition. . . ."

> *Question.* You say, then, that in 1877 you lost all hope of being able to remain in the South, and you began to think of moving somewhere else?
>
> *Answer.* Yes; we said we was going if we had to run away and go into the woods.
>
> *Question.* About how many did this committee consist of before you organized your council? Give us the number as near as you can tell.
>
> *Answer.* As many as five hundred in all.
>
> *Question.* The committee, do you mean?
>
> *Answer.* Yes; the committee has been that large.
>
> *Question.* What was the largest number reached by your colonization council, in your best judgment?
>
> *Answer.* Well, it is not exactly five hundred men belonging to the council that we have in our council, but they all agreed to go with us and enroll their names with us from time to time, so that they have now got at this time ninety-eight thousand names enrolled.

Adams noted that these names included blacks from Louisiana, Arkansas, Texas, Mississippi, and Alabama.

Samuel Perry, who was instrumental in planning the migration of blacks from North Carolina to Indiana, also testified before the Senate committee and pointed out that interest in migration began as early as 1872.

> *Question.* You have heard a good deal of this testimony with reference to this exodus from North Carolina. Now begin at the beginning and tell us all you know about it.
>
> *Answer.* Well, the beginning, I supposed was in this way: The first idea or the first thing was, we used to have little meetings to talk over these matters. In 1872 we first received some circulars or pamphlets from O. F. Davis, of Omaha, Nebraska.
>
> *Question.* In 1872?
>
> *Answer.* Yes, sir; in 1872—giving a description of government

lands and railroads that could be got cheap; and we held little meetings then; that is, we would meet and talk about it Sunday evenings—that is, the laboring class of our people—the only ones I knew anything about: I had not much to do with the big professional negroes, the rich men. I did not associate with them much, but I got among the workingmen, and they would take these pamphlets and read them over.

George F. Marlow, a black lawyer, maintained that the State Labor Union, made up of working-class black Alabamians, hired and sent him to Kansas in 1871 to inquire about the possibility of settling there. And Benjamin "Pap" Singleton, who claimed to be the "father of the exodus," said that he had been working to bring southern blacks to Kansas from as early as 1869. Senators Blair and Windom suggested that "here, then, we have conclusive proof from the negroes themselves that they have been preparing for this movement for years. Organizations to this end have existed in many States, and the agents of such organizations have traveled throughout the South. One of the organizations alone kept one hundred and fifty men in the field for years, traveling among the brethren and secretly discussing this among other means of relief. As stated by Adams and Perry, politicians were excluded, and the movement was confined wholly to the working classes."[63]

In their explication of the "causes of the exodus" Senators Blair and Windom felt obliged to point up the base falseness of the Democratic position that political outrages played no significant part in causing the migration.

> In the presence of most diabolic outrages clearly proven; in the face of the declaration of thousands of refugees that they had fled because of the insecurity of their lives and property at the South, and because the Democratic party of that section had, by means too shocking and shameful to relate, deprived them of their rights as American citizens; in the face of the fact that it has been clearly shown by the evidence that organizations of colored laborers, one of which numbered ninety-eight thousand, have existed for many years and extending into many States of the South, designed to improve their condition by emigration—in the face of all these facts the majority of the committee can see no cause for the exodus growing out of such wrongs, but endeavor to charge it to the Republicans of the North.[64]

The statements and reports of military commanders in the South, including General Philip Sheridan in Louisiana, were cited to underscore the point that beginning with the election of 1868 (if not before) a "reign of terror" existed in several Louisiana parishes and this led to the massacre of many Afro-Americans.

> These reports show that in the year 1868 a reign of terror prevailed over almost the entire State. In the parish of Saint Landry there was a massacre of colored people which began on the 28th of September, 1868, and lasted from three to six days, during which between two and three hundred colored men were killed. "Thirteen captives were taken from the jail and shot, and a pile of twenty-five dead bodies were found burned in the woods." The result of this Democratic campaign in the parish was that the registered Republican majority of 1,071 was wholly obliterated, and, at the election which followed a few weeks later not a vote was cast for General [Ulysses S.] Grant, while [Horatio] Seymour and [Francis P.] Blair received 4,787.
>
> In the parish of Bossier a similar massacre occurred between the 20th and 30th of September, 1868, which lasted from three to four days, during which two hundred colored people were killed. By the official registry of that year the Republican voters in Bossier Parish numbered 1,938, but at the ensuing election only *one* Republican vote was cast.
>
> In the Parish of Caddo during the month of October, 1868, over forty colored people were killed. The result of that massacre was that out of a Republican registered vote of 2,894 only one was cast for General Grant. Similar scenes were enacted throughout the State, varying in extent and atrocity according to the magnitude of the Republican majority to be overcome.[65]

The practice of bringing hundreds of white "regulators" (terrorists) into a district or parish to threaten, intimidate, whip, and murder black and white Republican voters was known as "bulldozing." The testimony before the Senate committee made it clear that bulldozing was directly responsible for causing some blacks to migrate. For example, Madison Parish, Louisiana, furnished one of the largest contingents of "Exodusters" to Kansas in the summer of 1879. William Murrell, a black Republican politician, testified in January that this would also be the case during the summer of 1880.[66]

> You have not read of any exodus yet as there will be from that section this summer, and the reason for it is that, for the first time since the war in Madison Parish, last December we had bulldozing there. Armed bodies of men came into the parish—not people who lived in the parish, but men from Ouachita Parish and Richland Parish; and I

can name the leader who commanded them. He was a gentleman by the name of Captain Tibbals, of Ouachita Parish, who lives in Monroe, who was noted in the celebrated massacre there in other times. His very name among the colored people is sufficient to intimidate them almost. He came with a crowd of men on the 28th of December into Madison Parish, when all was quiet and peaceable. There was no quarrel, no excitement. We had always elected our tickets in the parish, and we had put Democrats on the ticket in many cases to satisfy them. There were only 238 white voters and about 2,700 colored registered voters.

When David Armstrong, the black president of the Third Ward Republican Club, complained about these threats, "some white men heard of it, and got a squad by themselves and said, 'We'll go down and give that nigger a whippin.'"

So Sunday night, about ten o'clock, they went to his house to take him out and whip him. They saw him run out the back way and fired on him. One in the crowd cried out, "Don't kill him!" "It is too late, now," they said, "he's dead." The *Carroll Conservative,* a Democratic newspaper, published the whole thing; but the reason they did it was because we had one of their men on our ticket as judge, and they got sore about it, and we beat him. They killed Armstrong and took him three hundred yards to the river, threw him in the river, and left the sheet in the bushes.

Murrell tried to prevent further bulldozing by meeting with the local leaders of the Democratic Party, and suggested that he might be able to convince some of the Afro-Americans to vote for Democratic candidates. The Democrats were not appeased:

"Murrell, you know damned well the niggers in this parish won't vote the Democratic ticket—there is no use to tell me you will give us the clerk of the court, you know the niggers won't do it. You can't trust the niggers in politics; all your eloquence and all the speeches you can make won't make these niggers vote this ticket or what you suggest, even if we was to accept it. No, by God, Murrell, there's no use talking, we are going to carry this parish; we have found a way to carry it. There ain't no use talking any more about it. *No, by God, we are going to carry it.* "Why," he said, *"there is more eloquence in double-barreled shot-guns to convince niggers than there is in forty Ciceros."* I said to him, "Well, do you suppose the merchants and planters will back you up," and he said, "O, by God, they have got nothing to do with it. We have charge of it. *We three men, the Democratic committee, have full power to work."* (Italics in original)

In that district, which contained 2,700 registered Republican voters and only 238 Democrats, "the Democrats returned a majority of 2,300. The witness swears that not more than 360 votes were cast. Democratic shot-gun eloquence did its work. . . ."

The Louisiana State Convention of Colored Citizens that met in New Orleans in April 1879 accepted the following report of its business committee, which was charged with determining the reasons for the exodus.

> The Committee find that the primary cause of this lies in the absence of a republican form of government to the people of Louisiana. Crime and lawlessness existing to an extent that laughs at all restraint, and the misgovernment naturally induced from a State administration itself the product of violence, have created an absorbing and constantly increasing distrust and alarm among our people throughout the State. All rights of freemen denied and all claims to a just recompense for labor rendered or honorable dealings between planter and laborer disallowed, justice a mockery, and the laws a cheat, the very officers of the courts being themselves the mobocrats and violators of law, the only remedy left the colored citizen in many parishes of our State to-day is to emigrate. The fiat to go forth is irresistible. The constantly recurring, nay, ever-present, fear which haunts the minds of these our people in the turbulent parishes of the State is that slavery in the horrible form of peonage is approaching; that the avowed disposition of the men in power to reduce the laborer and his interest to the minimum of advantages as freemen and to absolutely none as citizen has produced so absolute a fear that in many cases it has become a panic. It is flight from present sufferings and from wrongs to come.[67]

Senators Blair and Windom did not believe it was necessary to present as detailed an examination of the conditions for poor blacks in Mississippi that spurred the exodus; "it would be but a repetition of the intolerance, persecutions, and violence which have prevailed in Louisiana. The same 'shot-gun eloquence' which was so potent for conversion of colored Republicans in one has proven equally powerful in the other. The same 'eloquence' which wrested Louisiana from Republicans also converted Mississippi. And in both the same results are visible in the determination of the colored people to get away.

> Nearly all the witnesses who were asked as to the causes of the

exodus answered that it was because of a feeling of insecurity for life and property; a denial of their political rights as citizens; long-continued persecutions for political reasons; a system of cheating by landlords and storekeepers which rendered it impossible for them to make a living no matter how hard they might work; the inadequacy of school advantages, and a fear that they would be eventually reduced to a system of peonage even worse than slavery itself.[68]

In their concluding observations, Blair and Windom summarized the reasons why by 1880 "black freedom" had come to mean only the ability of formerly enslaved Afro-Americans to flee the oppressive social, economic, and political conditions of the post-Civil War South.

> A long series of political persecutions, whippings, maimings, and murders committed by Democrats and in the interest of the Democratic party, extending over a period of fifteen years, has finally driven the negro to despair, and compelled him to seek peace and safety by flight. . . .
>
> In some States a system of convict hiring is authorized by law, which reinstates the chain-gang, the overseer, and the blood-hound substantially as in the days of slavery. . . .
>
> A system of labor and renting has been adopted in some parts of the South which reduces a negro to a condition but little better than that of peonage, and which renders it impossible for him to make a comfortable living, no matter how hard he may work. . . .
>
> The only remedy for the exodus is in the hands of Southern Democrats themselves, and if they do not change their treatment of the negro and recognize his rights as a man and a citizen, the movement will go on, greatly to the injury of the labor interests of the South, if not the whole country.[69]

The movement did go on in the face of strong and persistent opposition at every step of the journey. Plans continued to be made in secret, making full use of the Afro-American "ethos of mutuality," in hopes that the planter and merchant capitalists would remain unaware that their exploited and intimidated laborers were preparing to make a run for their lives. The local white militia (in its various disguises) was used to blockade points of embarkation and disembarkation, while the local constabulary mobilized to track down those who might be brought back to stand trial for some infraction of "white law." Even after the migrants or emigrants or "exodusters" arrived in Kansas or Indiana they were often hassled and made to feel unwelcome. For those unable to "tough it out" the first or second year in the new environment, there were other places to try where hopefully they could live free and prosper.[70]

The desire to realize their freedom through migration was also informed by strong Pan-Africanist values held by elements among the Afro-American masses. Thus rather than joining the caravans to Kansas or the steamers to Missouri, many black southerners investigated the possibility of acquiring a homestead in Messurado County, Liberia, or outside Freetown, Sierra Leone. As Nell Irvin Painter made clear, during the same years that so many oppressed Afro-Americans caught severe cases of "Kansas fever," many also contracted terminal cases of "Liberia fever" as well.[71] In Liberia, these long-separated sons and daughters of Africa hoped to find the personal liberty and freedom praised by Washington McDonogh in a letter in 1846 to his former owner. Washington was thankful that John McDonogh had freed him and his family and financially supported their emigration to Liberia. He stated that he would very much like "to see you once more before we leave this world, for it would be a source of great delight to me, *but I will never consent to leave this country for all the pleasures of America combined together, to live, for this is the only place where a colored person can enjoy his liberty, for there exists no prejudice of color in this country, but every man is free and equal.*"[72]

Although there was freedom and black self-determination in Liberia, there were also many hardships and disadvantages. And whereas the movement from Caddo Parish, Louisiana, or Madison Parish to Topeka, Kansas, in 1879 or 1880 was fraught with untold dangers and problems, the move from Caddo Parish to Monrovia, Liberia, was double or triple the trouble and expense, even for the well-financed, experienced traveler. There were the reports circulating of mysterious diseases, such as "African malaria," that swept through entire settlements of Afro-Americans, and there were the unfriendly natives and antagonistic European colonizers and slavers.[73] Nevertheless, the Liberian Exodus Joint Stock Steamship Company was organized in Charleston, South Carolina, in 1877, raised funds for transporting Afro-Americans to their homeland, and in March 1878 it acquired the ship *Azor,* which carried 206 black emigrants to Liberia. In 1878 and 1879 the American Colonization Society was inundated with letters of inquiry from Afro-Americans interested in emigration, especially after the demise of the Liberian Steamship Company in 1879. But during these years the Colonization Society was sending only one or two ships annually to West Africa, carrying mostly supplies, and could only accommodate fifty to one hundred passengers. Without strong financial backing from either their own people or white colonizers, it was very difficult for Afro-Americans, inspired by Pan-Africanist cultural values, to realize their dream of returning to the motherland.[74]

The impetus for migrating out of the rural South, however, did not subside in the 1880s. There was great movement within states from rural to urban areas, and there was great interstate traffic within the South. In their monograph *Black Migration in America: A Social Demographic History* (1981), Daniel Johnson and Rex R. Campbell found that "considerable interstate migration . . . occurred within the South during the post-Reconstruction decades. Among the more pronounced patterns were those linking the South Atlantic states of Virginia, North and South Carolina to the Gulf states of Louisiana, Mississippi, and Texas. These streams were, in large part, continuations of those formed in the latter years of the antebellum period. Thirty-five thousand blacks from South Carolina and Georgia moved to Arkansas and Texas in the decade following the Civil War. . . .

> The largest single out-migration from South Carolina during the post-Reconstruction period came from "bloody Edgefield," near the western border of the state, in the last week of 1881: an estimated 5,000 blacks left their homes for Arkansas. Political oppression was reportedly more severe in and around Edgefield than in other parts of the state; blacks complained that they could not vote in elections, or if they did, their ballots were not counted.[75]

During the 1890s there was an even larger migration out of the South to the industrial North than in previous decades. While the numbers moving to the West from the South decreased between 1890 and 1900, the number of blacks born in the South, but residing in the North, increased during that decade by 105,000. Economic recession and depressions, plus political persecution, combined to drive thousands of Afro-Americans from the South, primarily to the industrial states of Pennsylvania, New York, Illinois, New Jersey, Indiana, and Massachusetts.[76] But, as in the 1870s, emigration to Africa, as opposed to the North or West, also assumed great importance among the masses of Afro-Americans, and Bishop Henry McNeal Turner received more support for his emigrationist schemes in the 1890s and early 1900s than had the carriers of "Liberia fever" in the 1870s.[77]

As we have seen, Pan-Africanist values often underpinned the attempts of Afro-Americans to realize the cultural goals of advancement and self-determination. The African Union Society of Newport, Rhode Island, in the 1780s; the Haitian Emigration Societies of the 1820s; the conventions sponsored by Martin Delany, J. Theodore Holly, and other emigrationists, in the 1850s; "Liberia Fever" in the 1870s; and Bishop Turner's African Dream in the 1890s—all represented a continuous stream of Pan-Africanist activities that fed into the larger river of Afro-American freedom and self-determination. They served as the historical and cultural precedents for Marcus Garvey's campaign for African and Afro-American solidarity in the years after World War I.

It should be kept in mind, however, that returning to Africa was very likely the most difficult (some would say extreme) way that Afro-Americans could choose to achieve advancement and self-determination. There were other alternatives, available within the United States, for Afro-Americans to pursue in order to use their hard-won freedom to bring about greater control over their destiny and that of their children. All-black towns began to spring up in the 1880s and 1890s: Mound Bayou, Mississippi, Nicodemus, Kansas. As part of the "great black march westward" in Oklahoma in the 1890s, over twenty all-black communities were founded. The origins of these settlements can be traced directly to the chaos and upheaval associated with southern redemption and the removal of blacks from the political arena.[78] As the founder of Langston, Oklahoma, made clear, the purpose of the town was to create a place where the Afro-American could prosper and "rule supreme in his own community." Afro-Americans who settled in these towns wished to escape white domination and through this self-determinative activity they hoped to "elevate themselves under their own powers." They desired to be completely self-sufficient; as a resident of one of these towns in Oklahoma made clear: The white people "will respect you more if you are independent."[79]

With the influx of large numbers of rural blacks into northern and southern urban centers during the last two decades of the nineteenth century, complex social networks could develop. Within the urban black communities black churches, separate schools, fraternal institutions, voluntary associations, and advancement groups sprouted up to meet the social and cultural needs of expanding populations. "Jim Crow" was not merely a southern practice, it was "the American way," and Afro-Americans who settled in large and small cities to take advantage of increased employment opportunities found that they could become a part of a wide array of organizations in which blacks exercised complete control. As long as these institutions functioned, there was little need to confront the discrimination practiced in white-dominated public and private organizations.[80] It was not until the Great Depression of the 1930s, when thousands of black social organizations were forced to disband, that the Afro-American masses saw the wisdom of trying to integrate themselves into white-dominated programs and institutions, especially those programs offered by the New Deal.

"My remembrance sure is good," declared Mittie Freeman, a former slave interviewed by the Federal Writers Project in 1937. "The day freedom came I was fishing with Pappy. . . . Pappy jumps up, throws the pole and everything, and grabs my hand, and starts flying towards the house. 'It's victory,' he keep on saying. 'It's freedom. Now we're gwine be free.'" Mittie confessed, however, that "I didn't know what it all meant. It seem like it took a long time for freedom to come. Everything just kept on like it was. We heard that lots of slaves was getting land and some mules to set up for themselves. I never knowed any what got land or mules or nothing."[81] Afro-Americans enslaved in the United States lived and prayed for the day of deliverance. It came and went, and too many things remained the same as they were before emancipation. Land was not redistributed, citizenship was conferred without civil rights, the franchise was extended, then withdrawn, and Night Riders enforced white racial domination with such ferocity that it made some former slaves long for the days of "outrunning pattyrollers."

Initially, many Afro-Americans were disappointed with "Mister Lincum's freedom," but after a few years of testing its limits, masses of southern blacks decided that they would use their freedom to escape oppressive economic and political conditions to try to make a new start in the next city, county, or state. The Afro-American value of resistance required that they not submit to the depredations of white landowners and vigilantes, and hundreds (perhaps thousands) lost their lives as a result. For others the preferred form of resistance was migration to another area where they could purchase land, get an education, raise their families, and live in peace with their neighbors. Freedom and resistance eventually led to migration.

Lawrence Levine, in *Black Culture and Black Consciousness: Afro-American Folk Thought from Slavery to Freedom* (1977), examined a wide array of folk materials—songs, tales, stories—and concluded that during the slavery era they revealed an overarching preoccupation with religion and religious concerns. According to Levine, the religious or "sacred world-view" of enslaved Afro-Americans occupied the "central position" within slave folk culture. It was not until after the General Emancipation that Afro-American folk culture developed a "secular world-view." "If during slavery it was the secular songs that were occasional and the religious songs that represented the ethos of the black folk," Levine wrote,

in freedom the situation began to reverse itself. Secular song became increasingly important in black folk culture in the decades following freedom. Negroes were thrust into the larger world, and their response to their experience was couched more and more in explicitly worldly terms. The sacred world was not shattered immediately and decisively for all Negroes in the period after the Civil War; it continued, with different degrees of intensity and pervasiveness, to inform the consciousness and world view of large numbers of blacks both North and South. But never again was it to occupy the central position of the antebellum years.[82]

While few researchers would argue with Levine's contention that the "sacred world" was an important aspect of a slave folk culture, it is hardly accurate to place it in the "central position." In his research Levine chose to examine primarily the religious folk materials of antebellum Afro-Americans, as did Thomas Wentworth Higginson, William Francis Allen, Charles P. Ware, and Lucy McKim Garrison in the 1860s. And like these earlier collectors, Levine concluded that slave songs, tales, and music were overly preoccupied with "religious" concerns. But as was shown in Chapters Two and Three, evidence of a flourishing secular folk culture went largely unrecorded because Afro-Americans were reluctant to share these songs and stories with whites. These songs and tales reinforced values of resistance against the unjust oppression of slavery. Not all members of the slave community were religious, but all were enslaved, and it was on the basis of the common experience of slavery that Afro-Americans developed secular and sacred values of resistance and survival with dignity. The shared experience of racial oppression occupied the central position in defining the emerging value system of the Afro-American masses.

Levine believed that "freedom" or emancipation had a profound impact on Afro-American folk culture by making it less religious and more secular. Work songs, protest tunes, proverbs, jokes, and folktales, whose origins he traced to the post-emancipation era, Levine believed, had no counterpart in slave folk culture. But again, as was noted earlier, the enslaved Afro-Americans were as adept at "puttin' down ole massa" as they were at putting him on. Thomas Wentworth Higginson, William Allen, and others in the 1850s and 1860s reported hearing Afro-American work songs, and many of the Negro spirituals were "freedom songs." Musicologist Dena Epstein in her recent study, *Sinful Tunes and Spirituals: Black Folk Music to the Civil War* (1977), identified a great deal of religious music, but also found a wide variety of secular musical forms including worksongs, harvest tunes, street cries, field hollers, and "corn-shucking tunes," all quite popular within the slave and free black communities during the antebellum period.[83]

While emancipation brought about a profound change in the legal status of the vast majority of Afro-Americans, it did *not* bring about a significant change in the predominant cultural values and attitudes within the black community. But we would not anticipate great change in cultural values, unless there was some fundamental change in the material conditions and experiences of the masses of Afro-Americans. Since this change did not occur, there was great continuity in Afro-American cultural values from slavery to freedom. Under slavery, Afro-Americans valued survival with dignity, resistance against oppression, religious self-determination, and freedom. After emancipation, they continued to hold these ideals; and freedom, rather than being an end in itself, became a means for achieving other cultural goals that developed within the slave and free black communities.

Economists and economic historians have emphasized the continuities in the southern political economy from antebellum to postbellum periods, despite the dislocations wrought during that "tragic era." Richard Sutch, Roger Ransom, Jonathan Weiner, and Joseph Mandle examined the economic position of the masses of Afro-American laborers in the South, from a number of different angles and vantage points, and concluded that between 1850 and 1880 blacks remained exploited agricultural workers occupying the bottom rung of the southern socioeconomic ladder.[84]

When we examine the testimony of the former slaves, we find repeated statements of the need to escape not only the poverty and terrorism of the "Reconstructed South," but also the "enforced ignorance" that had been a cornerstone of the slave regime. As a direct result of the conditions that the masses of Afro-Americans faced during slavery and in the immediate postwar years, there developed within the Afro-American nation a preoccupation with literacy, schooling, and education in general. For thousands of newly emancipated Afro-Americans the acquisition of knowledge became as important an objective as holding on to their freedom.

FIVE

Education Is What We Need

When I done been 'deemed en done been tried,
I'll sit down side de lamb.
Can't you read? Can't you read?
When I done been ter heaven den,
I can read my title clear.
I's goin' ter git my lesson,
I's goin' ter read,
I's goin' ter read my title clear.

Afro-American folk song

The work of instructing my dear fellow-slaves was the sweetest engagement with which I was ever blessed. . . . These dear souls came not to Sabbath School because it was popular to do so, nor did I teach them because it was reputable to be thus engaged. Every moment they spent in that school, they were liable to be taken up and given thirty-nine lashes. They came because they wished to learn. Their minds had been starved by their cruel masters. They had been shut up in mental darkness. I taught them, because it was the delight of my soul to be doing something that looked like bettering the condition of my race.

FREDERICK DOUGLASS, 1845

FLOYD THORNHILL had been working as a sleeping-car porter on the Great Southern Railway Line for about three years, and he had "worked off and on for about two years on the Chesapeake and Ohio Railroad." Before that he had been employed for twelve years in a tobacco factory in Lynchburg, Virginia. Mr. Thornhill had been born and raised in slavery in Campbell County, Virginia: "I was sixteen years old when Lee surrendered." Floyd Thornhill strolled onto the historical stage while carrying the luggage and conversing with Senator Henry Blair (Republican, New Hampshire), who had just completed hearings in Boston in late October 1883 for the Senate's Committee on Education and Labor, and was now on his way to Birmingham, Alabama, for further investigations and hearings. Interested primarily in learning more about the working conditions for American laborers, black and white, Senator Blair was so favorably impressed with Floyd Thornhill's extensive knowledge of living and working conditions in the South that he decided to interview him and record his testimony right on the train.

Question. What do you call your present business?

Answer. Sleeping-car porter, running between Washington and New Orleans.

Question. Is this an important route between the North and the South?

Answer. Yes, sir; it is called the boss route—the boss Southern railroad.

Question. How long have you worked at your present business?

Answer. About three years.

Question. What pay do you get?

Answer. Twelve dollars a month.

Question. In addition to that you get something from the passengers, I suppose?

Answer. Yes, sir.

Question. How much does that amount to, on an average?

Answer. Well, I reckon, from time to time, I make here about $30 a month.[1]

Senator Blair's committee had been authorized by the full Senate in a resolution of 7 August 1882 to conduct an investigation of "the relations between labor and capital, the wages and hours of labor, the conditions of the laboring classes in the United States, and their relative conditions and wages as compared with similar classes abroad. . . ." Prompted by the increasing labor unrest in various parts of the country, the committee was also to investigate "labor strikes and to inquire into the causes thereof and the agencies producing the same." The members, as a group, were supposed to suggest "what legislation should be adopted to modify or remove such causes and provide against their continuance or recurrence, as well as other legislation calculated to promote harmonious relations between capitalists and laborers, and the interests of both, by the improvement of the condition of the industrial classes of the United States." The recent emergence of the Knights of Labor and the American Federation of Labor as strong workers organizations as well as the increase in labor disputes and disruptions in 1881 and 1882 led the Senate to call for an investigation to determine the overall role of the federal government in the industrial workplace.[2]

Senator Blair questioned Floyd Thornhill about the wages for black farm workers.

> *Question.* What wages do colored men generally receive working on the land in this part of the country or about Lynchburg?
> *Answer.* They get from $10 to $12 a month and board.
> *Question.* Do they also have houses and garden plots?
> *Answer.* Yes, sir; they generally have as much land as they want.
> *Question.* Do the women have anything to do?
> *Answer.* Yes, sir; they sometimes works for wages; sometimes they does washing, and sometimes they works out in the field.
> *Question.* How many hours do the men and women work generally?
> *Answer.* The women works along like the men, except that sometimes they have to stop and go home and get the meals.
> *Question.* What pay do the women get?
> *Answer.* About 50 cents a day.
> *Question.* Do the girls work on the land at all?
> *Answer.* Yes, sir; some of the girls work at it, and some of them go to school. When they aint going to school they work.
> *Question.* What sort of work do most of the girls do?
> *Answer.* The girls works the same as the old people do, weedin' corn or suckerin' tobacco or hoein' corn or bindin' wheat in the harvest field—most any kind of work.

Mr. Thornhill also mentioned that "a great many colored people have right smart little farms in Virginia," including his brother in Prince Edward County. "He has got fifty acres of land and a team. He has got good rich, land. He raises wheat, tobacco and corn."[3]

Although it was not part of the original charge, Senator Blair's committee also collected a great deal of information on the conditions of the public schools in the South, especially those for Afro-Americans. Senator Blair by 1883 had become one of the chief spokesmen for a nationwide movement to gain federal funds for the financially strapped public school systems throughout the country. Blair and many other Republican leaders (including Presidents James Garfield and Chester Arthur) had put forward the position that the lack of advancement of Afro-Americans in the southern states since the end of the Civil War could be traced directly to the failure of state legislatures to appropriate sufficient funds for black public education. Southern Democrats argued that, given the decrepit financial status of most of the southern state treasuries, plus the large (and in several states majority) black population in need of schooling, it would take some years to make a significant impact on southern "mass illiteracy." Several Democratic and Republican Senators had announced their support for the use of the current surplus in the federal treasury to assist local public school districts temporarily in opening new schools, especially in remote rural areas.[4]

In the wake of the widespread political violence, outrages, and mass migrations of Afro-Americans out of the South in the late 1870s, the "Southern Negro" and the "Southern Question" became one of the central political issues in the presidential campaign of 1880. In their platform the Republicans took great pride in "enumerating among its achievements, the suppression of the rebellion, the enfranchisements of 4,000,000 negroes [and] the suppression of the Fugitive Slave Law." James Garfield, their presidential nominee, stood firmly within the camp of the liberal wing of the GOP in his early years in the Congress, but by 1880 he responded more conservatively to the exposure of Ku Klux Klan depredations, or to the use of federal troops in the South to maintain law and order; and he generally remained unsure about the most appropriate "southern strategy" for the Republican party. To his way of thinking, wrote Garfield in 1875, southern politics was a contest between "a reckless set of scamps . . . on the one hand, and an armed negro-hating band of murderers on the other."[5]

Throughout the low-keyed campaign against Democratic candidate, General Winfield Scott Hancock of Pennsylvania, Garfield openly defended the right of suffrage for Afro-Americans in the South, and in the fall election managed to squeeze by his opponent by only 7,368 more popular votes, the closest presidential election in American history.[6] Moreover, at least one third of Garfield's inaugural address in March 1881 was devoted to the problems facing Afro-Americans in the South. For Garfield, there was a direct connection between freedom and black social advancement. "The elevation of the negro race from slavery to the full rights of the citizenship is the most important political change we have known since the adoption of the Constitution of 1787. . . .

The emancipated race has already made remarkable progress. With unquestioning devotion to the Union, with a patience and gentleness not born of fear, they have "followed the light as God gave them to see the light." They are rapidly laying the material foundations of self-support, widening their circle of intelligence, and beginning to enjoy the blessings that gather around the homes of the industrious poor. They deserve the generous encouragement of all good men. So far as my authority can lawfully extend, they shall enjoy the full and equal protection of the Constitution and the laws.

The new President then went on to discuss his position on black suffrage. "It is alleged that in many communities negro citizens are practically denied the freedom of the ballot.

In so far as the truth of this allegation is admitted it is answered that in many places honest local government is impossible if the mass of uneducated negroes are allowed to vote. These are grave allegations. So far as the latter is true, it is the only palliation that can be offered for opposing the freedom of the ballot. Bad local government is certainly a great evil, which ought to be prevented; but to violate the freedom and sanctities of the suffrage is more than an evil. It is a crime which, if persisted in, will destroy the Government itself. Suicide is not a remedy. If in other lands it be high treason to compass the death of the king, it shall be counted no less a crime here to strangle our sovereign power and stifle its voice.

Garfield was fearful of the "danger which arises from ignorance in the voter" because "it covers a field far wider than that of negro suffrage and the present condition of the race. It is a danger that lurks and hides in the sources and fountains of power in every state." Every attempt must be made to wipe out illiteracy, and since the federal government had decreed that the former slaves should be voters, the federal government should be willing to assist the southern states in providing schooling for the new citizens.

The census has already sounded the alarm in the appalling figures which mark how dangerously high the tide of illiteracy has risen among our voters and their children [over fifty percent].

To the South this question is of supreme importance. But the responsibility for the existence of slavery did not rest upon the South alone. The nation itself is responsible for the extension of the suffrage, and is under special obligations to aid in removing the illiteracy which it had added to the voting population. For the North and South alike there is but one remedy. All the constitutional power of the nation and of the States and all the volunteer forces of the people should be surrendered to meet this danger by the savory influence of universal education.

It is the high privilege and sacred duty of those now living to educate their successors and fit them, by intelligence and virtue, for the inheritance which awaits them.[7]

Regrettably, President James Garfield was shot on 2 July 1881 at the Baltimore & Potomac Railroad Station in Washington, D.C., by Charles Julius Guiteau, a disappointed office-seeker; and he died two months later. In many ways following through on the pledges of the martyred President, Senator Henry Blair introduced a bill into the Senate in April 1882 calling for federal aid for public school education in states with high rates of illiteracy.[8]

The Senate's Committee on Education and Labor, in its investigation into the "relations between capital and labor," collected thousands of pages of testimony (four volumes) from hundreds of Americans, blacks and whites, masses and elites, on the educational conditions in the South in the early 1880s. In the interrogation of Floyd Thornhill, Senator Blair elicited his perceptions of public school conditions in Lynchburg, Virginia.

> *Question.* How is it generally as to the attendance at school of the children, white and colored, in and about Lynchburg?
>
> *Answer.* Well, they both seem to attend school pretty well, both colors.
>
> *Question.* How long are the schools kept open each year?
>
> *Answer.* I think the session is about nine months in the year. They have a vacation of about three months, I think; I don't believe now but it is only two months, because I kind of remember that my little boy didn't stop going to school till some time in June.
>
> *Question.* Are the teachers white or colored?
>
> *Answer.* Some white and some colored.
>
> *Question.* Do you have colored teachers in the schools for the colored people?

Answer. There is one part white and another part colored.

Question. Are the schools mixed or separate?

Answer. They are separate.

Question. There are no white children in the colored schools, nor colored children in the white schools?

Answer. No, sir; not one.

The issue of "mixed versus separate" public schools in the post-Reconstruction South had been used to divert attention away from the real problem of providing a basic common school education for southern black and white children and adults.

Question. You don't want to have any white children in your schools, I suppose.

Answer. No, sir.

Question. How do the colored people generally feel about that?

Answer. They want their children to go to their own schools. I never heard one colored man say that he wanted his children to go to a white school.

Question. Why not?

Answer. Well it's just this: them children would not do to go to school together anyhow.

Question. Why not?

Answer. Well, now, I'll tell you. The white children, them that is big enough, knows we have been slaves that belonged to their parents, and there comes a great 'sturbment out of that. The white children *will* show authority over the nigger, and I don't believe they have any business to go to school together. That is my idea. Now, I am a mighty strange man. If I am working for you and you trust me good and pay me, that is all right, but you could not have me come and sit down in your dining room, because I have never been used to it, and I don't look to it, and the dinner is just as good after you are gone, and my feelings would feel freer to sit down by myself. Now them is facts.

Blair and Thornhill agreed that there was great potential for arguments and quarrels between blacks and whites in mixed public schools, thus they were to be avoided. But "going to school" was greatly valued among Afro-Americans, even among those individuals who were illiterate, such as Floyd Thornhill.

Question. Do you think it is of any consequence whether the children go to school or not?

Answer. Certainly; I tell you I believe in doing the best you can for the children. When a boy comes to be a man he will need it. I have managed to get along pretty well, but sometimes I imagine that if I could read and write it would be better. Many a time a passenger hands me a ticket; wants to know which way he is going, and I have to tell him, "I can't read, but if you will read it along I will tell you whether it is the Kenesaw route or not." I might take it myself and hum over it and make it out in a kind of a way, but not satisfactory. So I believe in children being educated and elevated somehow, because when they come to be men it is great help.

Question. Then you mean to keep your children at school, I suppose?

Answer. Yes, sir.

Question. Is that the feeling of the colored people generally?

Answer. Well, they seem to be tolerable earnest to keep the children going to school.[9]

When the Senate committee arrived in Birmingham, Alabama, the investigators began taking testimony on 12 November 1883. Both black and white citizens testified before the committee on the economic conditions for former slaves and their progress (or lack of it) since emancipation. For example, former Democratic governor Robert Patton, declared that "the young negroes, are not equal to those of the older generation who were trained by the whites." He believed that "in slavery times, the young negroes were raised under discipline and government, and the consequence was that they were better trained to industry and better able to do any kind of work with advantage to themselves as well as to their owners."[10] W. W. Gardner, a wealthy cotton merchant in Birmingham, complained about the "restlessness of negro labor," and as a result, "in the agricultural districts the relations between capital and labor are . . . neither satisfactory [n]or profitable." He noted that now, as opposed to the situation under slavery, the black farm worker "not infrequently leaves the plantation, leaves it at a time when it is almost impossible to replace his labors, and goes off to work by the day on a railroad or somewhere else." Gardner wanted legislation which "compels the observance of his contract by the laborer. . . ."[11]

Some of the witnesses, when questioned about the need for more public schools, were unsure that it could improve the conditions. For example, Albert C. Danner, president of the Bank of Mobile and large-scale capitalist in the lumber and coal business, believed that for most Afro-Americans, "a little learning is a dangerous thing. . . ."

Those of them that have a little school learning seem to be puffed up by it and made proud, and their parents are proud of it, but a good deal of their schooling is not of the practical kind. I think they should be taught to read and write, of course, but they should be taught also that labor is honorable and necessary. They have difficulty in connecting the idea of freedom and labor.

When Senator Henry Blair asked whether or not he thought education could improve the situation, Danner responded, "Yes, sir; if they are *properly* educated; if they are taught the necessity and value and dignity of labor."[12] Most Afro-Americans enslaved in the antebellum South clearly recognized the value of their labor to their owners, but they did not control it. When black workers began to exercise greater control over their labor following emancipation, wealthy capitalists, like Robert Patton, W. W. Gardner, and Albert Danner, complained about the "restlessness of negro labor."

A group of Afro-American citizens from Birmingham began testifying before the Senate's investigating committee on 16 November 1883 and provided detailed information on the state of public schooling in that city. From their perspective, there were many problems. Rev. Isaiah Welsh, pastor of the African Methodist Episcopal Church in Birmingham, complained that the school year was "too short now for children to make progress.

A child in some instances spends three months in the school and nine months out of school, so that when he is in school you may say he is always on review, and is never making any progress. By the time he gets started in the study the school is compelled to close from want of means or some other unavoidable circumstance, and while it is closed the pupils lose as much as they have gained during the short school term. Of course this state of things has a very injurious effect upon both races, especially the laboring classes. People in easy circumstances are able to establish private schools or to patronize such schools where they are already established, and in that way to overcome these difficulties under which the poorer people labor.

J. H. Thomasson, editor of the local black newspaper, was disturbed because "I don't think the appropriations are enough to pay good, competent teachers to teach in our schools, and some of our best young men and young ladies who have attended the schools, and have received their diplomas, have had to go away to other States to seek employment where salaries are better than they are in Alabama." Thomasson objected strongly to the hiring of "ignorant teachers and superintendents." "I have objection to their employing incompetent teachers. It seems to me from what I have observed that an incompetent teacher can get a place in a school more readily than one who is competent."

> *Question.* Do you mean that those who examine the teachers select the most incompetent?
> *Answer.* It has seemed to me that way, sir, in some places. Of course there are exceptions.
> *Question.* What do they do that for?
> *Answer.* That is what I don't know. I have wondered at it myself, and have often asked myself what they do it for, but of course I am unable to tell that.
> *Question.* How far does your observation extend?
> *Answer.* I have some knowledge of several counties in the northern part of the State. That is where I hail from. That is the case in the county I am from, that incompetent teachers are generally those who are first served in the matter of employment in the schools there, and it has been so for several years.
> *Question.* Do you mean colored teachers or white teachers?
> *Answer.* Colored. I never knew but one white man up there to teach a colored school. He was incompetent, and the colored people felt that if they had to have a white teacher they wanted one of better understanding than themselves; they do not care about mixing with them. He is about the only one that we ever had in our county in the public schools. [13]

W. W. Wilson, a white teacher and for ten years a member of the board of examiners for teachers in the Birmingham public schools, was later asked by Senator Blair, "How do you find the qualifications of the Colored teachers?"

> In the main I find the colored teachers very well qualified to teach. I find many of them better qualified than many of the white persons are who want to teach. I was on the board of examiners for Jefferson County here for three years, and I found that a large number of the colored teachers were incompetent—not a majority of them, but about one-fourth—at least, they were not so well qualified as they should have been. We indulged them for a time, and some of them came up to the standard, but others failed. Some of them dropped out each year. However, in many cases the teachers of the colored schools, as well as of the white schools, were very well qualified. On one occasion we had an examination, and it was not convenient that the negroes and the whites

should be examined in different rooms. It was our custom generally to give the negroes a more lenient examination than the whites, but on this occasion as we were about to examine them, two white persons came up to be examined, and we told them they could take the same examination if they chose, and they did so, and we found the negroes were equal to the whites in that case. I have had occasion to examine applicants for the Birmingham schools, and I have found the negroes—some of them, at least—pretty well qualified to teach.[14]

But even if the teachers were "qualified," they could accomplish little in a three-month school term. And since the public schools in Birmingham were not free, many poor students were unable to attend even for the three months. N. R. Fielding, a black bricklayer in the city, startled several members of the committee when he announced that he was "somewhat opposed to the school system."

I don't know who to find fault for it directly, but the poorer classes of colored people here are deprived of schools. The State or the county makes a little appropriation to start a school, but, as some people have already testified, we have very incompetent teachers, a good many of them; and the poorer children, that are not able to go to school, they are charged a "supplement," and they are not able to pay that, so they are not able to go to school on account of the supplement fund. They are charged 10 cents a week. Now, where a man has to work for $1 a day, and has to pay from $5 to $10 a month, and has five or six children to go to school, he cannot afford to send them to school and pay 10 cents a week extra for each of them; and if he is not able to pay that his children are not allowed to go to school, and he is deprived of the benefit of the public appropriation which the State makes for that purpose.

At this point the Democratic Senator from Alabama, James L. Pugh, interrupted Mr. Fielding's testimony.

Mr. Pugh. You are mistaken about that, I think.

The Witness. No, sir; I am not.

Mr. Pugh. Well, the mayor differs with you about it. He says that if the parents are not able to pay, the children are received in the schools at any rate.

The Witness. Well, they do not go, and they are refused admittance to the schools, and that has been so within the last thirty or sixty days.

Mr. Pugh. The mayor says that if they say that they are unable to pay they are admitted without pay.

The Witness. Well, I have always argued that they could not be deprived of going to school, but the teachers have undertaken to collect money from them, and if the parents don't pay they send the children home. I don't know whether it is done by authority or not, but I know it is done.

The Chairman. There is nothing to pay the teachers but that fund, is there?

The Witness. My idea is that if a school is being run in the name of the public, the poor children ought to get the benefit of it even if it does not run but one month. There is a heap of people that would send their children if they could pay.

Question. Do you think of anything else that you desire to state?

Answer. No, sir; nothing else.

These and other statements seemed to confirm Senator Blair's contention that there was a great need for federal aid to public schools for blacks and whites in the South. During the hearings Blair commented to one of the black witnesses from Birmingham: "You all seem to be thoroughly impressed with the idea that it is well and desirable to be better educated?" J. G. Going, a black barber in the city, answered; "Yes, sir, that is the thing that our people need mostly."[15]

But basic literacy training was not the only type of schooling that was suggested as necessary for the education of the poorer classes, black and white. The numerous complaints about the lack of a "disciplined labor force" in the South led to the suggestion by many capitalists (and a few noncapitalists) of the need to provide some sort of "industrial education" for the black and white lower classes. Initially, the scheme was put forward as a way of insuring that each child going through the public schools would emerge with some kind of practical skill or trade, as well as basic literacy. It was not enough merely to teach the Protestant work ethic through the grammars, spellers, and readers used in public school classrooms around the country; the children should also receive instruction in mechanical arts, drawing, surveying, carpentry, agriculture and any number of other "practical subjects." Before 1860, various types of manual training programs existed, and many industrial training classes were included in the regular college, secondary, and elementary school curricula. After the Civil War, however, as the common school ideal made its way slowly through the southern states, the suggestion was heard over and over again that the poor whites and blacks needed manual training as much as they needed to learn to read and write. Black and white southerners, for a wide variety of reasons, came to the conclusion by 1883 that "industrial education" should be included in the regular public school curriculum, especially for the lower classes.[16]

"Don't you think it would be well to combine instruction in the industrial arts with our public school education?" asked Senator Pugh. "I think so," answered former governor Robert Patton, who considered himself a "champion of industrial education" in that region. Patton wished "that all our schools were practical labor schools, to teach our people how to work to advantage, how to till the earth, how to run the spindle, and all the branches connected with industrial education. That is what we need, particularly in all this part of the country. When we have that education in the South, and when we learn to diversify our industries so as to give varied employment, and employment to all our people in the different branches of labor, we shall become a great people here; we shall have a great South."[17]

This was not the only quasi-political statement on industrial education included in the congressional testimony on the "relations between labor and capital." Witness after witness, black and white, recited a litany of the needs that would be fulfilled in Alabama and throughout the South once industrial education was provided. Senator Pugh asked J. H. Fitts, president of the J. H. Fitts Bank in Tuscaloosa, "What do you think would best promote the rapid development of cotton manufacturing in the South?" Fitts was emphatic. "The establishment of manufacturing schools, where boys and young men could learn the art of making all kinds of cotton fabrics. Such a school would supply the present need for skilled men in whom our capitalists have faith." Fitts, who was also president of the Tuscaloosa Cotton Mills, firmly believed that "the cause of the failure of so many mills at the South . . . may be attributed to the fact that the owner or stockholders are entirely ignorant of the business. . . ." And Senator Blair asked G. W. Walton, the black owner of a restaurant in Wetumpka, Alabama, "Is there anything else that you think ought to be done for the improvement of the condition of the people here; anything that you think Government ought to do?" Walton echoed the sentiments of former Governor Patton.

> *Answer.* I think that if there is any power in the Government to establish industrial schools in the South and get our people to come into them, and teach them how to make a living, save their money, and so on, I think the Government would help us on a great deal as a race of people by doing that.
>
> *Question.* Is that the main suggestion that you wish to make?
>
> *Answer.* Yes, sir; if I was going to suggest anything to do our people good here, I think, that would be the plan that I would suggest to the Government; to give us industrial schools all through the South, to teach our people industry and economy. That would do more good than anything else.[18]

The black and white witnesses at hearings before Senator Blair's Committee on Education and Labor in 1883 differed widely on whether there was a need for federal aid to public school districts in the South, but there was no disagreement about the need for some type of industrial education for the children of the laboring classes. Black and white supporters of universal common schooling were thus joined by wealthy capitalists in advocating training for industrial and agricultural workers for the rise of the "New South." But given the 50 percent illiteracy rate nationwide in 1880 (60 or 70 percent in the South), plus the general unwillingness of white southerners to tax themselves to support public education; the educational philanthropists, rich capitalists, and "New South" politicians who supported literacy and industrial training for lower class whites and blacks had a long way to go to achieve "universal literacy" in the Reconstructed South. [19]

And there was still another factor that had to be dealt with when discussing publicly supported educational opportunities for blacks and whites in the South in the 1880s and 1890s—white supremacy: the training provided for Afro-Americans in the public schools should not challenge the domination of whites over all areas of American life. Many white southerners opposed any sort of publicly supported schooling for blacks, and the compromise that was reached between common school enthusiasts and staunch white supremacists resulted in public educational systems throughout the South that were "woefully inadequate" for meeting the needs and demands of the Afro-American population. [20] The strong desire for education among Afro-Americans can be traced backed to the conditions and practices under slavery, and fortunately this "yearning for learning" was significantly stronger than white prescriptions. This may account for the historical reality that during the same period (1880–1910) when public expenditures for black public schooling in the southern states decreased significantly, most Afro-Americans living there became literate men and women.

Assistance Without Control

During the antebellum era, education and literacy were greatly valued among Afro-Americans enslaved in the United States because they saw in their day-to-day experiences—from one generation to the next—that knowledge and information helped one to survive in a hostile environment. In numerous ways, Afro-Americans came to understand that wisdom and knowledge were associated with freedom. An important part of the oppression of enslavement was depriving Afro-Americans of knowledge of their condition, and thus the ways to change it. But the desire for literacy and "book-learning" was often stronger than the prohibitions and persecutions associated with the slave regime, and as a result, in so many difficult and diverse fashions, enslaved Afro-Americans learned to read and write.[21]

Slave letters, narratives, and interviews reveal a broad range of experiences that resulted in literacy for the enslaved. Many Afro-American children learned to read by playing and studying on the plantation with the white children who were enrolled in schools and learning to read and write. Unfortunately, sometimes the slave children learned more quickly than the offspring of the master class. Margaret Terry was born in Charlottesville, Virginia, right before the beginning of the Civil War and used to study with the children of her owner, Alfred Benson. "We studied together and the old lady would hear them. I would know mine. Now she would say, 'I can't see why Margaret always knows her lesson and you all do not.' Pow, Pow, the strap would go." Then one day the mistress, Kitty Benson, came and told her, "Margaret, you stop studying with the children." But it was too late; a spark had been lit in Margaret's young and inquisitive mind: "I would find out where the lesson was and would get it just the same, but she didn't know it."[22]

Philip Ward, who was also enslaved in Virginia, recounted the following story to the interviewers from the Federal Writers Project about how a slave boy got a whipping because his master's son did not know his lessons.

> Marse had six children of his own. There was Charles, Russell, Henrietta, Lucy, Violet, and Elizabeth. All the children went to school, and Marse used to warn them about leaving their books around where we could get to see them. But they didn't pay any attention to him. One day Marse came down to the barn and found Russell whipping a little slave boy his own age, named Jerry. Marsa grabbed Russell and took the whip away from him. "Who tole you to whip that boy?" he asked. Russell started crying, "Well, that's what the teacher did to me today 'cause I didn't know my lesson. And he doesn't know it no better'n I do." All us slaves knew that Russell had been going over his lessons with Jerry a long time, but Marse didn't know it. He put a stop to it after that, though.[23]

In most of the interviews with ex-slaves, however, the encounters with literacy were described as even more traumatic and violent. Ferebe Rogers was over one hundred years old when he was interviewed in 1937 by Ruth Chitty, and he promised at the outset, "I'm goin' tell de truth. I don't tell no lies." As a slave in Baldwin County, Georgia, in the 1850s, Rogers understood the value of literacy, but "I had my right arm cut off at de elbow if I'd tried to learn to read and write. If dey found a nigger what could read and

write, dey'd cut your arm off at de elbow, or sometimes at de shoulder."
Rogers also recalled that the man who married him, Enoch Golden, was
called a "double-headed nigger" because "he could read and write, and he
knowed so much. On his dyin' bed he said he been de death o' many a nigger
'cause he taught so many to read and write."[24]

Mutilation (or death) could sometimes result when enslaved Afro-
Americans tried to become literate men and women. Abram Harris believed
"dere weren't none of de white folks in dem slavery times what would let dey
niggers have any learnin." In Greenville, South Carolina, where he was born
and raised, "you sure better not be cotch a tryin' to learn no readin' and
writin'. . . . Iffen a nigger was to be found what could write, den right
straight dey would chop his forefinger offen dat hand what he write with."[25]
Ellis Bennett, who was recorded in 1937 at the age of ninety-one while
regaling hospital personnel at an old soldiers' home in Virginia with his
stories, swore that the "white man let no niggah read 'fore the war."

> White men stan on poarch. See nigguh walking by wif buk in 'is 'and.
> White man call, "Nig-gu-h nigguh, God dam! Come heah!" Nigguh
> come. Wite man snatch buk. Say "Buk no fo' nigguh; buk fo' wite
> man." Kick nigguh in slack o pants say, "Git long wuk you son
> of a b - - - !"[26]

Many slaves did manage to get books and learned to read and write,
sometimes at great cost, and thus for those individuals learning to read was
one of the most profound experiences in their lives. In the narratives of John
Thompson, Moses Grandy, J. W. C. Pennington, and others, the struggle
for literacy and knowledge was often central to the stories they had to tell.[27]
The classic account of the meaning and significance of literacy to the enslaved
is found in *The Narrative of the Life of Frederick Douglass* (1845). At the age of
six or seven, when he first went to live with Mr. and Mrs. Thomas Auld in
Talbot County, Maryland, Mrs. Auld "commenced to teach me the A, B, C.
After I had learned this, she assisted me in learning to spell words of three or
four letters.

> Just at this point of my progress, Mr. Auld found out what was going
> on, and at once forbade Mrs. Auld to instruct me further, telling her,
> among other things, that it was unlawful, as well as unsafe, to teach a
> slave to read. To use his own words, further, he said, "If you give a
> nigger an inch, he will take an ell. A nigger should know nothing but
> to obey his master—to do as he is told to do. Learning would *spoil* the
> best nigger in the world. Now," said he, "if you teach that nigger

(speaking of myself) how to read, there would be no keeping him. It would forever unfit him to be a slave. He would at once become unmanageable, and of no value to his master. As to himself, it could do him no good, but a great deal of harm. It would make him discontented and unhappy."

The declaration by Mr. Auld exposed the true nature of the slave's predicament to the young Frederick. "These words sank deep into my heart, stirred up sentiments within that lay slumbering, and called into existence an entirely new train of thought.

It was a new and special revelation, explaining dark and mysterious things, with which my youthful understanding had struggled, but struggled in vain. I now understood what had been to me a most perplexing difficulty—to wit, the white man's power to enslave the black man. It was a grand achievement, and I prized it highly. From that moment, I understood the pathway from slavery to freedom.

Douglass later remarked that the "Mistress, in teaching me the alphabet, had given me the *inch* and no precaution could prevent me from taking the ell."[28]

Thus long before the end of slavery the ethos of education and literacy had been instilled in many Afro-Americans, who then passed it on to the next generation within the black community. And it was often the case that those who themselves were illiterate and unschooled held firmest the value of "education for advancement." Ex-slave Peggy Burton of Newport News, Virginia, like sleeping-car porter Floyd Thornhill, was illiterate; and when the Federal Writers Project researcher approached her for a second interview, she was annoyed; "I ain't got nothin' to tell you. I'se done told you all I knows." But in this brief summary of the important aspects of her life, Mrs. Burton provided us with a great deal of information about what she valued and thought was "serious."

I raise' my chillun—sent dem to school and give dem what education dey got, and I'se done raise' my grand chillun and help to educate dem—guess I'se done through. I try to give dem all de chances cause I never had privilege to go to school cause I come long during slavery days. Where de white folks spit in de nigger chillun's faces and dey couldn't help dem selves—dat dey did. . . . I was a slave and couldn't go to school, but if I had de chance dese young folks have now a days, I'd make good use of dem cause I always wanted an education so dat I could be somebody, but Lordy childe dese chillun ain't taking life serious now.[29]

Freedom and education were inextricably bound together in the cultural value system that developed among Afro-Americans enslaved in the United States. With the outbreak of the Civil War and the military campaigns in the South, Afro-Americans streamed across the Union lines into military encampments and fortifications and took advantage of relief supplies and other material benefits. They also flocked to the makeshift schoolhouses of black and white teachers and missionaries, and by 1865 throughout the former Confederacy we find what Booker T. Washington referred to as "a whole race trying to go to school."[30]

The records of the federal government, especially the Freedmen's Bureau, which was responsible for opening hundreds of schools for newly emancipated Afro-Americans, as well as the files and letters of the religious and secular relief and missionary societies, contain a vast amount of information relevant to understanding how the cultural values supporting education affected the behavior of the freedpeople. These sources also provide insights into the struggle for control over the form and content of freedmen's education during the Reconstruction era. Initially, the field was completely dominated by private schools founded by free blacks in the larger southern cities. Between 1861 and 1865 hundreds of "Sabbath Schools" were opened by black church congregations in both rural and urban areas. Then the northern black and white teachers and missionaries descended on the liberated areas in large numbers, and northern religious denominations and missionary boards moved to control the educational activities in particular sections, even those of all-black groups. The federal government entered the picture with the opening of the "Freedom Schools," and the officials of the Freedmen's Bureau worked closely with the missionary societies, especially the American Missionary Association (AMA). By 1868 nearly all the schools available to the freedpeople living in the South were controlled by these white-dominated agencies.[31]

Between the end of the Civil War and the overthrow of Radical Reconstruction (1877), Afro-Americans gradually lost control over most of the educational institutions and the content of the schooling being provided the masses of Afro-American children and adults living in the South. The officials of the AMA and other religious-missionary groups generally treated black teachers and students in a paternalistic fashion, and even tried to drive nonreligious or secular groups from the field of freedmen's education. The freedom schools sponsored by the federal government were more dependent on local participation and resources, and thus could not afford to be overly demanding and aggressive. But by 1871 most of the freedom schools had been turned over to either the AMA or local white public school officials, and in either case, the schools were placed under the control of individuals and groups that did not necessarily share the same values as the masses of Afro-Americans.[32]

Jacqueline Jones, in *Soldiers of Light and Love: Northern Teachers and Georgia Blacks, 1865–1873* (1980), examined the records of the AMA teachers and administrators and tried to document the day-to-day relations and interactions between AMA programs and personnel and the newly emancipated Afro-Americans. "The attitude of white northern officials towards blacks was one of paternalism," Jones concluded.

> When they began to work in Georgia, northern teachers and superintendents had preconceived notions about the role freedpeople should play in the overall education effort. They believed that black teachers lacked the formal training to be effective instructors and that enlightened white men and women must assume major responsibility for establishing—and to a great extent teaching in—black schools throughout the state. Representatives of freedmen's aid societies intended to oversee all aspects of black education. At the same time, few northerners felt inclined to provide substantial aid to local black communities without evidence that the people were able to raise a certain amount of money on their own.[33]

The self-contradicting nature of this response led to decisions and programs that were ultimately self-defeating.

> In rural areas, poverty-stricken communities were unable to make large cash contributions for the maintenance of schools. As a result, northern societies assumed that they had an insufficient appreciation of formal instruction and gradually withdrew aid from almost all rural areas. But, when blacks successfully established their own schools, as they did in some towns, northerners were shocked and offended at this lack of appreciation for white benevolence.

Whatever schooling that was provided the freedpeople by "white benevolence" would be controlled in most instances by white capitalists. Oftentimes the educational programs offered in these schools emphasized middle-class capitalistic values rather than those values and beliefs that were necessary (and would be necessary) to guarantee black survival and advancement in American society. In the schools opened by northern white teachers, according to Jones, "their preoccupation with order and obedience in the classroom put a premium on conformity, passivity, and deference to whites in authority." But the intention was merely to maintain decorum. "Most had to deal single-handedly with large numbers of pupils for several hours a day, and they enforced strict disciplinary procedures in an effort to prevent the whole situation from getting out of hand." The values, however, were those of nineteenth-century "Yankee schoolmarms"; and in their classrooms they emphasized the "Protestant work ethic" and "tried to instill in their pupils habits of hard work, punctuality, and sobriety that would make them tractable workers for their employers."[34]

In *Northern Schools, Southern Blacks, and Reconstruction: Freedmen's Education, 1862–1875* (1980), Ronald Butchart focused directly on the values and ideologies underpinning the educational programs sponsored by northern white missionaries and the federal government. Butchart also systematically examined "the content of southern black education." The various texts, readers, and grammars, published by the American Tract Society (ATS) of the AMA specifically for use in black missionary schools, were geared, according to Butchart, toward "the reformation of black life styles and the imposition of an alien cultural ideal." For example, John Alvord, a white superintendent of education in the Freedman's Bureau in 1869, presented his "pedagogical formula" for the "moral uplift" of the freedpeople.

> First: Moral culture should be paramout [sic] in our plans; the constant practical aim in our schools. This alone will neutralize the corrupt influences of slavery still remaining, and give to character a solid basis. Without this, indeed, there can be no right education of any people.
>
> Second: The various affairs and economics of every-day life should be taught: cleanliness, dress, home habits, social proprieties, uses of furniture, dwellings, though with rustic material; also with individual self-reliance; labor, productive of support and thrift; habits of saving, with right use of what is saved. We desire to make strong impressions on thees [sic] points.
>
> . . . Teachers, therefore, should not drill in mere technical scholarship; every point of character is to be rounded out, and the minutest habits which perfect the well-trained child are to be cared for.[35]

The reformation that was to take place was not merely confined to social and economic relations with the dominant white group, but was to permeate even the "primitive religious sensabilities" of Afro-Americans. In 1867 the AMA clearly explained its "guiding ideas" about the freedpeople.

> The emotional character of these people renders their religion impulsive, tending to mere excitement, while the terrible curse of slavery has well nigh divorced, in their minds, a practical morality from emotional

piety. This great evil can only be remedied by connecting most closely in all, and particularly the earlier stages of their progress, their intellectual and their religious training. In their homes, in the schools as well as in the church, must this blended teaching be maintained. This obvious necessity has largely dictated the policy of the Association in its efforts for their advancement. . . . .[36]

The culture that allowed Afro-Americans to survive the degradation of enslavement in the United States was considered by many white missionaries and teachers to be "grossly inferior to white culture." Professor Butchart concluded that "their educational emphasis, then, would constitute an assault on several facets of black culture—the nature of religious expression, home life, personal demeanor, social interactions, and work habits."[37]

The existence of these alien values and practices in the schools opened by white teachers and missionaries, however, meant that the masses of Afro-Americans generally preferred to attend schools conducted by Afro-American teachers and principals. There was not merely the generalized belief that Afro-American instructors would better relate and empathize with the students, but also the fact that educated blacks could serve as "role models" and leaders and contribute valuable service to their community. Jacqueline Jones, for example, pointed out in *Soldiers of Light and Love,* that the "freedpeople were sometimes willing to make a financial sacrifice to patronize schools taught by their neighbors. An AMA official lamented that same year [1866], 'Many (or rather I would say some) parents now prefer to send their children to col[ored] teachers and pay a dollar a month for tuition than to send them to our schools free.' This greatly irritated association teachers and administrators alike." Jones found that, as far as the masses of rural blacks were concerned, "in the absence of literate blacks who wanted to run a school, they were grateful for northern [white] teachers."[38]

Ronald Butchart in his much-too-brief discussion of "the black response to freedmen's education" also touched upon the substantial problems that arose when there was competition between black-controlled and northern white-sponsored schools operating in the same area. Afro-Americans living in Savannah, Georgia, organized the Savannah Education Association in 1865 and operated a system of schools that was "entirely self-supporting, relied exclusively on the local black community for their support, and had an all black faculty, including James Porter, the principal." Despite the existence of AMA and other white missionary schools in the city, William Channing Gannett, a white AMA teacher from New England, reported that "they have a natural praiseworthy pride in keeping their educational institutions in their own hands. There is jealousy of the superintendence of the

white man in this matter. What they desire is assistance without control."
Butchart mentioned several other instances of northern white missionaries
trying to gain control over black-initiated, self-help programs.[39]

The values of education, advancement, and self-determination underpinned the numerous efforts by Afro-American communities and organizations to open classrooms and schoolhouses for themselves and for their
children following the Civil War. But opening and maintaining a school was
an arduous task for an impoverished, illiterate community of ex-slaves and
free blacks, and thus they welcomed the support of northern white missionaries and teachers. Their acceptance of this support and attendance at
these missionary schools did not mean that Afro-Americans living in the
former Confederacy necessarily believed that "integrated" efforts would
achieve the type and level of advancement they wished to obtain. Most white
southerners did not openly oppose vigilante groups that terrorized the black
community, and there was just no significant evidence that most whites were
willing to assist Afro-Americans in their climb "up from slavery." Even the
labor unions and other worker organizations conspired to oppose the attempts of black workers to upgrade their skills and training and advance
themselves. Afro-Americans had to have their own social institutions that
were controlled by and for them. Afro-Americans wanted their own schools,
churches, social and fraternal organizations since they were excluded from
those provided for whites or for the public. White southerners did not want
to work on an "integrated" basis to solve the problems facing the region;
indeed, many whites argued that the possibility of integration was the
greatest threat to racial rapprochement. These differences in the perceptions
of black and white southerners about the value and possibility of integration
emerged in the cross-examination of Preston Brooks Peters. Although he had
been born a slave in Macon, Georgia, in 1855, he was, when he testified
before Senator Henry Blair's Committee on Education and Labor in November 1883, principal of the "public colored school" in Columbus, Georgia.
Senator Blair inquired, "When did you commence attending school?"

> *Answer.* I commenced the first year after the war. I suppose I was
> eleven years old.
> *Question.* Where did you live?
> *Answer.* I lived near Atlanta.
> *Question.* What sort of school did you attend?
> *Answer.* I commenced in the little school that they started there.
> The Yankee teachers, as we called them, came down and started a little
> school. I first learned my A B C's in a box-car which was used as a
> school house. Two years after that they built a house which was called

the Storrs school, named for some gentleman out West, I believe. I went through that school, the grammar school there; from there I went to the preparatory school in the Atlanta University which was established in 1869, though we did not get into the building until 1870. I finished that course, and then went out and taught four or five years, and went back after I was twenty-four and graduated.

Question. How long did you stay the last time?

Answer. Four years. I was twenty-seven when I graduated. I graduated in June and was elected here as principal of this school in September.

Like most northern white teachers working in the South, Peters believed that Afro-Americans were *equal* to white Americans in the capacity for intellectual development. "The colored man placed in similar circumstances with the white man would develop into as high a grade of intellectuality as the white man would. I believe that too. I believe that if we are given all the chances and help and encouragement that the whites have we will take advantage of them and improve accordingly." Unlike many northern white teachers, however, Peters also understood that the racial proscriptions placed on Afro-Americans in the South (and throughout the United States) *did* affect the motivation of black school children.

Question. Do these colored children that come to your school appear to be anxious to learn?

Answer. Yes, sir; there is a great deal of ambition among them, but our ambition is curbed because we cannot be anything but teachers and preachers. It is no use for us to educate ourselves for anything else; there is no other work for us to do. We cannot get employment in the higher branches of art or mechanics; we cannot be civil engineers or anything of that sort, we cannot even be operatives in factories, and consequently there is nothing for us to do but to teach or to preach or to lay brick or something of that sort.

Question. You are as badly off as the women?

Answer. Well, very nearly.

By *Mr. Pugh* [the Democratic Senator from Alabama]:

Question. How about carpentering?

Answer. Oh, well, we can be carpenters, or we can work in any of the trades of low grades. We cannot get into the higher grades, however. And this condition of things is not confined to the South; it is all over the country, everywhere that I have ever traveled. I find that everywhere the colored man is debarred from going into these different departments of trade that I have mentioned.

Question. If they were skilled engineers, do you think they could not find employment?

Answer. No, sir. If you would put a colored man on one of these roads here as an engineer all the white men would strike; they would not run with the colored man.

Question. That is merely your opinion; it never has been proved to be correct, has it?

Answer. Well, I do not think they would run with the colored men; that is my opinion about it.[40]

Peters was, of course, correct about the response of white skilled craftsmen in the American Federation of Labor and of white industrial and agricultural workers in various other labor organizations (including branches of the Knights of Labor) to competition from black workers.[41] The opposition of organized labor to participation and membership by Afro-Americans closed off numerous avenues for economic advancement and eventually stunted the growth of enthusiasm for "industrial education" among the black laboring classes by the beginning of the twentieth century.[42]

But in 1883, when Floyd Thornhill, Rev. Isaiah Welsh, N. R. Fielding, G. G. Going, Preston Brooks Peters, and other blacks testified before the Senate's Committee on Education and Labor, they unanimously supported separate public schools for Afro-American children in which they would be taught the basic literacy skills and industrial education. This position generally reflected the educational and self-determinist values within the Afro-American community, especially among the masses. The major problem, however, continued to be the cost of providing adequate schooling for the large and impoverished black population. The continued significance of the black vote in southern elections after Reconstruction led ultimately to the decision by white Democratic politicians and leaders to launch a campaign to disenfranchise the Afro-American population altogether, beginning with the Mississippi Constitutional Convention in 1890. Throughout the decade of the nineties there was increasing racial violence and terrorism as rabid racists assumed power in state after state in the ex-Confederacy; and by 1910, through "literacy tests," "understanding clauses," poll taxes, fraud, and intimidation, Afro-Americans were removed from participation in southern electoral politics. Given the heightened racial awareness of the southern white population, there was little "grass roots" white support for expanding public expenditures for black common school or industrial education in the 1890s or early 1900s.[43]

At the sixth annual meeting of the Atlanta University Conference on Negro Problems (1901), the conferees examined the issue of the Negro common school, and in the report, W. E. B. Du Bois, the editor, presented statistics and estimates of the financial expenditures for black and white public schools in sixteen southern states and Washington, D.C. In Mississippi, for example, Afro-Americans were 60 percent of the school-age population in 1899, but only 38.2 percent of these black pupils attended school regularly. The "regular school year" lasted only 101 days, or less than four months. Du Bois concluded that "the Negroes of Mississippi, forming 60 percent of the school population, receive less than 20 percent of the school expenditures, which were $1,306,186.17 in 1899. This would make the cost of Negro schools $250,000 or thereabouts." But according to Du Bois's estimates, black Mississippians paid over $282,000 in 1899 for "poll taxes," "state, county, and city taxes," and "pro-rata of indirect taxes and school funds." "The Negroes of Mississippi without doubt are paying for all their schools by their direct taxes and their just share of other sources of income; and are also contributing a considerable sum to the training of white children." In concluding Du Bois quoted from the report of the state superintendent of public education in 1899: "It will be readily admitted by every white man in Mississippi that our public school system is designed primarily for the welfare of the white children of the state, and incidentally for the Negro children."[44]

Conservative opponents of equal or adequate public expenditures for black public schooling would, of course, argue that Mississippi was a very poor state and that the citizens could ill-afford increased taxes. But what Du Bois found in Mississippi was part of the whole pattern of expenditures for black public education throughout the South. "It is fairly clear that in seven States [Delaware, Arkansas, South Carolina, Georgia, Alabama, Mississippi, and Louisiana], the Negro schools are not today costing the white tax-payers a cent." Du Bois found "in four other States [District of Columbia, Virginia, Florida, and Texas], the Negro schools are not costing the white taxpayers over 25 per cent of the total expense of such schools, and in many cases much less than this. . . . In four other States [West Virginia, Tennessee, Missouri, and North Carolina], something between one-fourth and one-half of the cost of Negro schools is borne by white taxpayers. . . . In the two remaining States, [Maryland and Kentucky], the Negro contributes at least 30 percent of the school fund." Du Bois's estimate of the amount blacks contributed to their own "public" education did not include "the supplemental funds" and "tuition payments" mentioned earlier.[45] It was fairly clear that in 1900 Afro-Americans in the South were paying more than their fair share for a public educational system that Du Bois characterized as "woefully inadequate." The only hope lay in federal aid to public education. Du Bois agreed with William Torrey Harris, U.S. Commissioner of Education, who wrote in 1893 that "the most serious obstacle to practical fulfillment of the school laws in the southern States . . . [is] the want of funds. It is not necessary to repeat here the proofs of the statement that the Southern States cannot of themselves bear the whole burden of the instruction and development of the Freedmen; the fact is admitted; the responsibility of the nation in the matter is admitted; there appear to be an overwhelming sentiment in the country in favor of appropriations from the national treasury to meet the emergency."[46]

Senator Henry Blair's bill for federal aid to local public school districts in states with high rates of illiteracy passed the Senate in 1881, 1884, and 1886, but was held up each time in the House of Representatives because, according to one writer, the Speaker of the House, John G. Carlisle of Kentucky (D), "unalterably opposed what he considered reckless spending of the treasury surplus, a practice he feared might lead to tariff increases." A fourth Blair bill was introduced into the Senate in March 1890, and was defeated there by a vote of 52 to 36. Conservative, agrarian Democrats and Republicans, North and South, joined together to defeat a bill many considered "unconstitutional" and a first step toward "federal control leading to a nationalized educational system."[47]

It should come as no surprise that, lacking federal funds, and with the Afro-American population almost completely disenfranchised, and amid increasing black poverty and overt white hostility to black advancement, the public educational services and facilities made available to southern black (and white) children in 1900 and 1910 were in many ways inferior to those public services provided back in 1890. At the sixteenth annual meeting of the Atlanta University Conference on Negro Problems, the participants again addressed the topic *The Common School and the Negro Americans* (1911). In the official resolutions issued by the conference, these black educators noted that they had "great concern over the condition of common school training among Negro Americans." It was only in the North where a small minority of black children lived that they were generally given facilities somewhat similar to those provided white students. In the larger cities in the border states, Maryland, West Virginia, and Delaware, black public schools were considered "good though crowded." But "in South Carolina, Georgia,

Florida, Alabama, Mississippi, Louisiana, and Arkansas, and in the country districts of the border states, elementary training for Negroes is in a deplorable condition.

> In the larger part of this area it is our firm belief that the Negro common schools are worse off than they were twenty years ago, with poorer teaching, less supervision and comparatively few facilities. In Virginia and North Carolina there are signs of improvement and in isolated instances in other states; but on the whole, thruout the lower South and to a large degree thruout the whole South these things are true:
>   1. The appropriations for Negro schools have been cut down, relatively speaking.
>   2. The wages for Negro teachers have been lowered and often poorer teachers have been preferred to better ones.
>   3. Superintendents have neglected to supervise the Negro schools.
>   4. In recent years few school houses have been built and few repairs have been made; for the most part the Negroes themselves have purchased school sites, school houses and school furniture, thus being in a peculiar way double taxed.
>   5. The Negroes in the South, except those of one or two states, have been deprived of almost all voice or influence in the government of the public schools.

The Atlanta University educators declared that if something was not done within a few years, "the problem of ignorance . . . will soon overshadow all other problems.

> The Negroes themselves are making heroic efforts to remedy these evils thru a wide-spread system of private, self-supported schools and philanthropy is furnishing a helpful but incomplete system of industrial, normal and collegiate training for children of the black race. In many parts of the South Negroes are paying into the school fund in the way of taxes much more than they are receiving in actual appropriations for their school facilities. Wherever this is true it may be said that the Negroes are helping to pay for the education of the white children while the states are depriving the Negro children of their just share of school facilities.

As was the case with the 1901 report, the resolutions ended with an appeal for federal appropriations for the support of public education in the South: "The Conference feels that in the case of continued failure on the part of the South to provide adequate school facilities for Negro children, permanent relief can be secured only from national aid to education with such safeguards as will insure the fair treatment of black children."[48]

What must also be noted at this point, however, is the generally accepted belief in 1910 that over the previous forty-five years, despite decreasing public expenditures for black public education, the masses of Afro-Americans had become literate. Du Bois, U.S. Census Bureau officials, and others accepted as basically accurate the statistical fact that the 70 percent illiteracy rate (defined as inability to write) among Afro-Americans in 1880 had dropped to about 30 percent in 1910.[49] In each decade between 1880 and 1910 the black population increased, but the number of illiterates in each age group decreased. For example, the black population 10 years of age and over increased during the decade 1900–1910 by 902,341 (out of a total population of 10,215,482). The number of illiterates in the black population decreased between 1900 and 1910 by 625,463. The U.S. Bureau of the Census reported that "classified by age, the Negro population in each age group increased and the number of illiterates decreased during the decade ending in 1910." This had also occurred in the two previous decades.[50]

Thus despite the lack of common school facilities, the disenfranchisement of the masses of black voters, the increasing white terrorism and lynchings, the Afro-American nation developing in the United States between 1880 and 1910 was becoming literate. To be educated and literate had an important cultural significance to Afro-Americans and was highly valued because of its association with advancement, self-determination, and freedom. Educational researchers and historians who have examined the rise and progress of "mass literacy" in western societies have found that oftentimes the "role of literacy in the life of the individual and society is contradictory and complex." Educational historian Harvey Graff found that "literacy was both act and symbol; it was neither neutral, unambiguous, nor radically advantageous or liberating. Its value, in fact, depended heavily on other factors, from ascribed social characteristics such as ethnicity, sex, or race, to the institutional, social, economic, and cultural contexts in which it was manifest."[51] Thus in trying to account for the increasing rates of literacy among Afro-Americans in the United States between 1880 and 1910, in the face of decreasing financial expenditures for black public schooling, we must look to the "cultural context" of literacy for Afro-America.[52]

Although a detailed analysis of the numerous cultural factors and agencies that were active in contributing to mass literacy among Afro-Americans is beyond the scope of this study, a few observations can be made. In most instances literacy was necessary for Afro-American economic, political, and cultural advancement. Although there were hundreds of occupations that did not require literacy for proficiency and success, oftentimes the ability to read and write was needed to advance from tenant farmer to landowner, and from day laborer to stevedore or millright. Whatever opportunities for upward social mobility that were presented to Afro-Americans in capitalist industry, commerce, or agriculture usually demanded literacy, if not specialized training.[53] At the same time, the white supremacist campaigns to drive black voters away from the polls in the 1890s often centered on the use of "literacy tests" to determine who could read and "properly interpret" the constitution and laws of the state. The disenfranchisement movement that swept the South in the 1890s and early 1900s served as another powerful incentive for black literacy.[54] And researchers who have examined the history of literacy in the West have all emphasized the significance of religion as the "dynamic force" behind the achievement of near-universal literacy. Kenneth Lockridge, in *Literacy in Colonial New England* (1974), concluded that "Protestantism was instrumental in whatever major changes that took place in literacy." Not merely in New England but throughout the Atlantic world in the eighteenth century, "the only areas to show a rapid rise in literacy to levels approaching universality were small societies whose intense Protestantism led them widely to offer or to compel in some way the education of their people."[55] Afro-Americans in the United States were among those Protestants who believed that the way to achieve salvation and personal deliverance was "to know the Word of God, and live it." Thus many Afro-Americans learned to read and write in various religious settings, such as Sunday School classes and Sabbath Schools, within their own communities. Afro-American families not only preserved and passed on cultural values supporting education and social advancement, but also taught their children to read and write as part of the parental responsibility for the "Christian education" of the younger generation.[56]

Literacy and education were also major objectives for an extremely important institution developing within Afro-America between 1880 and 1910—the black press. From the publication of the first black-controlled newspaper in New York City in March 1827, most black editors and journalists reflected and disseminated the cultural values of the emerging Afro-American nation and viewed their publications as more than mere "business enterprises," but important weapons in the ongoing struggle for knowledge and Afro-American self-determination in the United States.

To Plead Our Own Cause

"Education being an object of the highest importance to the welfare of society," wrote John Russwurm and Samuel Cornish, the editors of the first issue of *Freedom's Journal* in March 1827, "we shall endeavor to present just and adequate views of it and to urge upon our brethern the necessity and expediency of training their children, while young, to habits of industry, and thus forming them for becoming useful members of society." From the earliest newspaper, the black press pledged itself to a program of educating the Afro-American community. *Freedom's Journal* would publish "many practical pieces, having for their bases, the improvement of our brethren, . . . from the pens of many of our respected friends, who have kindly promised their assistance." The editors viewed it as "part of their duty to recommend to our young readers, such authors as will not only enlarge their stock of useful knowledge, but such as will also serve to stimulate them to higher attainments in science."[57]

The rise of the black press signaled the institutionalization of several of the emerging cultural values and beliefs of the Afro-American nation. The "black protest tradition" could easily be traced back to the eighteenth-century petitions and pamphlets of free blacks in New England and Pennsylvania, but the publication of black newspapers and other periodicals gave the Afro-American community an institution that would give voice to the issues and concerns of the group, and set the tenor and tone of Afro-American protest strategies against discriminatory treatment. Black-controlled publications were also examples of the operation of self-determinist values within the Afro-American community. "We wish to plead our own cause," wrote Russwurm and Cornish in that first issue of *Freedom's Journal*. "Too long have others spoken for us.

> Too long has the publick been decieved by misrepresentations, in things which concern us dearly, though in the estimation of some mere trifles; for though there are many in society who exercise towards us benevolent feelings; still (with sorrow we confess it) there are others who make it their business to enlarge upon the least trifle, which tends to the discredit of any person of colour; and pronounce anathemas and denounce our whole body for the misconduct of this guilty one. We are aware that there are many instances of vice among us, but we avow that it is because no one has taught its subjects to be virtuous; many instances of poverty, because no sufficient efforts accommodated to minds contracted by slavery, and deprived of early education have been made,

to teach them how to husband their hard earnings, and to secure to themselves comfort.

The black newspaper would serve the Afro-American community by fighting for black "civil rights."

> The civil rights of a people being of the greatest value, it shall ever be our duty to vindicate our brethern, when oppressed; and to lay the case before the publick. We shall also urge upon our brethern, (who are qualified by the laws of the different states) the expediency of using their elective franchise; and of making an independent use of the same. We wish them not to become the tools of party.[58]

The preoccupation with education, protest, civil rights, and self-determination characterized the black press in the United States throughout the nineteenth century. Martin Dann noted in his introduction to a compilation of hundreds of essays and articles that appeared in black newspapers and magazines between 1827 and 1895 that the press was instrumental in forging the Afro-American's "national identity." "This national identity was formed not merely by the American environment, but through the material conditions and experiences of the African diaspora in the United States." This peculiarly "Afro-American" cultural identity "involved an awareness of a collective responsibility, a resistance to racism, and a commitment to self-definition and self-determination." Afro-America should be considered "a nation within a nation" and this "quest for national identity takes place against the attempt by a white nation to enslave or destroy, to exploit or exclude a black nation in its midst." The black press emphasized "racial pride" and "ethnic solidarity" and "became along with the church, a central institution in the black community." Dann found that "black editors and their correspondents, as leaders in the community, not only were able to communicate information vital to the community and necessary for its cohesion, but also were often the only educational resources available."[59]

The national black press not only embodied emerging Afro-American cultural values, but the editors and publishers also supported social, political, and economic positions that reflected the interests of the vast majority—the masses—of Afro-Americans. But this, of course, was not always the case. As was noted in Chapter Three, when editor Frederick Douglass opposed the campaigns in the 1840s and 1850s for mass emigration outside the United States for freedom, advancement, and self-determination, Douglass's position did not reflect the predominant interests or opinions within the free black community at the time. Moreover, in the late 1870s and 1880s, from his position as Republican leader and elder spokesman for his race, Douglass opposed the mass migration of blacks out of the South. "I am opposed to this exodus," wrote Douglass in a widely publicized letter of 6 May 1879, "because it is an untimely concession to the idea that white people and colored people cannot live together in peace and prosperity unless the whites are a majority and control the legislation and hold the offices of the State." Douglass believed that the exodus "will pour upon the people of Kansas and other northern states a multitude of deluded, hungry, homeless people to be supported in a large measure by alms." He argued that "the conditions of existence in the Southern States are steadily improving, and that the colored man there will ultimately realize the fullest measure of liberty and equality accorded and secured in any section of our common country."[60]

The Afro-American masses who had been victimized by southern white exploitation, violence, and terrorism did not agree with Douglass, and neither did the vast majority of black editors and publishers. For the most part, the black press in serving as "the voice of the people" exposed the conditions that led to the migration, provided information on locations for possible settlement, and supported the efforts of the Colonization Council and other "grass-roots organizations" involved in assisting the Exodusters. Afro-American editors in black-controlled publications usually defined the "people" as the masses of Afro-Americans and tried to identify with their needs and interests.[61] Within this larger black institution, however, there were several different departments, all competing for the dominant position within the larger structure, plus all the financial and political success that would entail. The increased economic prosperity and higher rates of literacy and political awareness among Afro-Americans in the 1880s were accompanied by a sharp increase in the number of black-controlled publications. It became an "era of editors" who commanded respect and a following on the bases of the sharpness of their analysis and the range and quickness of their wit. Calvin C. Chase of the Washington *Bee*, W. J. White, editor of Atlanta's *Georgia Baptist*, John Mitchell of the Richmond *Planet*, Chris J. Perry of the *Philadelphia Tribune* and reporters Frances E. H. Harper, and Ida Wells-Barnett headed a large group of Afro-American journalists who saw themselves as "champions of the rights of the people." These editors often took the vanguard position in exposing and protesting the increasing social and political proscriptions being placed upon Afro-American citizens.[62]

Flamboyant journalist and editor T. Thomas Fortune was instrumental in the formation of the National Afro-American League in November 1889, whose purpose was to "successfully combat the denial of our Constitutional and inherent rights, so generally denied or abridged throughout the Republic. . . ." At the first annual convention held in Chicago in January 1890,

Fortune, who was secretary of the new organization, made clear the relationship between the League and the black masses.

> We have met here to-day as representatives of 8,000,000 freemen, who know our rights and have the courage to defend them. We have met here to-day to impress the fact upon men who have used us for selfish and unholy purposes, who have murdered and robbed and outraged us, that our past condition of dependence and helplessness no longer exists.[63]

The Afro-American League from its inception had the almost unanimous support of the black press and many black editors and publishers were active in the organization.[64]

The masses of Afro-Americans were workers, and the black press often urged the formation of all-black or integrated labor unions. T. Thomas Fortune, for example, confronted the increasing exploitation of southern black labor with the suggestion that the solution to the problem might be found in black participation in the larger "working class movement." "When it became known that the Knights of Labor were going to organize black laborers in the South," Fortune wrote in December 1886, "the most serious apprehensions were aroused throughout that section." He suggested that the issue of black labor in the South should be addressed by the new labor organizations in the face of the "unscrupulous and cruel" tactics of southern capitalists.

> The time is now when the laboring classes all over the country must take up the question of Southern labor and the methods by which it is defrauded, pauperized and tyrannized over before they can hope to accomplish the ends they have in view. The colored people of the South are gradually, as a class, sinking deeper and deeper into the cesspool of industrial slavery, and selfishness and greed are hedging themselves about by statutory enactments of the most unjust and iron-clad nature. What the end will be no man can safely say, but it is a comparatively easy matter to predict that the pathway thereto will be honeycombed with fraud, cruelty, and bloodshed. Capitalists and landowners, in all times and all countries . . . have been unscrupulous and cruel, yielding no inch to the sentiments of justice or humanity. The capitalists and landowners of the South of today will be found to be as stubborn and unjust as the ante-bellum slave holders. What they yield of justice and fair play will be at the command of organized and irresistible power; and none but knows just what this means in the last resort.[65]

Lack of financial support and endorsement by the leading black Republican politicians of the day, such as Blanche K. Bruce, Frederick Douglass, and P. B. S. Pinchback, led to the demise of the National Afro-American League by 1893. However, John Mitchell, William Monroe Trotter, W. E. B. Du Bois, Ida Wells-Barnett, and several other editors and reporters revived the organization in the form of the "National Afro-American Council" in September 1898. The new group's objectives were basically the same as those of the Afro-American League, though the movement that had begun in 1890 for the complete political disenfranchisement of Afro-Americans provided a new urgency to the campaigns for black advancement.[66] Moreover, by 1898, a new "black position" was being enunciated by Booker T. Washington, principal of Tuskegee Institute and influential black leader following his address in Atlanta at the opening of the Cotton States Exposition in 1895. Washington suggested that Afro-Americans accommodate themselves to the political realities of the South and be about the task of advancing themselves through black capitalist enterprises. Despite the fact that T. Thomas Fortune became one of Washington's closest friends, the "Afro-American Agitator" vehemently opposed the disenfranchisement movement and counseled resistance to the black masses. Fortune consistently expressed views contrary to those of Washington, the Great Accommodator. For example, in a letter published in the *Brooklyn Eagle* on 5 June 1900 there was not a trace of Washington's acquiescence to disenfranchisement and political subordination.

> When the law does not protect me, as it does not in the South . . . what am I to do? Accept it all meekly, without protest or resentment? . . . Slaves do that sort of thing, and are worthy to be slaves, but free men, American freemen! Who expects them to do it?

Fortune went on to declare that black victims of southern white attacks have a right and duty to use force to protect themselves.

> The black man's right of self-defense is identically the same as the white man's right of self-defense. Tell me that I shall be exterminated, as you do, if I exercise that right and I will tell you to go ahead and exterminate—if you can. That is a game that two can always play at. And suppose you do exterminate me, what of it? Am I not nobler and happier exterminated while contending for my honest rights than living a low cur that any poor white sneak would feel free to kick? The black race is not going to be exterminated for standing up for its rights. . . .

But if it continues to allow itself to be robbed of its manhood and womanhood rights, to be lynched and flayed and mutilated by frenzied mobs, to be degraded in legislative enactments which ramify all the relations of life; if it continues to be allowed all this without protest . . . then it will fall into . . . contempt.[67]

When Fortune, John Mitchell, Ida Wells Barnett, W. E. B. Du Bois, William Monroe Trotter, and other Afro-American editors, journalists, and writers called for protest and resistance against white supremacist violence and disenfranchisement campaigns; when they urged Afro-Americans to organize for mutual protection, self-defense, and advancement; or when they suggested that black workers join the struggles of the white laboring classes against the aggressive, exploitative industrial capitalists, and endorsed the migration of black agricultural workers out of the South; these spokespersons reflected both the values of the developing Afro-American nation and the objective social, political, and economic interests of the black masses. When Booker T. Washington and his associates in the National Negro Business League supported accommodation to political disenfranchisement and suggested that Afro-Americans "learn to live with Jim Crow"; or when Washington opposed the migration of the masses of poor southern blacks to northern urban areas to obtain freedom, advancement, and self-determination and suggested that blacks "cast down their buckets where they are"; or when he discouraged black participation in the organized labor movement because some unions practiced racial discrimination; the so-called "leader of the race" was advocating positions that were contrary to objective social, political, and economic interests of the vast majority of Afro-Americans in the United States.

In each significant area of black life at the turn of the century, Washington enunciated a "conservative position" that was not only against black interests, but was also contrary to Afro-American cultural values. Self-determinist values that had developed among the black masses meant that black control of black institutions was valued and sought. To most people Washington appeared to be the captain as well as the "wizard" of Tuskegee and his support for black-owned business and other capitalistic enterprises through the National Negro Business League appealed to the self-determinist values of the Afro-American masses. But at the same time, Washington's accommodating political positions were opposed to the Afro-American cultural values of survival with dignity and resistance against oppression. The experience of slavery had taught most Afro-Americans to resist the repressive practices of the white slave regime, and in many ways the

Klansmen and other white terrorists were more vicious and deadly than the slave patrollers. Resistance meant self-defense and self-protection; therefore T. Thomas Fortune argued in 1900 that it was useless to remain in the South and cry "Peace! Peace! when there is no peace. . . . [I]f the law can afford no protection, then we should protect ourselves, and if need be die in defense of our rights as citizens. The Negro can't win through cowardice."[68]

As far as Washington was concerned, blacks should demonstrate that they were "indispensable to the South" and should improve their skills through industrial education. Washington thus appealed to the Afro-American values of advancement and education when he promoted the Hampton-Tuskegee model of industrial education, but his educational program accommodated the white supremacist values of the New South. And rather than supporting what the masses of southern blacks seemed to want, that is, separate *and* equal educational facilities and programs; Hampton and Tuskegee Institutes provided a special type of "Negro industrial education" that basically consisted of literacy training, handyman crafts, and manual labor. Graduates from Hampton and Tuskegee before the 1920s could not compete with southern white skilled craftsmen and workers; they did not have the training. Basically, they were to serve as teachers in the southern public school systems and pass on to the younger generation of southern blacks the conservative attitudes and values they learned at the feet of the masters, General Samuel Armstrong and his prize student, Booker T. Washington.[69]

Mass testimony consistently revealed that separate educational facilities were preferred by southern blacks, but they expected these facilities to be equal in quality to that provided at public expense for whites. If whites had publicly supported state universities, law schools, and institutes of technology, then blacks should have the same. Washington advocated "Negro industrial education," and his was a minority position even in Alabama, his home state. Robert G. Sherer, in *Subordination or Liberation? The Development and Conflicting Theories of Black Education in Nineteenth Century Alabama* (1977), found that "nothing in the Tuskegee curriculum encouraged higher education." Washington often pronounced that he supported higher education "for black leaders . . . but he did nothing at Tuskegee to validate such statements except hire teachers from and send his children to black schools of higher education." But what was more interesting was the historical reality that other black educators *in Alabama* generally did not share Washington's educational views. Sherer examined the records of the black state teachers organizations, private colleges, other state-supported institutions in Alabama and found that, "by 1901, Washington's national political and philanthropic connections made him increasingly influential with many blacks. But even in 1916, the year after Washington died, most black secondary schools in Alabama still followed the lead of the AMA in offering college preparatory or liberal arts education.

> That most black educators in Alabama did not follow Washington's lead despite all his national prominence and connections has implications for understanding race relations and black history beyond Alabama. In his public roles *Washington was the representative and symbol of white interests* rather than being a truly indigenous black leader. Many blacks, even in Alabama, disagreed with Washington from the first although this opposition did not receive national attention until his struggle with W. E. B. Du Bois and William Monroe Trotter after 1903. . . . Even Washington's power and white patronage could not always force those who followed different strategies in trying to escape the web of subordination to adopt his program, even if this disagreement meant losing badly needed money such as the Slater Fund. (Italics added.)[70]

Washington's educational rhetoric and programs, according to Sherer, were rejected by the majority of black educators within his home state of Alabama because they would not lead to the type and level of social advancement that blacks desired.

The Afro-American editors who used their influence to educate the masses about their best interests were usually members of Du Bois's talented tenth. As Washington's power and influence grew throughout the nation, and his accommodationist doctrines became the guides to a "New South reconciliation," he was continually attacked in the so-called radical black press. In articles that appeared in national publications and in *The Souls of Black Folk* (1903) Du Bois questioned the acceptability of a position of accommodation. William Monroe Trotter's Boston *Guardian* and Henry C. Smith's Cleveland *Gazette* agitated for black civil rights and against Washington and his Tuskegee Machine. Eventually, through his power and money Washington sought to influence and determine the editorial statements of more friendly (and oftentimes less financially viable) black publications. Even before 1901, Washington had managed to gain control over the editorial positions of *Alexander's Magazine* and the *Colored Citizen* in Boston, the *Colored American* in Washington; and T. Thomas Fortune remained a somewhat troublesome ally at the New York *Age*.[71]

The buying of influence over the black press was only a minor issue compared to larger differences that separated Washington from the "radical intellectuals" of the race. In July 1905, a meeting was held at Niagara Falls, Canada, of about sixty Afro-American leaders and editors who opposed the growing power and influence of the Tuskegee Machine. Du Bois again spelled out the differences in the two positions. First, "we want manhood suffrage, and we want it now, henceforth, and forever. Second, we want discrimination in public accommodations to cease. Separation in railway and street cars, based simply on race and color is un-American, undemocratic and silly. We protest against all such discrimination." With regard to education, Du Bois argued that "we believe in work. We ourselves are workers, but work is not necessarily education. Education is the development of power and ideal. We want our children trained as intelligent human beings should be and will fight against any proposal to educate black boys and girls simply as servants and underlings, or simply for the use of other people. They have the right to know, to think, to aspire."[72] In pursuing these objectives, the Afro-American editors, ministers, and educators associated with the Niagara movement were advocating positions that upheld the objective political and economic interests of the black masses and reflected the cultural values that had been developing within the Afro-American nation in the United States from the eighteenth century.

CONCLUSION

The Challenge of Black Self-Determination

> We've come this far by faith,
> Leaning on the Lord;
> Trusting in his Holy Word,
> He's never failed us yet.
> Oh, can't turn around
> We've come this far by faith.
>
> Afro-American gospel song
> by ALBERT G. GOODSON

The eight million nonvoting Negroes are in the majority; they are the downtrodden black masses. The black masses have refused to vote, or to take part in politics, because they reject the Uncle Tom approach of the Negro leadership that has been handpicked for them by the white man.

These Uncle Tom leaders do not speak for the Negro majority; they don't speak for the black masses. They speak for the "black bourgeoisie," the brainwashed, white-minded, middle-class minority who are ashamed of black, and don't want to be identified with the black masses, and are therefore seeking to lose their "black identity" by mixing, mingling, intermarrying, and integrating with the white man.

The race problem can never be solved by listening to this white-minded minority.

MALCOLM X, 1963

"IT IS GENERALLY SAID that the Negro represents in America the man farthest down." Booker T. Washington had been sent to Europe in the summer of 1910 by the board of trustees of Tuskegee Institute for a much-needed rest, but the indefatigable Washington managed to turn his tour into sociological fieldwork. "In going to Europe I had in mind to compare the masses of the Negro people of the South with the masses in Europe in something like the same stage of civilization." He was interested in exploring "that portion of the world where the human family is farthest down, to see for myself how the 'man farthest down' was living and what was being done to improve his condition, and how this condition compared with that of the average black man in America." "The Man Farthest Down" was the title later given to the series of articles Washington published in *The Outlook* magazine, one of the leading news weeklies of the era. The essays contained Washington's, and his traveling companion and ghostwriter Robert A. Park's, perceptions of European life "from the bottom up." But given that by 1910 Booker T. Washington had become the most apologetic of the leading black "spokespersons for the race," it should come as no surprise that he found, over and over again, that the man farthest down in Europe generally looked up to the man farthest down in America.[1]

"I know no class among the Negroes in America," Washington reported following a stint in the British Isles, "with whom I could compare the man at the bottom in England. Whatever one may say of the Negro in America, he is not, as a rule, a beggar." He mentioned that "one does see, to be sure, too many idle and loafing Negroes standing on the street corners around the railway stations in the South; but the Negro is not as a rule, a degenerate."[2] Washington traveled to southern Italy, around Naples, and to Sicily. He was unimpressed by what he saw.

> I passed through the farming country south of Naples from which large numbers of emigrants go every year to the United States. It is a sad and desolate region. Earthquakes, malaria, antiquated methods of farming, and the general neglect of the agricultural population have all contributed to the miseries of the people. The land itself—at least such portion of it as I saw—looks old, worn-out, and decrepit; and the

general air of desolation is emphasized when, as happened in my case, one comes suddenly, in the midst of the desolate landscape, upon some magnificent and lonely ruin, representing the ancient civilization that flourished here two thousand years ago.[3]

Washington believed that Afro-Americans in the United States were better off than the Sicilians in all but one area: access to industrial education and skilled training. "Whatever may be the disadvantages of the people of Sicily in other respects, they have the advantage over the Negro in learning skilled trades, the value of which is difficult to estimate." This minor caveat in the description of despair and desolation he observed in Southern Europe was ultimately self-serving, for it allowed Washington to declare that Afro-Americans will never be as skilled as Sicilians until "the masses of the Negro people have secured a training of the hand and a skill in the crafts that correspond to those of other races."[4]

Given the thrust of these articles, it would of course follow that the "woman farthest down" in the United States would be better off than the "woman farthest down" in Europe. "While I was in Cracow, in Austrian Poland, I saw women at work in the stone quarries. The men were blasting out the rock, but the women were assisting them in removing the earth and in loading the wagons." When Washington visited Vienna he saw "hundreds of women at work as helpers in the construction of buildings; they mixed mortar, loaded it in tubs, placed it on their heads, and carried it up two or three stories to men at work on the walls." His comparisons were not subtly made. "In America Negro women and children are employed very largely at harvest time in the cottonfields; but I never saw in America, as I have seen in Austria, women employed as section hands on a railway, or digging sewers, hauling coal, carrying the hod, or doing the rough work in brick-yards, kilns, and cement factories." And unlike the woman in many parts of Europe, Afro-American women in this country had access to all of the educational opportunities available to black men. "The Negro women in America have a great advantage in this respect. They are everywhere admitted to the same schools to which the men are admitted. All the Negro colleges are crowded with women. They are admitted to the industrial schools and to training in the different trades on the same terms as men." Washington failed to note that the higher educational opportunities for Afro-American men and women were pitifully few in 1910.[5]

What is extremely interesting and important to our understanding of Washington's relationship to the masses of Afro-Americans in the United States is his article on "Races and Politics," in which he discussed the political, economic, and cultural similarities between the Poles and other

Slavic peoples in Europe and the black masses in the United States. "In many respects the situation of the Slavs in the Austro-Hungarian Empire and in Southern Europe generally is more like that of the Negroes in the Southern States than is true of any other class or race in Europe." The Slavic peasants in Hungary, Serbia, and Austria "worked on the soil, where they have been the servants of great landowners, looked down upon by the educated and higher classes as 'an inferior race.'" Within each society their political relationships were similar in that the Slavic peoples were generally dominated by cultur- ally different outside forces, institutions, and peoples. "Both in Austria and Hungary all the races are supposed to have all the same political privileges," but there were great economic inequalities due to "racial and traditional prejudices, as well as the wide differences in wealth and culture of the different peoples. . . ." As a result, the Slavic peoples from one generation to the next have remained powerless, and "political power" stayed "in Austria proper in the hands of the Germans, and in Hungary in the hands of the Magyars."

But here, for Booker T. Washington, the similarities between the economic, political, and cultural conditions for Afro-Americans in the United States and the Slavic peoples of Eastern Europe ended. For example, Washington believed that unlike the Slavs, "the Negro is not compelled to get his education through the medium of a language that is foreign to the other people by whom he is surrounded." In drawing these distinctions between Afro-Americans and Slavs, Washington clearly revealed his particu- lar understanding of Afro-Amercan cultural values, as well as the political and economic objectives of the black masses.

> The black man in the South speaks the same tongue and professes the same religion as the white people. He is not seeking to set up any separate nationality for himself nor to create any interest for himself which is separate from or antagonistic to the interest of the other people of the United States. The Negro is not seeking to dominate politically, at the expense of the white population, any part of the country which he inhabits. Although he has suffered wrongs and injustices, he has not become embittered or fanatical. Competition with the white race about him has given the Negro an ambition to succeed and made him feel pride in the successes he has already achieved; but he is just as proud to be an American citizen as he is to be a Negro. He cherishes no ambi- tions that are opposed to the interests of the white people, but is anxious to prove himself a help rather than a hindrance to the success and prosperity of the other race.[6]

Much of what Washington stated to his European audiences on this 1910 tour exaggerated the prosperity and progress that Afro-Americans were making in the United States at the time. As soon as reports began to appear of his statements, many other black leaders and spokespersons were outraged, and in October 1910 an "Open Letter to the People of Great Britain and Europe" was written by W. E. B. Du Bois and signed and circulated broadly, by twenty-one other black leaders, many of them veterans of the Niagara movement. The letter stated that "if Mr. Booker T. Washington or any other person, is giving the impression abroad that the Negro problem in America is in process of satisfactory solution, he is given an impression which is not true." The authors suggested that Washington's "large financial responsibilities have made him dependent on the rich charitable public and that, for this reason, he has for years been compelled to tell, not the whole truth, but that part of it which certain powerful interests in America wish to appear as the whole truth." The statement went on to paint a somewhat different portrait of contemporary conditions. Afro-Americans "meet discrimination based solely on race and color. . . . When we seek to buy property in better quarters we are sometimes in danger of mob violence. . . . We are forced to take lower wages for equal work, and our standard of living is then criticized. Fully half the labor unions refuse us admittance, and then claim that as 'scabs' we lower the price of labor." Afro-Americans were legally segregated in public accommodations and "worse than all this is the wilful miscarriage of justice in the courts. Not only have 3,500 black men [and women] been lynched publicly by mobs in the last twenty-five years without semblance or pretense of trial, but regularly every day throughout the South the machinery of the courts is used, not to prevent crime and correct the wayward among Negroes, but to wreak public dislike and vengeance. . . ." Fortunately, "against this dominant tendency strong and brave Americans, white and black, are fighting, but they need . . . the moral support of England and Europe in this crusade for the recognition of manhood . . . and it is a blow in the face to have one, who himself suffers daily insult and humiliation in America, give the impression that all is well. It is one thing to be optimistic, self-forgetful and forgiving, but it is quite a different thing, consciously or unconsciously, to misrepresent the truth."[7]

In the second volume of his prize-winning biography, *Booker T. Washington: The Wizard of Tuskegee, 1901–1915* (1983), Louis R. Harlan devotes almost a chapter to this tour and Washington's response to the public attack by black leaders, many of whom were associated with the newly organized National Association for the Advancement of Colored People (NAACP). Harlan reports that "Washington decided to make the signers of the appeal, and particularly Du Bois, as uncomfortable as possible," and "members of the Tuskegee Machine also abandoned restraint in their editorial attacks on the signers."[8] But what Du Bois and the co-signers of the appeal and Louis Harlan in his biography failed to note was that the accommodationist positions taken by Washington were contrary not only to the objective social, political, and economic interests of the southern black masses, but also to the predominant cultural values and objectives of the majority of Afro-Americans living in the United States. The public statements in Europe in 1910 (and the earlier books and articles) reflected Washington's general failure to articulate positions based on the cultural values that emerged from the Afro-American experience in the eighteenth and nineteenth centuries. These core values served as "cultural ideals" that underpinned the behavior, institutions, and social movements among the black masses in the early twentieth century as well.

Contrary to the perspectives presented by Washington, the particular version of Christianity adhered to by Afro-Americans in the South before World War I developed out of the material conditions and religious experiences of enslaved and free blacks in eighteenth- and nineteenth-century America. The cultural backgrounds, social experiences, and relationship to the mode of production for blacks and whites were vastly different throughout that period, as were their religious experiences. Both groups considered themselves Christian, but any superficial resemblances in formal religious practice did not generally extend to "religious meanings," which were embedded in a broader cultural context. As we have heard from the testimony, on the basis of their experiences Afro-Americans generally came to believe that Christianity was a religion of the oppressed and downtrodden in society. After having been exposed to the biblical stories of oppression, persecution, and enslavement of the Hebrews, God's Chosen People in the Old Testament, many Afro-Americans identified with Jews and came to consider themselves God's Chosen People in America.[9]

Also on the basis of what happened to them, Afro-Americans came to view slavery and other white terroristic acts as against the will of God. The slaveholder's preachers told the enslaved that to disobey the masters was sinful; and that particular emphasis of "slaveholding piety" the slaves rejected. To hold one's fellow man in perpetual enslavement was the greatest of sins, according to the enslaved; and if wrongdoers were not punished in this world, they would be subject to God's judgment and receive their "just deserts" in the next. Since many slaveholders opposed the religious instruction of slaves and banned slave religious meetings, enslaved Afro-Americans met amongst themselves in the woods and canebreaks in the evenings and at night "to praise God together," thus instilling in themselves and the next generation the basic value of Afro-American religious self-determination. Initially, blacks formed separate religious denominations because they were rejected by white Christian institutions. White supremacist values lay at the core of the Christian beliefs and practices among Euro-Americans, and they taught that it was "good" to ban Africans and Afro-Americans from white religious congregations or to tolerate their presence in a separate "nigger heaven" in predominantly white churches. After the African Methodist Episcopal and other black churches and denominations were formed, they often became *the* centers of social and cultural activities. From their independent base within the community, Afro-American religious institutions were able to participate in and often lead campaigns of resistance and protest against oppression and discrimination in antebellum America. As we have seen, black church groups were most active in the free black resistance movement, and they remained throughout the nineteenth and twentieth centuries central cultural institutions for Afro-America. The socially active and culturally aware black church congregation embodied the predominant values that emerged from the Afro-American experience in the nineteenth century. [10]

While the black church and the black press should be considered central cultural institutions for Afro-Americans, the "act of migration" (like "the condition of enslavement") should be considered a central event in the interpretation of Afro-American cultural history. The movement of tens of thousands of rural farm people to urban areas in the South and North was a "mass phenomenon" that was greatly influenced by economic conditions, but it was also driven by the individual and collective goals of the Afro-American population. The depressed material circumstances under which Afro-Americans were expected to eke out an existence consistently served as direct precipitating causes of this migratory response. The persistent failure to gain and hold land, the refusal of southern white leadership to deal fairly and equitably with black citizens with regard to public education and employment, the exclusion of Afro-Americans through fraud, extortion, intimidation, violence, and brutality from competition for the limited economic resources available meant that for far too many Afro-Americans the "New South" was a less hospitable environment than the "Old South," and they were forced to leave. As was pointed out in Chapter Four, emancipation provided "one kind of freedom," and in many instances it meant the freedom to flee the oppressive conditions "at home."

These acts of migration also represented "acts of self-determination" on the part of Afro-Americans. When black migrants set out from Alabama, Georgia, or South Carolina and ended up in Mound Bayou, Mississippi,

Boley, Oklahoma, or Monrovia, Liberia, West Africa, they demonstrated the desire of Afro-Americans to be separate from whites and free of white domination. The major difference between migrating to an all-black town in the nineteenth century and moving into a predominantly black section of a northern or southern city was the greater amount of control exercised by Afro-Americans over their own social, political, and economic circumstances in black towns. If the "highest stage of white supremacy" had been reached when segregation of the races was legally sanctioned, then "the highest stage of black self-determination" occurred when blacks controlled the legislative processes in a particular municipality.[11] In acts of migration Afro-Americans took control of their own destiny in a society bent on controlling and exploiting them and keeping them "in their place." The dominant white group wanted Afro-Americans to accommodate to their demands for supremacy, and many white Americans felt reassured and comforted by the pronouncements of Booker T. Washington, the white-sanctioned black spokesperson. Fortunately (or unfortunately), Washington did not represent the values and interests of the black masses and therefore should not be considered their "leader." Thus while Washington was counseling Afro-Americans to "cast down your buckets where you are," the southern black masses were launching the Great Migration.[12]

Frederick Douglass and W. E. B. Du Bois recognized and subscribed to the Afro-American values of survival with dignity, resistance against oppression, freedom, education, and advancement. However, both these leaders failed to appreciate and accept the self-determinist values developing among the masses of Afro-Americans. Whereas Booker T. Washington appealed to these values in his call for the support of black-controlled businesses, schools, and other social and economic institutions, Douglass in the 1830s and 1840s opposed "complexional" institutions and solutions to black problems and advocated "integrationist" strategies and programs. But integration would only work when, or if, white Americans were willing to participate in programs for black uplift. There were a few scattered examples in the nineteenth century of black-white alliances being formed to bring about the social or economic advancement of Afro-Americans. In the antislavery movement, in the post-Civil War educational campaigns and missionary societies, in the various farmers' organizations and the Populist movement of the 1880s and 1890s, blacks and whites worked together to achieve objectives desired by both groups. But these movements were short-lived and unsustained, and they often succumbed to the pull of white supremacy and thus served to reenforce the corresponding value of black self-determination.[13]

In the day-to-day experiences of the masses of Afro-Americans throughout the nineteenth century there were just too few examples of interracial cooperation to sustain "integration" as a viable strategy for realizing Afro-American cultural goals and objectives. Frederick Douglass and W. E. B. Du Bois supported integrationist strategies and objectives, but these values were generally not shared by the black masses because integration usually meant white domination. When confronted by the predominant cultural value of "white supremacy" in the society at large, Afro-Americans responded, "Yes, but not in black-controlled institutions." In nineteenth- and early twentieth-century America, the Afro-American masses opted for self-determination, and this value manifested itself in the thousands of black-controlled churches, schools, social organizations, and cultural institutions. As was noted, in the earliest years all-black institutions developed as a response to exclusion from white institutions and society in general, but gradually Afro-Americans came to value and appreciate the importance of having their own social organizations that they would control and would be geared toward their particular needs and desires.

The First World War created new opportunities for social advancement for Afro-Americans and greater possibilities for interracial contact and cooperation. Unfortunately, the increased contact and the need for cooperation did not necessarily lead to improved interracial understanding. Indeed, throughout the war years and immediately afterward, the level of interracial hostility and violence rose. Race riots broke out at East St. Louis, Illinois, and Chester, Pennsylvania in 1917, and at Philadelphia in 1918, following the growth of the local black population through in-migration from the South. Mob violence and the lynching of black citizens and soldiers (some still in uniform) continued during the war and increased after it. In 1915 a newly revitalized Ku Klux Klan, having as its objective "uniting native-born white Christians for concerted action in preservation of American institutions and the supremacy of the white race," appeared on the scene. Klan chapters sprouted up not merely in the Solid South, but in New England and New York State and throughout the Midwest. By the summer of 1919 interracial strife peaked; at least twenty-five race riots occurred throughout the United States between June and December of that year. [14]

These were the conditions under which Afro-Americans were living below and above the Mason-Dixon line when the young and ambitious Marcus Garvey arrived in the United States in March 1916. Garvey was originally attracted to the black capitalist themes and schemes of Booker T. Washington while still in Jamaica, and had begun corresponding with him in September 1914. [15] Garvey was planning to meet with Washington and his associates in the National Negro Business League to discuss possible joint economic ventures, but Washington died in November 1915, several months before Garvey arrived. Initially, Garvey was merely interested in a lecture tour around the United States to gain support for his Universal Negro Improvement Association (UNIA), a West Indian self-help society that he had founded in 1914. Garvey also wanted to raise funds "to establish an industrial and educational institute, to assist in educating the Negro youth" of Jamaica. Garvey traveled around the country lecturing, and was immediately impressed by the "racial progress" he saw. "I have traveled a good deal through many countries, and from my observations and study, I unhesitatingly and unreservably say that the American Negro is the peer of all Negroes, the most progressive and foremost unit in the expansive chain of scattered Ethiopia." He had visited New York, Boston, Philadelphia, Washington, Baltimore, and other cities and found black "banks, stores, cafes, restaurants, theaters and real estate agencies that fill my heart with joy to realize, in positive truth, and not by sentiment, that at one center of Negrodom, at least, the people of the race have sufficient pride to do things for themselves." Thus Garvey was quite aware of the particular "racial consciousness" that already existed among Afro-Americans in the United States and manifested itself in numerous black-controlled institutions and enterprises. "Industrially, financially, educationally, and socially, the Negroes of both hemispheres have to defer to the American brother, the fellow who has revolutionized history in race development . . . within the fifty years . . ." since the end of slavery.

In this same very early statement (January 1917) of his initial impression of the cultural and political situation of Afro-Americans in the United States, Marcus Garvey was extremely critical of blacks in the Caribbean and made it clear that they were *not* likely to lead the advancement of the race in the New World. "The West Indian Negro who has had seventy-eight years of emancipation has nothing to compare with your progress. Educationally, he has, in the exception, made a step forward, but generally he is stagnant. I have discovered a lot of 'vain bluff' as propagated by the irresponsible type of West Indian Negro who has become a resident of this country—bluff to the effect that conditions are better in the West Indies than they are in America. Now let me assure you, honestly and truthfully, that they are nothing of the kind." Garvey believed that the better-educated and ambitious West Indians emigrate to other countries rather than staying "at home and combat the forces that make them exiles. . . . We haven't the pluck in the West Indies to agitate for or demand a square deal and the blame can be attributed to no other source than indolence and lack of pride among themselves."[16]

Robert A. Hill suggested, in his introduction to the first volume of the

Marcus Garvey and Universal Negro Improvement Association Papers (1983), that Garvey was successful initially in attracting mass support in the United States because "the time was thus ripe for the convergence of the contrasting traditions of racial and social consciousness that the program and ethos of the UNIA would comprise."[17] But good timing was only a small part of the reason for his success. There were also important social and cultural factors that underpinned his triumphs. Garvey's movement appealed to the cultural values and economic interests of Afro-Americans both North and South.

In 1917 and 1918 Marcus Garvey was certainly not the only black leader trying to win the hearts and minds of the disgruntled black masses. W. E. B. Du Bois and James Weldon Johnson were leading spokespersons for the NAACP, and they were bidding strongly for "mass support" for their integrationist strategies and legalistic attacks on the expanding system of Jim Crow segregation. Indeed, membership in the NAACP was climbing during that period peaking at 91,203 in 1919; but it plummeted in the 1920s as Du Bois and other NAACP officials engaged in "literary battles" with Garvey. Then the integrationist group was losing membership.[18]

At the same time, socialists A. Philip Randolph and Chandler Owen were appealing through the *Messenger* magazine to the black working class to join with their white brothers in bringing about an end to capitalist exploitation of workers, which, according to Randolph and Owen, was the major reason for racist discrimination against black workers. Though Randolph succeeded at last in organizing the predominantly black Brotherhood of Sleeping Car Porters, in 1925, most blacks remained anti-union through the end of the decade because nearly all labor organizations remained anti-black.[19]

Garvey's leadership among the masses was more directly threatened by Cyril V. Briggs and the African Blood Brotherhood. Whereas Garvey's brand of black "nationalism" was greatly influenced by Irish nationalism, especially the Irish Rebellion of 1916 and 1917, other more-leftist Afro-Americans were inspired by the example of V. I. Lenin and the successful Bolshevik revolution in Russia. The West Indian communists challenged Garvey's leadership and tried unsuccessfully to lure him and his mass following away from the capitalist path.[20] The integrationists in the NAACP, the socialists in the labor movement, and the West Indian communists, all competed with Garvey for the support of the black masses in the postwar era, but Garvey was the most successful primarily because his ideology and programs strongly appealed to both the interests and cultural values that had developed among Afro-Americans from the late eighteenth century.

Marcus Garvey appealed to the self-determinist values in Afro-

American culture, as did Booker T. Washington. But Garvey's programs and approaches came to encompass many more aspects of the Afro-American belief-system and life-style in this country than did Washington's. Garvey's movement had a military air about it. In its rituals and symbols, and in the groups it sponsored, such as the African Legion and other military brigades and militias, the UNIA communicated militant resistance and self-defense against physical abuse; and it appealed to the Afro-American cultural value of resistance. Washington's pleas for accommodation were generally ignored by the masses of blacks, but Garvey's militant nationalism was not. And Garvey believed in and sponsored programs for the education of black people. His commitment to raising the levels of political and cultural consciousness of the masses manifested itself in the numerous publications, including *Negro World,* the weekly newspaper, and later *The Blackman* magazine, as well as in the many debating and literary societies the UNIA sponsored. It should be noted again that one of the original motives for Garvey's initial trip to the United States was to raise financial support for the opening of a "Little Tuskegee Institute" in Jamaica. Garvey's educational vision was much broader than Washington's, however, and encompassed areas many other black leaders were unwilling to pursue.[21]

Garvey's was not a "religious" movement, but the particular beliefs and meanings associated with Afro-American Christianity were incorporated into the basic ideological thrust of the UNIA. "African Redemption," the nineteenth-century ideal that Africa's stolen children would participate in the christianizing and elevation of the motherland, was one of the major political goals of the Garveyites. Garvey himself often claimed that he was not a "religious leader," but his political objective of "Africa for the Africans" indirectly appealed to the missionary instincts of many black Christians. Moreover, Garvey quite often discussed religion and religious issues, and even toyed with the idea of making Bishop Alexander McGuire's African Orthodox Church the official UNIA denomination.[22] For example, in the first volume of *Philosophy and Opinions of Marcus Garvey* (1923), there is a brief discussion of "the image of God." "If the white man has the idea of a white God, let him worship his God as he desires." Garvey proclaimed, "We, as Negroes, have found a new ideal. Whilst our God has no color, yet it is human to see everything through one's own spectacles, and since the white people have seen their God through white spectacles, we have only now started out (late though it be) to see God through our own spectacles. . . . We Negroes believe in the God of Ethiopia, the everlasting God—God the Father, God the Son, and God the Holy Ghost, the one God of all ages. That is the God in whom we believe, but we shall worship Him through the spectacles of Ethiopia."[23] This powerful image of viewing the Almighty through the weary eyes of the children of Africa offered a classic statement of Garvey's black nationalist Christianity, which also had roots in the nineteenth-century practices and beliefs of many predominantly black religious denominations. Garvey saw the UNIA, however, as "one great Christian confraternity" and tried to keep his religious statements general and to remain above the sectarian feuds within black Christiandom.[24]

This emphasis on militant resistance, education, and Afro-American religious nationalism meant that the Garvey movement appealed to the predominant values of the Afro-American culture and thus attracted a mass following. But Garvey's vision was somewhat distorted by a lack of appreciation of other Afro-American cultural practices. Robert Hill has suggested that Garvey was unsympathetic toward and unaware of the significance and meanings of jazz, spirituals, dialect poetry, and other mass cultural forms. "In Garvey's view, any support to the aesthetic revival of black folk culture had to be rejected, and he viewed such exercises as further perpetuating the cultural and political humiliation of Africa." Garvey also utilized European cultural standards in judging African and Afro-American cultural practices, and "held up to blacks the system of European civilization as a mirror of racial success. In this context Garvey expressed strenuous opposition to black folk culture, which he viewed as inimical to racial progress and as evidence of the retardation that for generations had made for racial weakness."[25] Although these assertions need to be supported by more direct evidence from Garvey, it certainly can be argued that Garvey's lack of awareness of the meanings and beliefs in black folk traditions in the United States accounts for his most grievous political error—the meetings with leaders of the Ku Klux Klan in 1922.

Through violence, brutality, and terrorism, the Night Riders had seared into the consciousness of thousands of southern blacks the true meaning of "white supremacy." The Klan had violently opposed the continuation of basic civil rights for Afro-Americans. (The Klan's spreading their hatred to include southern European immigrants, Catholics, Asians, and Jews did not diminish the black community's feelings and sentiments about their self-professed enemy.) In his struggles with other black leaders and the federal government, Garvey came to characterize his movement as the one that stood for "black racial purity" as well as self-determination; hence, through the "spectacles of a West Indian" there appeared to be nothing wrong with meeting the leaders of the major organization that believed in "white racial purity." But to Afro-Americans in the United States the Klan represented much more historically, economically, socially, and culturally than white racial purity. Garvey's opponents could justifiably ask whether or not he was a "traitor to the race." A great deal of jealousy, envy, and misunderstanding went into the "Garvey Must Go" campaigns of 1923, but Garvey left himself wide open to attack when he argued that there was some sort of "common cause" between the KKK and UNIA.[26]

This grave flaw in the Garvey movement was not fatal in itself, but it did undermine support within the black community and permit systematic attacks by the United States government. Recently published documents and statements from the records of the U.S. Department of Justice reveal a concerted effort, beginning in 1919, to undermine Garvey and his movement. By 1927 these federal officials, led by J. Edgar Hoover, had succeeded in bringing about Garvey's deportation.[27] Without the leader the movement became wracked with dissension. It never reestablished itself as a significant force in the campaigns for Afro-American political, social, or economic advancement in the United States.

That the movement was short-lived and its leader's perceptions flawed should not diminish the significance of Garvey's accomplishment. His was the largest and most significant mass movement among Afro-Americans before the coming Civil Rights-Black Power movement of the 1960s. Indeed, there are more similarities than differences between these two black mass movements. Although it is beyond the scope of this study to examine the complex set of social and economic circumstances that led up to Martin Luther King's nonviolent direct-action protest campaigns, it is clear that, at its height in the early 1960s, the Civil Rights movement also spoke to the "core values" of the Afro-American experience. Freedom, resistance against oppression, Afro-American religious and educational values, all were part of the direct appeal to the Afro-American masses to support and join the movement to end second-class citizenship and Jim Crow. Through his use of the old Negro spirituals and other traditional religious themes King revealed the sources of his vision for a changed America. While the echoes of Garvey's black nationalist rhetoric were more clearly discernible in the speeches of Malcolm X and the activities of the Nation of Islam, King and Malcolm presented overlapping appeals: Both were calling for resistance, education, and black responsibility for black advancement. Both attracted wide and committed followings. King's movement was more successful in the short run because his support of integrationism closely corresponded to the contemporary social, political, and economic realities for Afro-Americans in the 1960s.[28]

The complex changes in the American economy between 1930 and 1960 greatly affected not only the material conditions of Afro-Americans but also their predominant cultural values. Beginning with the horrendous economic conditions created for Afro-Americans by the Great Depression, both masses and elites began to understand the value of being "integrated" into the larger society. Since blacks were in no way responsible for the economic disaster, but were arguably its worst victims, Afro-Americans came to believe that it was "good" to be integrated into the federal government's programs for national recovery. When war broke out in Europe in 1939 and this country mobilized, Afro-American leaders and followers saw the value of being integrated into the training programs and employment opportunities created through the significant increase in federal contracts to produce military goods and services. Mobilization began among black organizations, led by A. Phillip Randolph, and the "March on Washington" movement was instrumental in getting President Franklin D. Roosevelt to issue Executive Order 8802, creating the Fair Employment Practices Commission in July 1941. The March on Washington movement sought the support of sympathetic whites, but it was an all-black movement that had integrationist objectives. Gradually, during the years after World War II the Afro-American masses (not just the elites, as was the case in the 1920s) came to recognize that integrationist strategies and objectives were necessary to achieve the cultural goal of black self-determination.[29]

With the support of Supreme Court decisions and thousands of white religious leaders, activists, and students, Martin Luther King was able to develop a mass movement that was dedicated to the destruction of all visible signs of the Jim Crow system. Integration was added to the value system of the Afro-American masses and was accepted as a strategy to bring about the advancement that they desired. Unfortunately, although most Afro-Americans eventually came to support "integrationism," it also became clear by the end of the 1970s and early 1980s that this strategy would not bring about the needed social, political, and economic advancement for the *majority* of Afro-Americans. Why was this the case? How did it happen? There are, of course, numerous theories and explanations of why Afro-Americans have not reached economic or political parity with Americans of European descent. These theories range from Arthur Jensen's assertion of the genetic inferiority of blacks to whites to suggestions that the problems lay with the black family, which is increasingly headed by women and impoverished. But the argument that appears to have the heaviest historical weight emphasizes institutional racism and the shifts in the American capitalist economy between 1964 and 1984. The expansion of the war in Vietnam in 1965 increased economic opportunities across the board. Thus Afro-American demands for inclusion could be met by "expanding the pie" and integrating blacks into those developing sectors of the economy. In post-Vietnam America, however, economic expansion had ceased in most industrial areas, and those where it continued were highly specialized technical areas requiring great amounts of initial capital outlay and skilled personnel. The increased competition for the limited technological resources had put Afro-Americans at a disadvantage, and the economic recessions of the 1970s and 1980s became for Afro-America another "Great Depression."[30]

In the search for alternatives to the continual decline in the economic status of Afro-Americans, some leaders have begun to appeal to the basic cultural value system of the black masses. Black politicians and capitalists argue that the potential for economic advancement still rests with the capitalist system and that Afro-Americans must use their power as *consumers* to gain the economic foothold needed to climb upward. Jesse Jackson's "Crusade for Economic Justice" of the early 1980s came closest to an attempt to organize the consuming habits of the Afro-American masses in order to bring about their own social and economic advancement. Unfortunately, Jackson dropped this strategy and moved on to another before the boycott was able to realize its full potential for gaining collective (as opposed to individual) objectives.[31] In the 1984 presidential election campaigns, candidate Jesse Jackson appealed to both the integrationist and self-determinist values of the black masses and generated a political campaign that raised the political consciousness of many Americans, black and white. But Jackson did not move beyond the narrow confines of American capitalism. He did not provide serious alternatives to the economic malaise that now afflicts nearly all Afro-Americans. Jesse Jackson's failure to recognize that it might be in the economic interest of the masses of Afro-Americans in the United States to pursue socialist alternatives to the unemployment and economic underdevelopment within the Afro-American community means that Jackson has only begun to accept the challenge of black self-determination.[32]

For those individuals who have aspired to leadership of the black community, the challenge of black self-determination has been to provide programs and strategies that were embedded in Afro-American values and cultural traditions *and* reflected mass (as opposite to elite) economic interests. Booker T. Washington appealed to some of these values—self-determination and education—but he did not understand the significance of the Afro-American religious tradition to black advancement, and supported economic positions that were antithetical to the interests of the southern black masses.[33] On the other hand, Marcus Garvey appealed to the sacred and secular values of the black masses and his capitalistic economic programs held out the possibility in the 1920s for advancement for thousands of lower status Afro-Americans, North and South. Martin Luther King also appealed to the core values of the Afro-American experience, and his integrationist strategies and objectives clearly coincided with the economic interests of most Afro-Americans. By the 1960s it was unmistakably clear that if Afro-Americans were to advance economically, they would have to be integrated into the dominant social, political, and economic structures in American society. King accepted the challenge of black self-determination and developed a "mass movement" on the basis of Afro-American cultural values and economic interests.

The Afro-American cultural vision was forged in the crucible of slavery, in the slave quarters and southern woods, where enslaved Africans and Afro-Americans came together to pray and plot their future. The vision was nurtured by the successful end of enslavement and the creation of viable black-controlled institutions that were geared specifically to the needs and desires of the Afro-American community. The vision was clarified and sharpened by organized resistance against oppression during and after slavery in the form of flight and migration. Afro-Americans saw themselves as God's Chosen People in America and maintained a covenant with the Almighty to bring about his kingdom on earth. Theologian and philosopher Cornel West, in *Prophesy Deliverance! An Afro-American Revolutionary Christianity* (1982), maintained that Afro-Americans espoused a type of "prophetic Christianity" that taught both "existential freedom" and "social freedom." "Existential freedom is the effect of the divine gift of grace which promises to sustain persons through and finally deliver them from the bondage of death, disease, and despair. Social freedom is the aim of Christian political practice, a praxis that flows from the divine gift of grace; social freedom results from the promotion and actualization of the norms of individuality and democracy." West believes that prophetic Christianity has as its objective "the self-realization of individuality within the community," and "must insist upon both this worldly liberation and other worldly salvation as the proper logic of Christianity."[34]

West argued that the "progressive vision" of Afro-American prophetic Christianity is quite compatible with progressive Marxist thought in that both foresee the ultimate liberation of mankind in this world or the next. The Marxist emphasis on "self-fulfillment, self-development, and self-realization" and "steadfast hope in an earthly paradise" means that Marxism and Christianity "share a similar moral impulse." Whereas Marxists are concerned primarily with "socioeconomic well-being," Christians are preoccupied with "spiritual well-being." In its more orthodox formulations in the nineteenth- and early twentieth centuries, Marxism failed to emphasize "the ways in which culture and religion resist oppression. . . . The orthodox Marxist analysis of culture and religion that simply relates racist practices to misconceived material interests is only partially true, hence deceptive and misleading." West believes that "these practices are fully comprehensible only if one conceives of culture, not as a mere hoax played by the ruling class on workers, but as the tradition that informs one's conception of tradition, as social practices that shape one's idea of social practice." As we have seen, the particular cultural values of Afro-Americans that informed their vision and behavior emerged from the material conditions under which they lived and were oppositional to the beliefs and values stressed by the dominant white ruling class. In the past, "orthodox Marxist analysis refuse[d] to acknowledge the positive, liberating aspects of popular culture and religion, and their potential for fostering structural social change."[35]

If the Afro-American nation in the United States is to move beyond its present condition of comparative economic inequality and political subordination, the cultural vision of the masses of Afro-Americans must be tied to a progressive economic program. That economic scheme must have the realization of each individual's potential and socioeconomic well-being, as well as the preservation of particular cultural perspectives and traditions, as its primary objectives. To date, black and white capitalists (and the American capitalist system in general) have failed to accept the challenge of black self-determination. Perhaps it is time that Afro-Americans began to pursue alternative economic visions for realizing their full social, political, and cultural potential in the United States.

EPILOGUE

Self-Determination and African-American Ideologies

At this moment then the Negroes must begin to do the very thing they have been taught they cannot do. They still have some money, and they have needs to supply. They must begin immediately to pool their earnings and organize industries to participate in supplying social and economic demands. If the Negroes are to remain forever removed from the producing atmosphere, and the present discrimination continues, there will be nothing left for them to do.

CARTER G. WOODSON, 1933

One of the questions we as Black people have the most difficulty dealing with is our response to capitalism, and most particularly our lack of collective response to the way in which consumer capitalism has changed the nature of anything we could call Black life or Black experience. We want to act as though we have managed to hold on to traditional Black folk culture, with its ethical value system, while we participate wholeheartedly in consumer capitalism. We have been reluctant, as a people, to say that capitalism poses a direct threat to the survival of an ethical belief system in Black life.

BELL HOOKS, 1991

THROUGHOUT THE 1980S and into the 1990s a debate has raged inside and outside government circles over whether or not the economic strategies pursued by the Republican administrations of Ronald Reagan and George Bush would bring about improvements in the economic status of African Americans. The Reagan-Bush conservative economic initiative basically boiled down to the deregulation of the marketplace, together with tax cuts for the wealthy to stimulate production (the "trickle-down" theory) and reduced spending for social services and programs. This strategy was wholeheartedly endorsed by a well-publicized group of black conservatives who argued that government intervention to improve the social and economic status of African Americans and other "historically oppressed" groups is unnecessary and in some cases detrimental because it encouraged economic dependency and distorted the market forces that create economic opportunities. Conservative black capitalists completely rejected the civil rights establishment's historical "liberal agenda," which sought black social and economic advancement through government-sponsored social programs and political mobilization.

In a series of books and articles published in the 1970s and 1980s, economist Thomas Sowell argued that too many African Americans have become dependent on government programs. He compared the social and economic status of European, Asian, and Caribbean immigrants with that of African Americans, particularly over the last three decades, and concluded that members of the former groups have been upwardly mobile without the assistance of government-sponsored welfare programs. Sowell believes that the tendency of the traditional civil rights leadership in the United States to place the blame for black social and economic disadvantages on "white racism" does not explain the social and historical realities. African Americans from the Caribbean were also victimized by racist attitudes and practices on entering American society, and yet they have made significant social and economic advancements. For Sowell and other conservatives, the existence of white racism in American society does not explain the depressed social and economic conditions of blacks in the United States either historically or in the contemporary period.[1]

Black conservatives also dispute the nature of changes within the African-American community brought about by the successful civil rights campaigns of the 1950s and 1960s. Thomas Sowell, Walter Williams, Robert Woodson, and other conservative social scientists have argued that the strategies for advancement advocated by the leadership of the NAACP, the National Urban League, People United To Save Humanity (PUSH), and other civil rights groups assist primarily middle-class blacks rather than the black poor. While these conservatives concede that the civil rights movement was important for ending the legal barriers to black advancement in American society, they also believe that the liberal programs calling for minority set-asides in government contracts and affirmative action in employment gave middle-class women and minorities preferential treatment while failing to assist African Americans who were uneducated and trapped in a cycle of poverty.[2]

Elizabeth Wright, publisher of the conservative magazine *Issues and Views,* suggested in an interview in *The New York Times* that the black civil rights leadership has paid too little attention to economic self-help activities and programs. "The civil rights crew diverted us, because it was the easier way out for their clique. It's easier to beat on the door of the white man to let you into I.B.M. than to go into business with your brother or cousin and open up a little grocery store or hat shop that builds up the black community. That's a long arduous task, and it doesn't give the prestige so many middle-class blacks crave." And Robert Woodson, director of the Center for Neighborhood Enterprise, has argued that the civil rights leadership has in the past ignored strategies that would provide poor blacks the opportunity to control their own lives and economic institutions through cooperative ventures with large scale businesses.[3]

While many would question the conservatives' contentions that affirmative action programs were originally designed to help primarily middle-class blacks or that the opening of "mom and pop" grocery stores is a viable way of dealing with massive black unemployment, a wide range of spokespersons—liberal, conservative, and radical—have suggested that African Americans in the 1990s need to do more to help themselves to advance socially and economically in the United States. It is not merely the black "petit-bourgeois capitalists" who have pointed to the need for more self-determination among African Americans. Many black physicians, ministers, social workers, educators, and other professionals have argued that African Americans must come together and take greater responsibility for improving the depressed social conditions within their communities.[4]

Black conservatives gained the national spotlight in the 1980s by pointing out over and over again that African Americans needed to do more the help themselves. However, today's black conservatives have no monopoly on black self-determination. On the contrary, this cultural value, which is deeply rooted in the African-American experience, has served as the ideological basis for liberal and radical, not just conservative, social movements among African Americans throughout our history. While conservatives hark back to the black self-help strategies associated with Booker T. Washington at the turn of the century, they forget that in the 1920s radical Socialists A. Philip Randolph and Chandler Owen also appealed to the self-determinist values of black workers. Randolph and Owen, confronting the antiblack attitudes of white unions and the antiunion attitudes within the black community, organized the Brotherhood of Sleeping Car Porters. In 1932 it became the first all-black union to gain a charter from the American Federation of Labor.[5]

From his position within the national labor movement Randolph was called upon in 1935 to assume the leadership of the National Negro Congress (NNC), whose purpose was to monitor the conditions for African Americans in the federally-sponsored New Deal programs, to help organize black workers, and to develop pro-union sentiment within the black community. Other prominent black leftists, including John P. Davis, James Ford, and Benjamin Davis, supported the NNC in its strategy of mobilizing all-black social and religious groups to work for improvements in the status of black workers and for recognition within the larger working-class movement.[6]

Randolph's experiences in the NNC solidified his commitment to self-determinist strategies to obtain integrationist objectives. Initially, integrationist strategies failed to bring about the kind of economic improvements that African Americans desired, and Randolph again appealed to the core value of black self-determination. In December 1940, after he had resigned as president of the NNC over ideological differences with Communist-backed leaders of trade unions active in the organization, Randolph issued a call for a march on Washington of ten thousand African American citizens to protest the discrimination practiced by employers who were receiving national defense contracts from the federal government. Randolph made it clear that this was something that African Americans had to do for themselves. "One thing is certain," Randolph declared in his first public statement calling for the march, "if Negroes are going to get anything out of this national defense . . . WE MUST FIGHT FOR IT AND FIGHT

FOR IT WITH OUR GLOVES OFF."[7] Randolph recognized the potential strength of a black united front in the attempts to overcome black oppression.

> Power and pressure are at the foundation of the march of social justice and reform . . . [and] power and pressure do not reside in the few, an intelligentsia, they lie in and flow from the masses. . . . Power is the active principle of only the organized masses, the masses united for a definite purpose.

Although the march scheduled for July 4, 1941 never took place because President Franklin D. Roosevelt issued his ban on employment discrimination by companies and businesses that received government contracts, the March on Washington Movement clearly demonstrated the commitment of African Americans on the left to black self-determination. Indeed, an appreciation of the appeal of self-determinist values is essential for gaining a true understanding of the history of the black labor movement in the United States.[8]

In December 1955, when Rosa Parks was arrested for not giving up her bus seat to a white passenger, African Americans in Montgomery, Alabama began their boycott of the city's public transit system and organized the Montgomery Improvement Association (MIA) to coordinate the movement. Initially, there were few white supporters or participants. The Inter Civic Council (ICC), organized in 1956 by African Americans in Tallahassee, Florida, and the Alabama Christian Movement for Human Rights (ACMHR), formed by blacks in Birmingham to coordinate the boycott and other protests against businesses and government agencies that discriminated against African Americans, were virtually all-black organizations. A few liberal white ministers joined and supported these groups, but at this point these campaigns could not be described as examples of "integration" or black-white cooperation. These boycotts and protests were effective because they appealed to the self-determinist values of southern blacks. Eventually, thousands of progressive whites in the north and south would support and join this black-initiated social movement.[9]

Moreover, in his early statements and addresses Rev. Martin Luther King, Jr., who throughout his period of national prominence represented the center of the African-American ideological spectrum, also appealed to the self-determinist values in African-American culture. Most southern blacks already subscribed to the traditional Christian belief that "God helps those who help themselves." However, Dr. King believed that participation in the civil rights campaigns would produce a new sense of pride and self-respect among African Americans. "This growing self-respect has inspired the Negro with a new determination to struggle and sacrifice until first class citizenship has been attained," he said. Ultimately, he felt change had to be brought about primarily by African Americans acting together. "In the final analysis," King told the participants in a National Urban League conference in November 1960, "if first class citizenship is to become a reality for the Negro, he must assume the primary responsibility for making it so. The Negro must not be victimized with the delusion of thinking that others should be more concerned than himself about his citizenship rights."[10]

Martin Luther King, Jr. was a product of the African-American church and knew the importance of all-black organizations and institutions. But he also understood the necessity of gaining the support of white allies and he welcomed the participation of white Americans in the civil rights campaigns. By 1960 King's movement was committed ideologically to integrationist strategies to obtain integrationist objectives.[11]

At the same time, however, as the Southern Christian Leadership Conference (SCLC), the Congress of Racial Equality (CORE), and other civil rights groups became more and more associated with the goal of integration, the Nation of Islam took up the challenge of black self-determination. By 1960, with Martin Luther King, Jr. firmly ensconced in the political center, Elijah Muhammad and the Black Muslims came to dominate the conservative end of the black ideological spectrum and launched an attack on the proponents of black-white solidarity. The Muslims were separatists, as the supporters of Marcus Garvey's Universal Negro Improvement Association (UNIA) had been in the 1920s, but the Muslims gained a large following primarily through their advocacy of black self-defense in the face of unprovoked attack. This was a very popular position in the 1960s because many African Americans who recognized the need to destroy the legal barriers to black movement into the mainstream of American society were nonetheless unwilling to participate in *nonviolent* direct action protests, such as those they saw on television taking place in Mississippi and Alabama in 1962 and 1963.[12]

In the early 1960s Malcolm X, the leading spokesperson for the Nation of Islam, presented an alternative ideological perspective to the one being offered by Martin Luther King and the civil rights leadership. Malcolm unequivocally upheld the right of African Americans to defend themselves against physical and verbal attacks. At conventions and meetings, in college lecture halls, mosques, churches, and on street corners, he railed against the idea that African Americans need to become more integrated into American society. While Malcolm condemned the racist practices that helped to create many social problems for African Americans, the Muslims believed that there was little that white Americans could do to change and improve the situation. Whereas Martin Luther King, Roy Wilkins, A. Philip Randolph, and other civil rights leaders actively sought non-black support for their protests and campaigns, Elijah Muhammad and the Muslims created cooperatively owned businesses and other enterprises whose economic viability was dependent solely on African Americans.

In the early 1960s, however, the pro-integrationist position was considered more progressive, and historically it was linked to the "anti-capitalism" of the Socialist and Communist parties that called for a redistribution of the wealth from the haves (capitalists) to the have nots (workers). According to these Marxist-derived theories, racist behavior exhibited by the white working class was part of the residue of capitalism; if society would get rid of capitalism and the unfair competition that it encourages, racial hostilities between black and white workers would end. Before 1963 Malcolm X's positions were often reactionary and depended on black separatist strategies that had proven ineffective for mass economic advancement in the past. After 1963 and his much-publicized break with Elijah Muhammed and the Nation of Islam, however, Malcolm also came to accept the more progressive notion that black-initiated movements for social change could benefit from alliances with predominantly white organizations and movements committed to bringing about an end to racist or capitalist exploitation of the laboring classes.[13]

The civil rights campaigns were successful in bringing about an end to legalized American apartheid with the passage of the 1964 Civil Rights Act. Segregation was outlawed in public accommodations, and the Equal Employment Opportunity Commission was created to investigate complaints of discrimination in hiring on the basis of race, creed, color, religion, or sex. The act also forbade discrimination by any federally assisted program and called for the termination of federal funding to programs that failed to comply. The U.S. Office of Education was authorized to provide technical assistance to public school districts around the country engaged in desegregation.[14]

The 1965 Voting Rights Act, which came in the wake of the marches and protests in Selma, Alabama, suspended the use of any "test or devise," such as literacy qualifications, as a prerequisite for voting in any state or county where less than fifty percent of the adults were registered to vote. In counties where there was abundant evidence of discriminatory voting practices, the U.S. Attorney General was authorized to send in federal employees to register voters.[15]

The significance of the civil rights campaigns of the late 1950s and early 1960s is that they depended on self-determinist *and* integrationist strategies for their success. Civil rights leaders represented the center and left wing of the ideological spectrum, and they appealed to the African American core values of freedom, resistance, and self-determination. Moreover, these leaders were able to build a mass movement because the objectives they sought would improve the daily lives of all African Americans, not just the middle class. The black middle class may have been better able to take advantage of the economic opportunities created by the new legislation designed to end discrimination, but the social circumstances for women and minorities of every social class background were improved by the passage of the civil rights laws.

The civil rights legislation and the increased government intervention and social welfare programs that culminated in President Lyndon B. Johnson's War on Poverty and Great Society legislation also laid the groundwork for the phenomenal increase in black political power and influence. In 1966, for example, there were only ninety-seven African Americans in state legislatures across the country and six in the U.S. Congress. By 1969, following the voter registration campaigns launched in the deep South by the SCLC, NAACP, CORE, the Student Nonviolent Coordinating Committee (SNCC), and other groups, the number of black voters increased dramatically, and more than one thousand African Americans held elective office throughout the country.[16]

One of the reasons for the increase in the number of black elected officials was that black political mobilization became closely associated with the new demand for "Black Power." After Stokely Carmichael, chairman of SNCC, introduced the black power slogan in June 1966 during the march from Greenwood to Jackson, Mississippi following the shooting of James Meredith, it was taken up by black militants and the mass media and projected throughout the country. Initially, black power was a slogan without a program, and the concept was publicly denounced by Martin Luther King, A. Philip Randolph, Roy Wilkins, and other civil rights leaders who feared that it would alienate white supporters of the movement.[17]

Eventually, activists of every ideological persuasion defined the term according to their own particular political agendas. Black militants in radical groups such as the Black Panthers saw black power as the means for mobilizing black communities along Socialist lines in a defensive move against further capitalist exploitation. Black conservatives eventually came to accept the concept of black power as a rationale for black capitalistic ventures and the development of new relationships between black business-men and corporate America. Black educators who recognized black power's potential for raising political consciousness and making the college curricu-lum more relevant to the needs of black students were influential in the development of Black Studies programs at colleges and universities across the country. Black students and professors developed "Afro-centric" courses and programs that focused primarily on the history and cultures of African peoples in Africa and throughout the diaspora.[18]

Given the huge increase in the black vote by the early 1970s, black power became the rallying cry in cities and towns across the country where African Americans were seriously underrepresented in elective offices. Self-determinist slogans and strategies were utilized by African Americans seeking political office, and the response from the black electorate was overwhelmingly positive. A high point was reached in March 1972 when a national black political convention was held in Gary, Indiana, bringing together African Americans from the left, center, and right to plan the mobilization of black voters. Some at the Gary convention even called for the creation of a separate black political party. Black politicians at the local level appealing directly or indirectly to the desire for black power were elected in record numbers; by 1975 there were more than three thousand black elected officials in the United States.[19]

The vast majority of these newly elected black officials were members of the Democratic party and thus the idea of creating a separate black political party quickly lost its appeal. Many of these black officeholders were veterans of the civil rights campaigns, and they saw their elections as fulfilling the movement's integrationist objectives. Consequently, despite some early differences over whether to endorse the candidacy of former Georgia governor Jimmy Carter for president in 1976, most black politi-cians eventually climbed aboard the Carter bandwagon. To a very great extent, the election of Jimmy Carter and his appointment of a number of African Americans to high-ranking positions within federal agencies was considered vindication of the integrationist ideals and strategies of the new black politicians.[20]

For a number of social, political, and economic reasons, Jimmy Carter failed to gain reelection in 1980. The election of Ronald Reagan in 1980 signaled the beginning of the "conservative revolution" and a new preoccupation with the virtues of capitalism and free market economics. No longer was the federal government to be overly concerned with issues of social justice and civil rights, and the idea of less government interference in the market and in the lives of individuals became the guiding premise of Republican officials. Business and industries were deregulated, taxes on the wealthy decreased, and government-sponsored social programs were eliminated or drastically reduced.[21]

By the end of the decade the results of these government policies had become apparent. Wealth was concentrated in the hands of the top half of one percent of the U.S. population. Kevin Phillips, in *The Politics of Rich and Poor: Wealth and the American Electorate in the Reagan Aftermath,* points out that "in 1988 approximately 1.3 million individual Americans were millionaires by assets, up from 574,000 in 1980, 180,000 in 1972, 94,000 in 1964, and just 27,000 in 1953." The number of billionaires went from 26 in 1981 to 52 in 1988. At the same time, however, wages, the principal source of income for the middle and lower classes, stagnated. "Most of the Reagan decade," writes Phillips, "was the heyday for unearned income as rents, dividends, capital gains, and interest gained relative to wages and salaries as a source of wealth and increasing economic inequality." Real hourly wages for nonsupervisory workers in 1987 were the same as they were in 1980. After 1987 real hourly wages began to drop so that by the first quarter of 1988, "they were 2.4 percent *below* where they had been in 1980 and falling at a rate in excess of 1 percent a year."[22]

The official unemployment rate of 5.3 percent throughout the decade was misleading because large numbers of unemployed Americans were not even counted. The underclass made up of the unemployed and unemployable expanded exponentially, but these individuals were not included in official unemployment statistics. Thousands of homeless people roamed the downtown sections of America's large cities. This was clearly a new development associated with the government's desire to allow market forces to determine what types of housing would be made available to the public. Moreover, with the soaring prices for homes, home ownership began to decline for the first time in forty years. Young people under the age of thirty-five found it more and more difficult to save enough money for down payments and the escalating closing costs involved in the purchase of a home.[23]

The destructive impact of the Reagan revolution on black Americans significantly undercuts the black conservatives' arguments in support of these policies. Since the vast majority of African Americans receive their incomes from wages and salaries, they were seriously affected by the decline in real wages. Median family income for African Americans in 1989, in adjusted dollars, was slightly below its 1969 level. The scaling back of federally funded social programs adversely affected lower-class blacks who received these services and middle-class blacks who provided them. Female-headed households among blacks rose to over 50 percent, and one out of every two black children lived in poverty. What was most alarming was the decrease in the proportion of African Americans attending and graduating from college, which meant these social problems would very likely be carried over into the next generation.[24]

Since Ronald Reagan had won the presidency without the black vote or the support of any well-known black politicians, he felt no need to address African-American issues or even to meet with black Democratic leaders. Moreover, black conservatives claimed that the policies and programs put forward by the traditional black leadership encouraged a "welfare mentality" and did not emphasize the need for African Americans to do more to help themselves. Black conservatives relentlessly attacked the civil rights agenda of the so-called black leadership family and suggested that the policies and programs it pursued reflected the incestuous nature of the relationship between black political leaders and the Democratic party. They charged that black politicians appeared more interested in gaining reelection and delivering the black vote to the Democratic party than in meeting the needs of the African-American community.

In the 1990s many African-American cultural institutions are in serious trouble. The black family has been ravaged by unemployment, inadequate health care, and decreasing public expenditures for social services. The financial crisis in many cities and states has meant that the budgets for African-American museums, theater companies, art centers, and other cultural institutions have been slashed. The public schools in which the vast majority of African-American children are enrolled have become little more than holding cells where young people are kept in "protective custody." While the black conservatives are correct in emphasizing that African Americans need to do more to change these social conditions, they should also realize that the consumer capitalism and free market economics that were pursued in the 1980s have diminished African Americans' ability to help themselves.[25]

The problems facing African Americans in the 1990s are formidable, but not insurmountable. African Americans were not the only victims of

Reaganomics, and many other social and cultural groups have come to recognize the need to pursue a new social agenda. African Americans have an important role to play in the development of progressive political coalitions whose objectives would be economic justice and the improvement of the quality of life for all Americans. The African-American cultural heritage places heavy emphasis on self-determination, but the social problems that must be addressed will require a united effort by a wide range of social and cultural groups committed to a more progressive vision for America's future.

NOTES

Introduction, pages 1–10

1. John Langston Gwaltney, *Drylongso: A Self Portrait of Black America* (New York, 1980), pp. xxiv–xxvi.
2. "The Narrative of Hannah Nelson," in ibid., pp. 4–5.
3. Several recent studies have closely examined the impact of African cultural beliefs and practices upon Afro-American culture. See, for example, Herbert G. Gutman, *The Black Family in Slavery and Freedom, 1750–1925* (New York, 1976); Albert J. Raboteau, *Slave Religion: The "Invisible Institution" in the Antebellum South* (New York, 1978); George E. Simpson, *Black Religions in the New World* (New York, 1978); Samuel Charters, *The Roots of the Blues: An African Search* (New York, 1981); Alfred P. Pasteur and Ivory L. Toldson, *Roots of Soul: The Psychology of Black Expressiveness* (New York, 1982); Janice E. Hale, *Black Children: Their Roots, Culture, and Learning Styles* (Provo, Utah, 1982); Robert Farris Thompson, *Flash of the Spirit: African and Afro-American Art and Philosophy* (New York, 1983); Charles Joyner, *Down By the Riverside: A South Carolina Slave Community* (Urbana, Ill., 1984).
4. For discussion, see Rupert Emerson, *From Empire to Nation: The Rise of Self-Assertion of Asian and African Peoples* (Cambridge, Mass., 1960); Frantz Fanon, *The Wretched of the Earth* (New York, 1963); David C. Gordon, *Self-Determination and the History of the Third World* (Princeton, N.J., 1971); A. Rigo Sureda, *The Evolution of the Right of Self-Determination: A Study of United Nations Practice* (Leiden, The Netherlands, 1973); and Michael Hechter, *Internal Colonialism: The Celtic Fringe in British National Development, 1536–1966* (Berkeley, Calif., 1975).
5. E. P. Thompson, *The Making of the English Working Class* (1963; reprint ed., New York, 1966) pp. 9–11.
6. George M. Fredrickson, *White Supremacy: A Comparative Study in American and South African History* (New York, 1981), pp. 70, 71–75, passim.
7. Following the success of the campaigns of the Civil Rights movement to "desegregate" American society, supporters of black self-determination became less preoccupied with getting "black faces in high places" and more concerned about making sure that social, political, and economic decisions affecting the black masses were also made in the interest of the majority of Afro-Americans, not merely a "professional elite." For an excellent analysis of the potential divergences in mass versus elite perceptions of political

and economic issues within the African context, see Chinweizu, *The West and the Rest of Us: White Predators, Black Slavers, and the African Elite* (New York, 1975).

8. Dov Ronen, *The Quest for Self-Determination* (New Haven, 1979), p. 39.

9. Ronen discusses "black separatists" on pp. 35–36, but does not discuss Native Americans in North America. The European settlers and later the United States government erected a legal facade of self-determination to cover their dealings with the various Native American (Indian) cultural groups. But there was little substance to these legalistic arrangements, and Native Americans rarely exercised control over decisions that affected both Indians and white Americans. For documentary information, see L. Carlson and G. A. Colburn, eds., *In Their Place: White America Defines Her Minorities, 1850–1960* (New York, 1972), pp. 1–54; see also F. S. Cohen, *Handbook of Federal Indian Law* (Albuquerque, N.M., 1942); W. E. Washburn, *Red Man's Land; White Man's Law* (New York, 1971); U.S. Commission on Civil Rights, *The Navajo Nation: An American Colony* (Washington, D.C., 1975); Ronald Takaki, *Iron Cages: Race and Culture in Nineteenth-Century America* (New York, 1979), pp. 55–65; Benjamin B. Ringer, *"We the People" and Others: Duality and America's Treatment of Racial Minorities* (New York, 1983), pp. 116–51.

10. James Forman, *Self-Determination and the African-American People* (Seattle, Wash., 1981), pp. 10–12. See also V. I. Lenin, *The Right of Nations to Self-Determination: Selected Writings* (New York, 1951); Harry Haywood, *Negro Liberation* (New York, 1948); and George Padmore, *Pan-Africanism or Communism? The Coming Struggle for Africa* (London, 1956), pp. 303–17.

Chapter One, "The Souls of Black Folk Revisited," pages 11–26

1. Most of Du Bois's early works, including the Atlanta University Studies, are still available in reprint editions. See *The Suppression of the African Slave Trade, 1678–1870* (1896; reprint ed., New York, 1968); *The Philadelphia Negro: A Social Study* (1899; reprint ed., New York, 1967); and *Atlanta University Studies (1898–1914)* reprint ed., (New York, 1968).

2. Du Bois's most important statement on race during this period was an essay, "The Conservation of the Races," published as an *Occasional Paper* by the American Negro Academy (Washington, D.C., 1897).

3. Review of *The American Negro, The Dial* 30 (16 April 1901): 262–64; reprinted in *Book Reviews by W. E. B. Du Bois*, comp. and ed. Herbert Aptheker (Millwood, N.Y., 1977), pp. 1–3.

4. Du Bois, "The Evolution of Negro Leadership," a review of B. T. Washington, *Up from Slavery, The Dial* 31 (16 July 1901): 53–55; reprinted in *Book Reviews by W. E. B. Du Bois*, pp. 3–5.

5. *The Autobiography of W. E. B. Du Bois: A Soliloquy on Viewing My Life from the Last Decade of Its First Century* (New York, 1968), p. 245.

6. *The Souls of Black Folk*, with introductions by Nathan Hare and Alvin Poussaint (1903, reprint ed., New York, 1969). All quotations are from this edition, hereafter cited as *Souls*.

7. Arnold Rampersad, *The Art and Imagination of W. E. B. Du Bois* (Cambridge, Mass., 1976), p. 68.

8. Du Bois, *Souls*, p. 169.

9. For discussions of elitism in *Souls*, see Rampersad, *Art and Imagination*, pp. 65–67; Houston Baker, "The Black Man of Culture: W. E. B. Du Bois and *The Souls of Black Folk*," *Long Black Song: Essays in Black American Literature and Culture* (Charlottesville, Va., 1972), pp. 102–6; Robert Stepto, *From Behind the Veil: A Study of Afro-American Narrative* (Urbana, Ill., 1979), pp. 86–91.

10. For a brief discussion of the preoccupation with "social advancement," see V. P. Franklin, *The Education of Black Philadelphia: The Social and Educational History of a Minority Community, 1900–1950* (Philadelphia, 1979), pp. 182–84. See also Chapter 5 of this study for a detailed analysis of the relationships between education and advancement.

11. Houston Baker has an extended discussion of the "remarkable similarity between Du Bois's point of view and the outlook of Booker T. Washington" in "The Black Man of Culture," pp. 99–106.

12. In Greek mythology, Atalanta was the daughter of Iasus and Clymene of Arcadia and is generally considered a by-form or composite of the goddess, Artemis, the huntress. According to legend Atalanta was averse to marriage and declared that she would marry only someone who could beat her at a foot race. Melanion or Hippomenes, her first cousin, challenged her, and received three golden apples from the goddess, Aphrodite, which he threw in Atalanta's path, thus delaying her and winning the race. Unfortunately, Hippomenes forgot to pay Aphrodite for the apples and slept with Atalanta in a holy place. For this impiety they were both turned into lions. See N. G. Hammond and H. H. Scullard, eds., *Oxford Classical Dictionary*, 2nd ed. (Oxford, 1970), p. 136.

13. Du Bois, *Souls*, p. 119.

14. Du Bois, ed., *The College-Bred Negro: Report of a Social Study Made under the Direction of Atlanta University* (Atlanta, 1900), pp. 65 and 114. For discussion, see V. P. Franklin, "W. E. B. Du Bois and the Education of Black Folk," *History of Education Quarterly* 16 (Spring 1976): 111–18.

15. Henry L. Morehouse, "The Talented Tenth," *Independent*, 23 April 1896, quoted by James MacPherson, *The Abolitionist Legacy: From Reconstruction to the NAACP* (Princeton, N.J., 1975) p. 222. MacPherson of course makes it clear that "nowhere near a tenth of the Negro population benefited from higher education. In 1909–1910 there were approximately 3000 black students in colleges and professional schools and probably not more than 3,500 living college graduates in a total black population of nearly 10 million. Less than one-third of 1 percent of college-age blacks were attending college in 1910, compared with more than 5 percent among whites," p. 223.

16. Du Bois, "The Talented Tenth," in *The Negro Problem* (New York, 1903), pp. 33, 74–75.

17. For recent discussions of the origins of Harvard College and the common school system of Massachusetts, see Lawrence A. Cremin, *American Education: The Colonial Experience* (New York, 1970) pp. 180–210; and Sheldon S. Cohen, *A History of Colonial Education, 1607–1776* (New York, 1972), pp. 40–69.

18. Du Bois, *Souls*, pp. 136–37.

19. Ibid., pp. 234–242. When Alexander Crummell returned to the United States from Liberia, he was instrumental in founding the American Negro Academy, whose purpose was to promote intellectual activity and refute "the Aryan who attacks the Negro by malicious and false accusations." See Alfred Moss, *The American Negro Academy: Voice of the Talented Tenth* (Baton Rouge, La., 1981), esp. pp. 35–92.

20. Washington had sufficient support for black capitalism within the black community in 1900 to found the National Negro Business League, with himself as president. For discussion, see Louis R. Harlan, *Booker T. Washington: The Making of a Black Leader, 1856–1901* (New York, 1972), pp. 266–71.

21. Du Bois, *Souls*, pp. 86 and 91.

22. Ibid., pp. 88–89.

23. Carlyle's "Great Man Theory" is set forth in his famous essay, *On Heroes and Hero Worship*, (London, 1967), with introduction by W. H. Hudson, pp. x–xv. For an examination of the theory, see B. H. Lehman, *Carlyle's Theory of the Hero: Its Sources, Development, History and Influence on Carlyle's Work* (Durham, N.C., 1928); See also Arnold Rampersad, *Art and Imagination*, pp. 66–67.

24. *The Autobiography of W. E. B. Du Bois*, pp. 133 and 228. Du Bois's second thoughts

about the ability of the talented tenth to "save the race" are detailed in David Lewis, *When Harlem Was in Vogue* (New York, 1981), pp. 176–78.

25. Du Bois, *Souls*, p. 274.
26. For a detailed examination of the reviews and responses to the publication of *The Souls of Black Folk*, see Herbert Aptheker's Introduction to Kraus-Thomson edition (Millwood, N.Y., 1973), pp. 5–46.
27. Du Bois, *Souls*, p. 85.

Chapter Two, "The Gospel According to Enslaved Afro-Americans," pages 27–68

1. W. E. B. Du Bois, "The Religion of the American Negro," *New World* 9 (December 1900): 614–25.
2. Du Bois, *The Souls of Black Folk* (1903, reprinted, New York, 1969), p. 211.
3. Ibid., p. 218. For a more recent discussion of the African influence on slave religion, see Albert Raboteau, *Slave Religion: The "Invisible Institution" in the Antebellum South* (New York, 1978), pp. 3–93.
4. Du Bois, *Souls*, p. 219.
5. Ibid., p. 222–25.
6. Du Bois, ed., *The Negro Church: Report of a Social Study Made Under the Direction of Atlanta University* (Atlanta, 1903), pp. 1–29.
7. Carter G. Woodson, *The History of the Negro Church* (Washington, D.C., 1945), p. 279. This was a reprint of the 1921 edition.
8. Benjamin E. Mays and Joseph W. Nicholson, *The Negro's Church* (New York, 1933), pp. 224–25.
9. Ibid., p. 59.
10. Ibid., pp. 86–89.
11. Benjamin Mays, *The Negro's God as Reflected in His Literature* (Boston, 1938), p. 14.
12. Ibid., pp. 14–15.
13. Ibid., pp. 24–25.
14. *Dwight's Journal of Music* 19 (September 7, 1861): 182, quoted by Dena Epstein, *Sinful Tunes and Spirituals: Black Folk Music to the Civil War* (Urbana, Ill., 1977), pp. 244–45.
15. Robert Toll, *Blacking Up: The Minstrel Show in Nineteenth Century America* (New York, 1974), p. v.
16. Ibid., pp. 65–103. See also Carl Wittke, *Tambo and Bones: A History of the American Minstrel Stage* (Durham, N.C., 1930), and Gary D. Engle, *This Grotesque Essence: Plays from the American Minstrel Stage* (Baton Rouge, La., 1978).
17. *National Anti-Slavery Standard* 22 (December 21, 1861): 1, quoted by Epstein, *Sinful Tunes and Spirituals*, pp. 245–46.
18. Thomas Wentworth Higginson, "Negro Spirituals" *Atlantic Monthly* 19 (June 1867): 685.
19. Higginson, *Army Life in a Black Regiment* (1870; reprint ed., Ann Arbor, Mich., 1960). See the Introduction by Howard M. Jones for background information on Higginson.
20. Higginson, "Negro Spirituals," p. 687.
21. Ibid., pp. 689–90, 694.
22. Ibid., pp. 693–94.
23. William Francis Allen, Charles P. Ware, and Lucy McKim Garrison, eds., *Slave Songs in the United States* (1867; reprint ed., New York, 1929).
24. "William Francis Allen," *Dictionary of American Biography*, vol. 1, p. 211.
25. "Excerpts from the Diary of William Francis Allen," reprinted in Epstein, *Sinful Tunes and Spirituals*, Appendix, p. 352.
26. Allen, Ware, and Garrison, *Slave Songs in the United States*, pp. vi and vii.
27. Ibid., p. x.

28. Ibid., p. xviii. See also Charles Nichols, *Many Thousand Gone: The Ex-Slaves' Account of Their Bondage and Freedom* (Leiden, The Netherlands, 1963), pp. 99–105.

29. Quoted by James MacPherson, *The Struggle for Equality: Abolitionists and the Negro in the Civil War and Reconstruction* (Princeton, N.J. 1964), pp. 149–50.

30. Allen, Ware, and Garrison, *Slave Songs in the United States*, p. viii.

31. See, for example, E. Franklin Frazier, *The Negro Church in America* (1953; reprint ed., New York, 1963), pp. 14–25.

32. Du Bois, *Souls* pp. 267–70.

33. For example, see William Harris, *Keeping the Faith: A. Philip Randolph, Milton Webster, and the Brotherhood of Sleeping Car Porters, 1925–1937* (Urbana, Ill., 1977); Wilson Record, *The Negro and the Communist Party* (New York, 1971); Stanford Lyman, *The Black American in Sociological Thought* (New York, 1972).

34. Frazier, *Negro Church in America*, pp. 19–21.

35. The historical reality that many of the Negro spirituals were "purely African" songs is discussed in detail in John Lovell, *Black Song: The Forge and the Flame, The Story of How the Afro-American Spiritual Was Hammered Out*, (New York, 1972), pp. 24–75, 84–88.

36. See Henry Mitchell, *Black Preaching* (Philadelphia, 1970), pp. 194–95.

37. James Cone, *A Black Theology of Liberation* (Philadelphia, 1970), p. 17; and idem, *Black Theology and Black Power* (New York, 1969).

38. Cone, *Black Theology of Liberation*, pp. 22–23.

39. Ibid., pp. 75–76.

40. Ibid., p. 59.

41. Gayraud Wilmore, *Black Religion and Black Radicalism*, (New York, 1972), p. xii.

42. Ibid., pp. 2–3.

43. Ibid., p. 36. For a comprehensive examination of the leading thinkers and thoughts in Black Theology, see Gayraud Wilmore and James H. Cone, eds., *Black Theology: A Documentary History, 1966–1979*. (Mary Knoll, N.Y., 1979).

44. Quoted by Sterling Brown, "Negro Folk Expression: Spirituals, Seculars, Ballads, and Work Songs," A. Meier and E. Rudwick, eds., *The Making of Black America* (New York, 1969) p. 215.

45. Ibid., p. 216.

46. Quoted by James Cone, *The Spirituals and the Blues* (New York, 1972), pp. 69–70.

47. Ibid., p. 34.

48. Aaron, *The Light and Truth of Slavery* (1843); quoted by Thomas Webber, *Deep Like the Rivers: Education in the Slave Quarter Community* (New York, 1978), p. 84.

49. Stephen Butterfield, *Black Autobiography in America* (Amherst, Mass., 1974), p. 15.

50. Webber discussed this rejection of "religious instruction" by the slaves in *Deep Like the Rivers*, pp. 43–58. See also Raboteau, *Slave Religion* pp. 243–75.

51. Frederick Douglass, *The Life and Times of Frederick Douglass* (1893; reprint ed., New York, 1962), p. 157.

52. John W. Blassingame, ed., *Slave Testimony: Two Centuries of Letters, Speeches, Interviews, and Autobiographies* (Baton Rouge, La., 1977), pp. 404 and 407.

53. Norman Yetman, ed., *Life Under the "Peculiar Institution": Selections from the Slave Narrative Collection* (New York, 1970), pp. 12–13, 262.

54. Henry Bibb to Albert Silbey, 7 October 1852; reprinted in Blassingame, *Slave Testimony*, pp. 52–53.

55. Frederick Douglass, *Narrative of the Life of Frederick Douglass, An American Slave*, ed. Benjamin Quarles (Cambridge, Mass., 1960), pp. 155–56.

56. Yetman, *Life Under the "Peculiar Institution,"* p. 116.

57. Ibid., pp. 182–83. See also the interviews of ex-slaves conducted by Mary White Ovington in 1910 and published in Blassingame, *Slave Testimony*, pp. 538–39.

58. Yetman, *Life Under the "Peculiar Institution,"* p. 308.

59. Quoted by Raboteau, *Slave Religion*, p. 294.
60. "Narrative of James Curry (1840)," reprinted in Blassingame, *Slave Testimony*, p. 131.
61. John Brown, *Slave Life in Georgia: A Narrative of Life, Sufferings, and Escape of John Brown, a Fugitive Slave* (1855; reprint ed., Savannah, Ga., 1972) pp. 166–67.
62. Cone, *Spirituals and the Blues*, p. 84.
63. Henry Bibb to Albert Silbey, 7 November 1852; reprinted in Blassingame, *Slave Testimony*, p. 55.
64. Benjamin Drew, *The Refugee: A North-Side View of Slavery* (1855; reprint ed., Reading, Mass, 1969), p. 56.
65. Blassingame, *Slave Testimony*, p. 135.
66. William Craft, "Running a Thousand Miles for Freedom; or, The Escape of William and Ellen Craft from Slavery" (1860); reprinted in Arna Bontemps, ed., *Great Slave Narratives*, (Boston, 1969), p. 275.
67. Yetman, *Life Under the "Peculiar Institution,"* p. 118–19.
68. Blassingame, *Slave Testimony*, p. 654.
69. Yetman, *Life Under the "Peculiar Institution,"* p. 280.
70. "Judgment Will Find You So," in G. D. Pike, *The Jubilee Singers and Their Campaign for Twenty Thousand Dollars* (Boston, 1872) p. 202.
71. "Come Along, Moses," in Allen, Ware, and Garrison, *Slave Songs in the United States*, p. 104.
72. Cone, *Spirituals and the Blues*, p. 35.
73. "Oh, Brothers, Don't Get Weary," in Allen, Ware, and Garrison, *Slave Songs in the United States*, p. 95.
74. Moses Roper to Thomas Price, 27 June 1836, in Blassingame, *Slave Testimony*, pp. 24–25.
75. John B. Cage, "Out of the Mouths of Ex-Slaves," *Journal of Negro History* 20 (July 1935): 295, 328–31.
76. Ibid., p. 329–30.
77. Yetman, *Life Under the "Peculiar Institution,"* pp. 263–64.
78. Ibid., pp. 254 and 231.
79. Ibid., pp. 36, 312–13. See also Roboteau, *Slave Religion*, pp. 212–43.
80. Yetman, *Life Under the "Peculiar Institution,"* p. 308.
81. Eugene Genovese, *Roll, Jordan, Roll: The World the Slaves Made* (New York, 1974), pp. 6–7.
82. Paul Escott, *Slavery Remembered: A Record of Twentieth Century Slave Narratives* (Chapel Hill, 1979), p. 95. Escott presents a detailed critique of Genovese's notion of "southern paternalism," see pp. 18–35.

Chapter Three, "Let Your Motto Be Resistance!," pages 69–102

1. Norman Yetman, ed., *Life Under the "Peculiar Institution": Selections from the Slave Narrative Collection*, (New York, 1970), pp. 226–27.
2. Angela Y. Davis, "The Legacy of Slavery: Standards for a New Womanhood," *Woman, Race, and Class* (New York, 1981), quotes pp. 15 and 23. In this essay Ms. Davis discusses the need for a comprehensive history of the black female slave in the antebellum South. See also Bell Hooks, *Ain't I a Woman: Black Women and Feminism* (Boston, 1981), pp. 15–49; Erlene Stetson, "Studying Slavery: Some Literary and Pedagogical Considerations on the Black Female Slave," in G. T. Hull, P. B. Scott, and B. Smith, eds., *But Some of Us Are Brave: Black Women's Studies* (Old Westbury, N.Y., 1982), pp. 61–84; and Jacqueline Jones, "My Mother Was Much of a Woman: Black Women, Work, and the Family Under Slavery," *Feminist Studies* 8 (Summer 1982): 235–69.
3. Yetman, *Life Under the "Peculiar Institution,"* p. 228.

4. For the idea that Afro-Americans accommodated to slavery and that this produced the "Sambo personality," see Stanley Elkins, *Slavery: A Problem in American Institutional and Intellectual Life.* (Chicago, 1959). For the debate Elkins triggered, see Ann Lane, ed., *The Debate over Slavery: Stanley Elkins and his Critics* (Urbana, Ill., 1971), and V. P. Franklin, "Slavery, Personality and Black Culture: Some Theoretical Issues," *Phylon* 35 (March 1974): 54–63.

5. Yetman, *Life Under the "Peculiar Institution"*, p. 229–30.

6. Charles S. Johnson, Introduction to Clifton H. Johnson, ed., *God Struck Me Dead: Religious Conversion Experiences and Autobiographies of Ex-Slaves* (Philadelphia, 1969), p. xvii. Some researchers believe these conversion experiences among Afro-Americans can be traced back to African religious practices; see, for example, Albert Raboteau, *Slave Religion: The "Invisible Institution" in the Antebellum South* (New York, 1978), pp. 132–33 and 266–71.

7. Yetman, *Life Under the "Peculiar Institution,"* p. 229.

8. Frederick Douglass, *Narrative of the Life of Frederick Douglass, An American Slave,* ed. Benjamin Quarles (Cambridge, Mass.; 1960), pp. 104–5.

9. For a discussion of the impact of these individual acts of resistance upon Brown, Thompson, Northrup, Grandy, and Ward, see Stephen Butterfield, *Black Autobiography in America* (Amherst, Mass., 1974), pp. 18–22. In the Federal Writers Project interviews, acts of resistance are discussed in Yetman, *Life Under the "Peculiar Institution,"* pp. 11–12, 40, 130–33, 142, passsim.

10. Frederick Douglass, *The Life and Times of Frederick Douglass* (1892; reprint ed., London, 1962) p. 52.

11. Yetman, *Life Under the "Peculiar Institution,"* p. 226–27.

12. Ibid., p. 228.

13. Herbert Aptheker, *American Negro Slave Revolts* (New York, 1943), p. 140.

14. Leslie Howard Owens, *This Species of Property: Slave Life and Culture in the Old South* (New York, 1976), pp. 92–93.

15. Vincent Harding, *There Is a River: The Black Struggle for Freedom in America* (New York, 1981), p. 58.

16. Ibid., p. 74. See also Raymond A. Bauer and Alice Bauer, "Day to Day Resistance to Slavery," in J. Bracey, et al., eds., *American Slavery: The Question of Resistance* (Belmont, Calif., 1971), pp. 37–60.

17. Some secular songs of resistance are discussed in George Rawick, *From Sundown to Sunup: The Making of the Black Community* (Westport, Conn., 1972), pp. 95–121; Thomas Webber, *Deep Like the Rivers: Education in the Slave Quarter Community, 1831–1865* (New York, 1978), pp. 207–23; and William F. Cheek, *Black Resistance before the Civil War* (Beverly Hills, Calif., 1970), pp. 60–68, 129–34. For a detailed examination of resistance themes in slave folktales, see Lawrence Levine, *Black Culture and Black Consciousness: Afro-American Folk Thought From Slavery to Freedom* (New York, 1977), pp. 102–35.

18. Yetman, *Life Under the "Peculiar Institution,"* p. 93.

19. W. F. Allen, C. P. Ware, and L. M. Garrison, eds., *Slave Songs in the United States,* (1867; reprint ed., New York, 1929), p. 89.

20. Yetman, *Life Under the "Peculiar Institution,"* p. 128.

21. Ibid., p. 49. Peter Kolchin suggested in "Reevaluating the Antebellum Slave Community: A Comparative Perspective," *Journal of American History* 70 (December 1983): 579–601, that, compared to slaves in the Caribbean and serfs in Russia, Afro-Americans enslaved in the United States "in their resistance to slavery . . . showed substantially less collective spirit than was evident elsewhere" (p. 600). Unfortunately, Kolchin provides no direct slave testimony to support this assertion. The evidence from slave testimony suggests that running away and other forms of organized resistance *had* to be collective, rather than individual, forms of resistance to be effective.

22. Yetman, *Life Under the "Peculiar Institution,"* p. 297. See also Davis, "The Legacy of Slavery," pp. 16–24.
23. Yetman, *Life Under the "Peculiar Institution,"* p. 180.
24. Quoted by John W. Blassingame, ed., *Slave Testimony: Two Centuries of Letters, Speeches, Interviews and Autobiographies* (Baton Rouge, La., 1976), 641 and 656.
25. Yetman, *Life Under the "Peculiar Institution,"* p. 149.
26. Ibid., p. 253.
27. William D. Pierson, "Puttin' Down Ole Massa: African Satire in the New World," in Daniel J. Crowley, ed., *African Folklore in the New World* (Austin, Tex., 1977), pp. 30–31. For a more recent examination of the legal issues inherent in slave flight and transit, see Paul Finkelman, *An Imperfect Union: Slavery, Federalism, and Comity* (Chapel Hill, N.C., 1981).
28. Yetman, *Life Under the "Peculiar Institution,"* p. 113–14.
29. Ibid., pp. 291–92.
30. The most exhaustive collection of legal cases that dealt with Afro-Americans and slavery is Helen T. Catterall, ed., *Judicial Cases Concerning American Slavery and the Negro*, 5 vols. (1926–37; reprint ed., New York, 1968). For a more recent analysis of the legal status of the fugitive slaves, see Mary Frances Berry, *Black Resistance/White Law: A History of Constitutional Racism in America* (New York, 1971), pp. 72–77.
31. The classic study of the organized resistance against slavery was Wilbur Siebert, *The Underground Railroad from Slavery to Freedom* (New York, 1898). See also Larry Gara, *The Liberty Line: The Legend of the Underground Railroad* (Lexington, Ky., 1961), and Charles Blockson, *The Underground Railroad in Pennsylvania* (Jacksonville, N.C., 1981).
32. For biographical information on those individuals active in the antislavery resistance movement, see Jane H. Pease and William H. Pease, *Bound with Them in Chains: A Biographical History of the Anti-Slavery Movement* (Westport, Conn., 1972).
33. Leon F. Litwack, *North of Slavery: The Negro in the Free States, 1790–1860* (Chicago, 1961), pp. 15–16.
34. Alexis de Tocqueville, *Democracy in America*, quoted by Litwack, *North of Slavery*, p. 65.
35. See, for example, Ira Berlin, *Slaves Without Masters: The Free Negro in the Antebellum South* (New York, 1974). Given the social network that Berlin documents for free blacks in the antebellum South, it appears that his title is also misleading in characterizing the conditions for that group as well.
36. Litwack, *North of Slavery*, p. 40.
37. William Robinson, ed., *The Proceedings of the Free African Union Society and the African Benevolent Society, Newport, Rhode Island, 1780–1824* (Providence, R.I., 1976).
38. "Preamble of the Philadelphia Free African Society, 12 April 1787," in Herbert Aptheker, ed., *A Documentary History of the Negro People in the United States: From Colonial Times to the Founding of the NAACP in 1910* (New York, 1969), pp. 17–18.
39. "Petition of Peter Bestes, Sambo Freeman, Felix Holbrook and Chester Joie, Boston, 20 April 1773," in Dorothy Porter, ed., *Early Negro Writing, 1760–1837* (Boston, 1971), pp. 254–55.
40. "Petition to the Massachusetts Legislature, 1787," quoted by Philip S. Foner, *History of Black Americans: From Africa to the Emergence of the Cotton Kingdom* (Westport, Conn., 1975), pp. 579–80.
41. The early emigrationist activities of blacks in Newport and Providence, Rhode Island, are discussed in Floyd Miller, *The Search for a Black Nationality: Black Emigration and Colonization, 1787–1863* (Urbana, Ill, 1975), pp. 5–20.
42. See, for example, "Petition to the Massachusetts Legislature, 1787," in Foner, *History of Black Americans*, p. 579.
43. Charles H. Wesley, *Richard Allen: Apostle of Freedom* (Washington, D.C., 1935), pp. 59–61; Carol V. R. George, *Segregated Sabbaths: Richard Allen and the Emergence of Independent*

Black Churches, 1760–1840 (New York, 1973) pp: 51–55; V. P. Franklin, *The Education of Black Philadelphia: The Social and Educational History of a Minority Community, 1900– 1950* (Philadelphia, 1979), pp. 5–7.

44. Gayraud Wilmore, *Black Religion and Black Radicalism* (Garden City, N.Y., 1972), pp. 108–9.
45. Benjamin Quarles, *Black Abolitionists* (New York, 1969), p. 4.
46. American Colonization Society, *African Repository* (1825), vol. 1, p. 68; quoted by Litwack, *North of Slavery*, p. 21.
47. *Report of the American Colonization Society* (ACS), 1832; quoted by Robert C. Dick, *Black Protest: Issues and Tactics* (Westport, Conn., 1974), pp. 11–12.
48. Quoted by Quarles, *Black Abolitionists*, p. 7.
49. Miller, *Search for a Black Nationality*, p. 11.
50. Ibid., pp. 74–82. Miller provides a detailed account of the Haitian emigration activities of free blacks during the 1820s.
51. Ibid., p. 82. See also A. Meier and E. Rudwick, "Introduction," *Black Nationalism in America*, ed. John Bracey, A. Meier, and E. Rudwick (Indianapolis, Ind., 1970), pp. xxv–lvi.
52. *Minutes and Proceedings of the Second Annual Convention for the Improvement of the Free People of Color in the United States . . . June 1832* (1832; reprint ed., New York, 1969), pp. 35–36. The published *Minutes* of the national black conventions were all edited by Howard H. Bell.
53. The best brief discussion of the different camps within the radical abolitionist movement is found in Carlton Mabee, *Black Freedom: The Non-violent Abolitionists from 1830 through the Civil War* (London, 1970), pp. 1–7.
54. *Minutes of the Fifth Annual Convention for the Improvement of the Free People of Color in the United States . . . June, 1835* (1835; reprint ed., New York, 1969), pp. 26–27.
55. For discussion, see Howard H. Bell, "The American Moral Reform Society, 1836– 1841," *Journal of Negro Education* 27 (Winter 1958): 34–40.
56. Samuel Cornish, *The Colored American*, 2 February 1839; quoted by Howard H. Bell, *A Survey of the Negro Convention Movement, 1830–1861* (New York, 1969), p. 53.
57. Ibid., p. 55.
58. Ibid., p. 66. See also, "New York State Convention of Colored Citizens, Troy, August 25–27, 1841," in Philip S. Foner and George E. Walker, eds., *Proceedings of the Black State Conventions, 1840–1864*, 2 vols. (Philadelphia, 1979), 1: 27–30.
59. Henry Highland Garnet, "An Address to the Slaves in the United States" (1843), in Sterling Stuckey, ed., *The Ideological Origins of Black Nationalism*, (Boston, 1972), pp. 168–69.
60. Ibid., pp. 172–73.
61. *Minutes of the National Convention of Colored Citizens, Held at Buffalo . . . August, 1843*, (1843; reprint ed., New York, 1969), p. 13. The Douglass-Garnet conflict extended into the positions they took on international antislavery strategies; for a detailed discussion of this conflict, see R. J. M. Blackett, *Building an Antislavery Wall: Black Americans in the Atlantic Abolitionist Movement, 1830–1860* (Baton Rouge, La., 1983), pp. 142–45.
62. Quoted by Bell, *Survey of the Negro Convention Movement*, p. 90.
63. For detailed information on Garnet and his political activities during this period, see Earl Ofari, *Let Your Motto Be Resistance: The Life and Thought of Henry Highland Garnet* (Boston, 1972) pp. 34–39; and Joel Schor, *Henry Highland Garnet: A Voice of Black Radicalism in the Nineteenth Century* (Westport, Conn., 1977), pp. 28–87.
64. *Proceedings of the National Convention of Colored People, and Their Friends Held in Troy, New York . . . October 1847* (1847; reprint ed., New York, 1969), pp. 31–32.
65. *Report of the Proceedings of the Colored National Convention, Held at Cleveland, Ohio . . . September 6, 1848* (1848; reprint ed., New York, 1969), pp. 14–15.

66. Ibid., pp. 18–20.
67. The most detailed account of the passage and enforcement of the Fugitive Slave Law of 1850 is Stanley Campbell, *The Slave Catchers: Enforcement of the Fugitive Slave Law, 1850–1860* (Chapel Hill, N.C., 1970).
68. Virginia General Assembly quoted in ibid., p. 8.
69. Ibid., pp. 15–25.
70. Quarles, *Black Abolitionists*, p. 150.
71. Quarles, "The Black Underground," ibid., pp. 151–67.
72. Larry Gara, *The Liberty Line*, p. 102.
73. Several writers have called attention to Douglass's temporary tilt toward "violent insurrection," including Gara, *The Liberty Line*, pp. 106–7; Quarles, *Black Abolitionists*, pp. 228–29; and Dick, *Black Protest*, pp. 146–47.
74. *Proceedings of the Colored National Convention Held in Rochester, July . . . 1853* (1853; reprinted New York, 1969), p. 4.
75. John Mercer Langston is quoted by Bell, *Survey of the Negro Convention Movement*, p. 139. See also "Minutes and Address of the State Convention of the Colored Citizens of Ohio, Convened at Columbus, January 10–13th, 1849," in Foner and Walker, *Proceedings of the Black State Conventions*, 1: 218–35.
76. Bell, *Survey of the Negro Convention Movement*, pp. 138–53. See also Miller, *Search for a Black Nationality*, pp. 112–15. Liberia became an independent, black-controlled nation in 1847.
77. Bell, *Survey of the Negro Convention Movement*, p. 153.
78. Miller, *Search for a Black Nationality*, pp. 138–41.
79. *Proceedings of the Colored National Convention . . . 1853*, p. 18.
80. Miller, *Search for a Black Nationality*, pp. 136–37.
81. Some writers have spent too much time tracing the twists and turns in the ideological positions of black leaders and too little time examining the responses of Afro-American masses to these convoluted ideologies. See Miller, *Search for a Black Nationality*, pp. 139–56; Leonard Sweet, *Black Images of America, 1784–1870* (New York, 1976), pp. 82–100; and Wilson Jeremiah Moses, *The Golden Age of Black Nationalism, 1850–1925* (Hamden, Conn., 1978), pp. 32–55.

Chapter Four, "Keep Your Mind on Freedom," pages 103–146

1. Patsy Mitchner is quoted by Paul Escott, *Slavery Remembered: A Record of Twentieth Century Slave Narratives* (Chapel Hill, N.C., 1979), p. 160.
2. Escott provides a general discussion of "freedom" in these slave narratives, ibid., pp. 119–42.
3. Norman R. Yetman, ed., *Life Under the "Peculiar Institution": Selections from the Slave Narrative Collection* (New York, 1970), pp. 234–35.
4. Charles L. Perdue, Jr., Thomas Barden, and Robert K. Phillips, eds., *Weevils in the Wheat: Interviews with Virginia Ex-Slaves* (Charlottesville, Va., 1976), p. 117.
5. Ibid., pp. 58–59.
6. Ibid., pp. 128–29. See also James M. McPherson, *The Negro's Civil War: How American Negroes Felt and Acted During the War for the Union* (New York, 1965), pp. 55–68.
7. Perdue, Barden, and Phillips, *Weevils in the Wheat*, p. 268.
8. Ibid., p. 44. Paul Escott included a discussion of the former slaves' impressions of their "Yankee Liberators" in *Slavery Remembered*, pp. 123–27.
9. Yetman, *Life Under the "Peculiar Institution*," p. 226.
10. Ibid., p. 309.
11. Ibid., pp. 219–20. See also Louis S. Gerteis, *From Contraband to Freedman: Federal Policy Toward Southern Blacks, 1861–1865* (Westport, Conn., 1973), pp. 33–48; and Leon

Litwack, *Been in the Storm So Long: The Aftermath of Slavery* (New York, 1979), pp. 167–291, passim.

12. For a discussion of the conditions in Fortress Monroe and other camps in Virginia immediately after the war see Robert Engs, *Freedom's First Generation: Black Hampton, Virginia, 1861–1890* (Philadelphia, 1979), pp. 3–44 passim.

13. "The Interview," *The Liberator,* 24 February 1865; reprinted in Herbert Aptheker, ed., *A Documentary History of the Negro People in the United States: From Colonial Times to the Founding of the NAACP in 1910* (New York: The Citadel Press, 1969), p. 497.

14. Mary Frances Berry, *Military Necessity and Civil Rights Policy: Black Citizenship and the Constitution, 1861–1868* (Port Washington, N.Y., 1977), pp. 82–84. For figures on Union soldiers, see Ira Berlin, et al., eds., *Freedom: A Documentary History of Emancipation,* Series II, Volume I, (New York, 1982), p. 733.

15. Herbert Aptheker, "Introduction to Documents on the Memphis Murders and the New Orleans Massacre," *A Documentary History of the Negro People,* p. 522. See also, W. E. B. Du Bois, *Black Reconstruction in America, 1860–1880* (1935; reprint ed., Cleveland, Ohio, 1964), pp. 313–15.

16. There still needs to be written a comprehensive history of the Union Leagues in the South immediately following the Civil War. Some information, however, is provided in Vernon Wharton, *The Negro in Mississippi, 1865–1890* (Chapel Hill, N.C., 1947), pp. 165–66; and James M. McPherson, *The Struggle for Equality: Abolitionists and the Negro in the Civil War and Reconstruction* (Princeton, N.J., 1964), pp. 123–24, 207–8.

17. Quoted by Daniel A. Novak, *The Wheel of Servitude: Black Forced Labor after Slavery* (Lexington, Ky., 1978), p. 2.

18. John Hope Franklin, *From Slavery to Freedom: A History of Negro Americans,* 4th ed. (New York, 1974), pp. 241–42. See also ibid., pp. 1–8; and Theodore B. Wilson, *The Black Codes of the South* (University, Ala., 1965).

19. For more detailed analysis of "Radical Reconstruction," see Harold M. Hyman, ed., *The Radical Republicans and Reconstruction, 1861–1870* (Indianapolis, Ind., 1967); Hans L. Trefousse, *The Radical Republicans: Lincoln's Vanguard for Racial Justice* (New York, 1969) and Herman Belz, *A New Birth of Freedom: The Republican Party and Freedmen's Rights, 1861–1866* (Westport, Conn., 1976), especially pp. 35–50.

20. The four Reconstruction Acts of 1867–68 are reprinted in Hans L. Trefousse, *Reconstruction: America's First Effort at Racial Democracy* (New York, 1971), pp. 103–13, 128–29.

21. Allen Trelease, *White Terror: The Ku Klux Klan Conspiracy and Southern Reconstruction* (New York, 1971), p. xlvi.

22. For detailed background information on the duties and operation of the slave patrols, see Gladys-Marie Fry, *Night Riders in Black Folk History* (Knoxville, Tenn., 1975), pp. 82–86.

23. Yetman, *Life Under the "Peculiar Institution,"* p. 117.

24. John B. Cade, "Out of the Mouths of Ex-Slaves," *Journal of Negro History* 20 (July 1935): 323.

25. Leonard Franklin is quoted by Fry, *Night Riders,* p. 88.

26. Marie Ardella Robinson is quoted, ibid., p. 93.

27. Perdue, Barden, and Phillips, *Weevils in the Wheat,* p. 290.

28. Mandy Cooper is quoted by Fry, *Night Riders,* pp. 100–101.

29. Joseph Hines is quoted, ibid., p. 96.

30. Ibid., p. 95. Fry included an extended interview with Floyd Warlaw Crawford about his grandfather's descriptions of the patrollers, pp. 107–109.

31. Herbert Aptheker, *American Negro Slave Revolts* (New York, 1943), p. 141.

32. Fry, *Night Riders,* pp. 96–102.

33. Ibid., pp. 88 and 92.

34. Trelease, *White Terror,* p. xlvii.

35. For discussions of black and white Republicans during the era, see David Donald, "The Scalawag in Mississippi Reconstruction," *Journal of Southern History* 40 (November 1944): 447–60; Allen W. Trelease, "Who Were the Scalawags?" *Journal of Southern History* 29 (November 1963): 445–68; Thomas Holt, *Black over White: Negro Political Leadership in South Carolina During Reconstruction* (Urbana, Ill., 1977); and Charles Vincent, *Black Legislators in Louisiana During Reconstruction* (Baton Rouge, La., 1976).

36. Trelease, *White Terror*, p. xlviii. For a recent study of this issue, see George C. Rable, *But There Was No Peace: The Role of Violence in the Politics of Reconstruction* (Athens, Ga., 1984).

37. U.S. Senate, *Report of the Joint Select Committee to Inquire into the Condition of Affairs in the Late Insurrectionary States* (Washington, D.C., 1872), 42nd Congress, 2nd sess., Report No. 41, pt. 11, pp. 1–3. (Hereafter referred to as *Report on KKK.*)

38. Trelease, *White Terror*, p. 392.

39. *Report on KKK, Mississippi*, pp. 891–93.

40. Ibid., pp. 1083–85.

41. Ibid., pp. 899–901.

42. *Report on KKK, Georgia*, pp. 374–77, 386–88, 501–4.

43. Ibid., p. 502.

44. Edward Magdol, *A Right to the Land: Essays on the Freedman's Community* (Westport, Conn., 1977), pp. 18–34.

45. Bayley Wyat is quoted by Ronald E. Butchart, *Northern Schools, Southern Blacks, and Reconstruction: Freedmen's Education, 1862–1875* (Westport, Conn., 1980), p. 178. See also, Eric Foner, *Nothing but Freedom: Emancipation and Its Legacy* (Baton Rouge, La., 1983), p. 56.

46. Magdol, *Right to the Land*, pp. 11–12, 35–61 passim. See also Claude F. Oubre, *Forty Acres and a Mule: The Freedmen's Bureau and Black Land Ownership* (Baton Rouge, La., 1978).

47. Ibid., pp. 212–13; Wharton, *Negro in Mississippi*, pp. 61–62.

48. W. E. B. Du Bois, *Souls of Black Folk* (1903; reprint ed., New York, 1969), p. 48.

49. U.S. Senate, *Report and Testimony of the Select Committee of the United States Senate to Investigate the Causes of the Removal of the Negroes from the Southern States to the Northern States* (Washington, D.C., 1880), 46th Congress, 2nd sess., Report No. 693, pp. 190–92. (Hereafter cited as *Report on Negro Exodus.*)

50. Ibid., pp. 177–78. See also Nell Irvin Painter, *Exodusters: Black Migration to Kansas after Reconstruction* (New York, 1977), pp. 71–81.

51. *Report on Negro Exodus*, pt. 2, pp. 114, 128.

52. Ibid., pp. 185–86.

53. Ibid., p. 108.

54. Henry Adams to U.S. Attorney General Charles Devens, 11 November 1878; quoted by Painter, *Exodusters*, pp. 97–98.

55. U.S. Senate, *Report of the United States Senate Committee to Inquire into Alleged Frauds and Violence in the Elections of 1878, with Testimony and Documentary Evidence* (Washington, D.C., 1879), 45th Congress, 3d Session, Report No. 855, p. i.

56. Ibid., pp. xlii–xlvi.

57. *Report on Negro Exodus*, pp. xx–xxi; Painter, *Exodusters*, pp. 146–47; 184–85.

58. Quoted in "The Senate Report on the Exodus of 1879—Documents," *Journal of Negro History* 4 (January 1919): 57–58.

59. *Report on Negro Exodus*, pp. iv–v.

60. Ibid., pp. vi–vii. For other statements that support the position of the exodus put forward in the majority report, see "Proceedings of a Mississippi Migration Convention, Vicksburg, Mississippi" and "How the Negroes Were Duped"—from *Vicksburg Commercial Daily Advertiser*, 6 May 1879; reprinted in *Journal of Negro History* 4 (January 1919): 51–55.

61. *Report on Negro Exodus,* p. ix.
62. Ibid., p. xi. For additional information on the Colonization Council, see Painter, *Exodusters,* pp. 82–95.
63. *Report on Negro Exodus,* pp. xii–xiv.
64. Ibid., p. xv.
65. Ibid., p. xviii.
66. Ibid., p. xx.
67. Ibid., pp. xxi–xxii. See also Painter, *Exodusters,* pp. 210–16; and Robert G. Athearn, *In Search of Canaan: Black Migration to Kansas, 1879–80* (Lawrence, Kan., 1978), pp. 225–41.
68. *Report on Negro Exodus,* p. xxii.
69. Ibid., p. xxv.
70. Magdol, *Right to the Land,* pp. 200–210; Painter, *Exodusters,* pp. 256–61; Athearn, *In Search of Canaan,* pp. 243–58.
71. Painter, *Exodusters,* pp. 137–45.
72. Washington W. McDonogh to John McDonogh, ? October 1846, King Will's Town, Liberia; in Bell I. Wiley, ed., *Slaves No More: Letters from Liberia, 1833–1869* (Lexington, Ky., 1980), pp. 141–42.
73. The best, most recent study of the conditions for Afro-Americans who emigrated to Liberia is Tom W. Shick, *Behold the Promised Land: A History of Afro-American Settler Society in Nineteenth Century Liberia* (Baltimore, Md., 1980).
74. George B. Tindall, *South Carolina Negroes, 1877–1900* (Columbia, S.C., 1952), pp. 153–68; and idem, "The Liberian Exodus of 1878," *South Carolina Historical Magazine* 53 (July 1952): 133–45.
75. Daniel Johnson and Rex R. Campbell, *Black Migration in America: A Social Demographic History* (Durham, N.C., 1981), pp. 60–61. See also Tindall, *South Carolina Negroes,* pp. 169–70.
76. Johnson and Campbell, *Black Migration in America,* pp. 62–70.
77. For information on Bishop Henry McNeal Turner's movement, see Edwin Redkey, *Black Exodus: Black Nationalist and Back-to-Africa Movements, 1890–1910* (New Haven, 1969). See also William E. Bittle and Gilbert Geis, *The Longest Way Home: Chief Alfred C. Sam's Back-to-Africa Movement* (Detroit, 1964).
78. See William Bittle and Gilbert Geis, "Racial Self-Fulfillment and the Rise of an All-Negro Community in Oklahoma," *Phylon* 17 (Summer 1956): 247–60; and Norman L. Crockett, *The Black Towns* (Lawrence, Kan., 1979).
79. Mozell C. Hill, "The All-Negro Society in Oklahoma" (Ph.D. diss., University of Chicago, 1946), pp. 31 and 161; and idem, "The All-Negro Communities of Oklahoma: The Natural History of a Social Movement," *Journal of Negro History* 31 (July 1946): 254–68.
80. The earliest study of the social network that developed in an urban black community in the late nineteenth century is, of course, W. E. B. Du Bois, *The Philadelphia Negro: A Social Study* (1899; reprint ed., New York, 1967).
81. Yetman, *Life Under the "Peculiar Institution,"* p. 131.
82. Lawrence Levine, *Black Culture and Black Consciousness: Afro-American Folk Thought from Slavery to Freedom* (New York, 1977), p. 191.
83. Dena Epstein, *Sinful Tunes and Spirituals: Black Folk Music to the Civil War* (Urbana, Ill., 1977), pp. 161–90.
84. Roger L. Ransom and Richard Sutch, *One Kind of Freedom: The Economic Consequences of Emancipation* (Cambridge, 1977); Jonathan Werner, *Social Origins of the New South: Alabama, 1860–1885* (Baton Rouge, La., 1978); and Jay R. Mandle, *The Roots of Black Poverty: The Southern Plantation Economy after the Civil War* (Durham, N.C., 1978). For a discussion of the continuities in the southern political economy examined by these and

other authors, see Peter Kolchin, "Race, Class, and Poverty in the Post-Civil War South," *Reviews in American History* 7 (December 1979): 515–26.

Chapter Five, "Education Is What We Need," pages 147–186

1. U.S. Senate, Committee on Education and Labor, *Report of the Committee of the Senate Upon the Relations Between Labor and Capital and Testimony Taken by the Committee,* 5 vols., 48th Congress (Washington, D.C., 1885). (Hereafter cited as *Report on Labor and Capital.*) Only four of the five volumes are available; Volume 5, the Report of the Committee, was never published. Floyd Thornhill's testimony may be found in Vol. 4, pp. 3–12.
2. The Senate Resolution of 7 August 1882 is reprinted in ibid., 1: 3. For background information on labor unrest in the late 1870s and early 1880s, see Philip S. Foner, *History of the Labor Movement in the United States,* vol. 2 (New York, 1947), and idem, *The Great Labor Uprising of 1877* (New York, 1977).
3. *Report on Labor and Capital,* 4: 5–6.
4. Gordon C. Lee, *The Struggle for Federal Aid; First Phase: A History of the Attempts to Obtain Federal Aid for the Common Schools, 1870–1890* (New York, 1949), pp. 88–98; Allen J. Going, "The South and the Blair Education Bill," *Mississippi Valley Historical Review* 44 (September 1957): 267–90.
5. James Garfield to Irvin McDonnell, 8 January 1875; quoted by Allan Peskin, "President Garfield and the Southern Question: The Making of a Policy That Never Was," *Southern Quarterly* 16 (July 1978): 381. See also Vincent P. De Santis, "President Garfield and the Solid South," *North Carolina Historical Review* 36 (October 1959): 442–65; and Stanley P. Hirshson, *Farewell to the Bloody Shirt; Northern Republicans and the Southern Negro, 1877–1893* (Bloomington, Ind., 1962), pp. 79–83.
6. Statistics on election of 1880 from Justus D. Doenecke, *The Presidencies of James A. Garfield and Chester A. Arthur* (Lawrence, Kan., 1981), pp. 29–30.
7. Inaugural address of James Garfield, 4 March 1881, in James Richardson, ed., *A Compilation of the Messages and Papers of the Presidents, 1789–1917,* (New York, 1917), 10: 4598–4600.
8. Lee, *Struggle for Federal Aid,* pp. 88–94.
9. *Report on Labor and Capital,* 4: 5–6. For a detailed discussion of the social purposes to be served in opening segregated and desegregated public schools, see V. P. Franklin, "American Values, Social Goals, and the Desegregated School: A Historical Perspective," in V. P. Franklin and James Anderson, eds., *New Perspectives on Black Educational History* (Boston, 1978), pp. 193–211.
10. *Report on Labor and Capital,* 4: 48–49.
11. *Ibid.,* 4: 68–69.
12. *Ibid.,* 4: 107–8.
13. The testimony of the black delegation from Birmingham, Alabama may be found in ibid., 4: 372–405.
14. The testimony of W. W. Wilson may be found in *ibid.,* 4: 464–68.
15. *Ibid.,* 4: 403–5.
16. For background information on the industrial education movement in the nineteenth century, see Melvin L. Barlow, *History of Industrial Education in the United States* (Peoria, Ill., 1967), pp. 30–50; Bernice M. Fisher, *Industrial Education: American Ideals and Institutions* (Madison, Wisc., 1967), pp. 14–49.
17. *Report on Labor and Capital,* 4: 42.
18. *Ibid.,* 4: 395, 485–86.
19. For a recent examination of various aspects of schooling in the southern states following the Civil War, see Ronald Goodenow and Arthur White, eds., *Education and the Rise of the New South,* (Boston, 1981).

20. George Fredrickson provides a brief discussion of the relationship between public school-ing and white supremacy in late nineteenth-century South Africa and the United States, in *White Supremacy: A Comparative Study in American and South African History* (New York, 1981), pp. 270–80.

21. For a general discussion of the desire to learn to read and write among enslaved Afro-Americans, see Thomas L. Webber, *Deep Like the Rivers: Education in the Slave Quarter Community, 1831–1865* (New York, 1978), pp. 131–38.

22. Charles L. Perdue, Jr., Thomas Barden, and Robert K. Phillips, eds., *Weevils in the Wheat: Interviews with Virginia Ex-Slaves,* (Charlottesville, Va., 1976), pp. 285–86.

23. *The Negro in Virginia: Compiled by Workers of the Writers Program of the Work Projects Administration in the State of Virginia* (1940; reprint ed., New York, 1969), p. 44.

24. Norman R. Yetman, ed., *Life Under the "Peculiar Institution": Selections from the Slave Narrative Collection* (New York, 1970), p. 257.

25. *Ibid.,* p. 161.

26. Perdue, Barden, and Phillips, *Weevils in the Wheat,* p. 29.

27. The encounters with literacy in the slave narratives of Thompson, Grandy, and Penning-ton are examined by Stephen Butterfield in *Black Autobiography in America* (Amherst, Mass., 1974), pp. 25–27. For an analysis of the significance of the search for literacy and education in Afro-American autobiographical writing in general, see Robert Stepto, *From Behind the Veil: A Study in Afro-American Narrative* (Urbana, Ill., 1979), pp. 128–94.

28. Frederick Douglass, *Narrative of the Life of Frederick Douglass, An American Slave* (1845), ed. Benjamin Quarles (Cambridge, Mass., 1960), pp. 58–59, 64.

29. Perdue, Barden, and Phillips, *Weevils in the Wheat,* p. 65.

30. Booker T. Washington, in *Up From Slavery, An Autobiography* (New York, 1902), pre-sents a vivid description of the freedmen's rush for schooling, pp. 26–37.

31. For the early black schools in the South, see Henry Bullock, *A History of Negro Education in the South: From 1619 to the Present* (Cambridge, Mass., 1967) pp. 21–35. See also Leon Litwack, *Been In the Storm So Long: The Aftermath of Slavery* (New York, 1979), pp. 472–501; and Mary Frances Berry and John Blassingame, *Long Memory: The Black Experience in America* (New York, 1982), pp. 261–67.

32. For discussions of these early black schools, see A. F. Beard, *A Crusade of Brotherhood: A History of the American Missionary Association* (Boston, 1909), pp. 119–94, passim; George Bentley, *A History of the Freedman's Bureau* (Philadelphia, 1955), pp. 169–84; Martin Abbott, *The Freedmen's Bureau in South Carolina, 1865–1872* (Chapel Hill, N.C., 1967), pp. 82–98; William P. Vaugh, *Schools for All: The Blacks and Public Education in the South, 1865–1877,* (Lexington, Ky., 1974), pp. 9–23, passim; and James Anderson, "Ex-Slaves and the Rise of Universal Education in the New South, 1860–1890," in Goodenow and White, *Education and the Rise of the New South,* pp. 1–25.

33. Jacqueline Jones, *Soldiers of Light and Love: Northern Teachers and Georgia Blacks, 1865–1873* (Chapel Hill, N.C., 1980), pp. 68–69.

34. Ibid., p. 139. See also Chap. 5, "Schooling," pp. 109–39.

35. John Alvord is quoted by Ronald Butchart, *Northern Schools, Southern Blacks, and Recon-struction: Freedman's Education, 1862–1875* (Westport, Conn., 1980), p. 156.

36. American Missionary Association, 21st Annual Report (1867), quoted, ibid., p. 157.

37. Ibid., p. 157–58. See also Jones, *Soldiers of Light and Love,* Chap. 6, "To Teach Them How to Live," pp. 140–66.

38. Jones, *Soldiers of Light and Love,* pp. 69–70.

39. William Channing Gannett is quoted by Butchart, *Northern Schools, Southern Blacks, and Reconstruction,* p. 173. Butchart's chapter "The Black Response to Freedmen's Educa-tion," pp. 169–79, is more insightful on this issue than Robert Morris's recent book, *Reading, 'Riting, and Reconstruction: The Education of Freedmen in the South, 1861–1870* (Chicago, 1981), in which Morris concludes (p. 129) that "black teachers . . . tended to

share . . . the values of their white counterparts." Morris's own evidence does not support the position; see pp. 119–30.

40. The testimony of Preston Brooks Peters may be found in the *Report on Labor and Capital,* 4: 566–71.

41. Two studies that attest to the correctness of Peters's observations are Philip A. Foner, *Organized Labor and the Black Worker, 1619–1981,* 2nd ed. (New York, 1982), and William Harris, *The Harder We Run: Black Workers Since the Civil War* (New York, 1982). See also Gerald H. Gaither, *Blacks and the Populist Revolt: Ballots and Bigotry in the New South* (University, Ala., 1977).

42. The reasons for the poor quality of "Negro industrial education" will be discussed below, but the classic description of the actual programs offered at the agricultural and mechanical, land grant, and private colleges for Negroes during the period is Thomas Jesse Jones, *Negro Education: A Study of the Private and Higher Schools for Colored People in the United States,* 2 vols. (Washington, D.C., 1917).

43. Rayford Logan, *The Betrayal of the Negro: From Rutherford B. Hayes to Woodrow Wilson,* new ed. (New York, 1965), remains the most comprehensive general study of the conditions for Afro-Americans in the United States between 1876 and 1915.

44. W. E. B. Du Bois, ed., *The Negro Common School* (Atlanta, 1901), pp. 77–78.

45. Ibid., pp. 90–91.

46. William Torrey Harris is quoted, ibid., p. 42.

47. The rise and fall of the Blair bills for federal aid to public education is recounted in Lee, *Struggle for Federal Aid,* pp. 80–98, and Going, "The South and the Blair Education Bill," pp. 267–290.

48. W. E. B. Du Bois, ed., *The Common School and the Negro American* (Atlanta, 1911), pp. 7–8.

49. Du Bois discussed "illiteracy" between 1870 and 1910 in ibid., pp. 14–16.

50. U.S. Dept. of Commerce, Bureau of the Census, *Negro Population, 1790–1915* (Washington, D.C., 1918), pp. 406–7.

51. Harvey Graff, *The Literacy Myth: Literacy and Social Structure in a Nineteenth-Century City* (New York, 1979), p. 19.

52. See also Harvey Graff, "Introduction," *Literacy and Social Development in the West: A Reader,* ed. Harvey Graff (Cambridge, 1981), p. 19. This reader contains fifteen essays assessing the impact of literacy on various western societies. See also Roger S. Schofield, "Dimensions of Illiteracy, 1750–1850," *Explorations in Economic History* 11 (October 1973): 437–54; Ivar Berg, *Education and Jobs: The Great Training Robbery* (Boston, 1971); E. P. Thompson, *The Making of the English Working Class* (New York, 1963); Christopher Jencks et al., *Inequality* (New York, 1972), and idem, *Who Gets Ahead? The Determinants of Economic Success in America* (New York, 1979).

53. The Atlantic University Studies provide the most comprehensive information on the activities of Afro-Americans to advance themselves economically and socially during the second half of the nineteenth century. In particular, see *Some Efforts of American Negroes for Their Own Social Betterment* (Atlanta, 1898); *The Negro in Business* (Atlanta, 1899); and *Efforts for Social Betterment Among Negro Americans* (Atlanta, 1910). All these studies were edited by W. E. B. Du Bois.

54. For the white supremacist, disenfranchisement movement, see C. Vann Woodward, *Origins of the New South, 1877–1913* (Baton Rouge, La., 1951), pp. 321–49; and John Cell, *The Highest Stage of White Supremacy: The Origins of Segregation in South Africa and the American South* (New York, 1982), pp. 82–170.

55. Kenneth Lockridge, *Literacy in Colonial New England: An Inquiry into the Social Context of Literacy in the Early Modern West* (New York, 1974), pp. 99–119. See also Graff, *Literacy Myth,* pp. 22–25.

56. Discussions of the relationship between religion and Afro-American educational activities may be found in Carter G. Woodson, *The Education of the Negro Prior to 1861* (Washington, D.C., 1919), pp. 179–204; and V. P. Franklin, *The Education of Black Philadelphia: The Social and Educational History of the Minority Community, 1900–1950* (Philadelphia, 1979), pp. 87–101. The author is preparing a study on the "cultural context of learning and education" at the family and community levels among Afro-Americans in nineteenth- and twentieth-century America.

57. *Freedom's Journal* 16 March 1827; reprinted in Martin E. Dann, ed., *The Black Press, 1827–1895: The Quest for National Identity,* (New York, 1971), pp. 33–34.

58. Ibid., pp. 34–35.

59. Dann, "Introduction," *Black Press,* p. 13.

60. Letter of Frederick Douglass, 7 May 1879; reprinted in "Documents," *Journal of Negro History,* 4 (July 1919): 56–57. See also Frederick Douglass, "The Negro Exodus from the Gulf States," *Journal of Social Science* 9 (May 1880): 1–21. For the opposing viewpoint, see Richard T. Greener, "The Emigration of Colored Citizens from the Southern States," *Journal of Social Science* 9 (May 1880): 22–35.

61. For a large sampling of the support among black editors for the exodus of 1879–80, see Dann, *Black Press,* pp. 269–91.

62. Biographical information on these and dozens of other black journalists of the 1880s may be found in I. Garland Penn, "Sketches and Portraits of Afro-American Editors," *Afro-American Press and Its Editors* (1891; reprint ed., New York, 1969), pp. 133–332. See also V. P. Franklin, "Voice of the Black Community: The Philadelphia Tribune, 1912–41," *Pennsylvania History* 51 (October 1984).

63. T. Thomas Fortune is quoted, ibid., by Penn, *Afro-American Press,* p. 532.

64. Penn published the "Constitution of the National Afro-American League" (1889) in *Afro-American Press,* pp. 530–33. He also included a large number of statements from black journalists supporting the league, see pp. 534–38.

65. T. Thomas Fortune, *New York Freeman,* 25 December 1886; reprinted in Dann, *Black Press,* pp. 225–26.

66. The National Afro-American League and the Afro-American Council are discussed in Emma Lou Thornbrough, *T. Thomas Fortune: Militant Journalist* (Chicago, 1972), pp. 105–18, 180–81, and passim. See also Alfreda M. Duster, ed., *The Autobiography of Ida B. Wells; Crusade for Justice* (Chicago, 1970), pp. 254–58, 260–66.

67. T. Thomas Fortune to *Brooklyn Eagle,* 5 June 1900, quoted by Thornbrough, *T. Thomas Fortune,* p. 200.

68. Quoted by Thornbrough, *T. Thomas Fortune,* pp. 198–99.

69. For detailed information on the actual programs offered at Hampton Institute and later Tuskegee, see James Anderson, "The Hampton Model of Normal School Industrial Education, 1868–1900," in V. P. Franklin and James Anderson, eds., *New Perspectives on Black Educational History,* (Boston, 1978), pp. 61–96; and Robert G. Sherer, *Subordination or Liberation? The Development and Conflicting Theories of Black Education in Nineteenth Century Alabama* (University, 1977), pp. 45–58, 119–33.

70. Sherer, *Subordination or Liberation?,* p. 148.

71. August Meier, "Booker T. Washington and the Negro Press," *Journal of Negro History* 38 (January 1953): 67–90; Louis Harlan, *Booker T. Washington: The Making of a Black Leader, 1865–1901* (New York, 1972), pp. 254–71; and Abby A. Johnson and Ronald M. Johnson, *Propaganda and Aesthetics: The Literary Politics of Afro-American Magazines in the Twentieth Century* (Amherst, Mass., 1979), pp. 3–17.

72. W. E. B. Du Bois, *The Autobiography of W. E. B. Du Bois: A Soliloquy on Viewing My Life from the Last Decade of Its First Century* (New York, 1968), pp. 236–53. The resolution of 1905 is reprinted on pages 249–51.

Conclusion: "The Challenge of Black Self-Determination," pages 186–207

1. Booker T. Washington (BTW), "The Man Farthest Down: The Man at the Bottom in London," *The Outlook* 98 (6 May 1911): 23. BTW's personal secretary, Emmett Scott, and Robert Park were the "ghostwriters" for many of Washington's books and articles during this period. With regard to the "Man Farthest Down," Louis Harlan, Washington's biographer, claimed that "both men took notes, discussed them and then Washington could dictate a draft to a stenographer for Park to further refine by additional research." *Booker T. Washington: The Wizard of Tuskegee, 1901–1915* (New York, 1983), p. 292.

2. BTW, "The Man Farthest Down," pp. 22–23.

3. Idem, "Naples and the Land of the Emigrant," *The Outlook,* 98 (10 June 1911): 296.

4. Ibid., pp. 298–99.

5. BTW, "The Women Who Work in Europe," *The Outlook,* 98 (1 July 1911): 498–99. For an incisive analysis of the "pitiful state" of higher education for Afro-American men and women during this period, see James M. McPherson, *The Abolitionist Legacy: From Reconstruction to the NAACP* (Princeton, N.J., 1975), esp. pp. 354–67.

6. BTW, "Races and Politics," *The Outlook,* 98 (3 June 1911): 262–63.

7. "An Open Letter to the People of Great Britain and Europe by William Edward Burghardt Du Bois and Others," 26 October 1910, reprinted in *The Booker T. Washington Papers,* 10, 1909–10, ed. Louis R. Harlan and Raymond Smock (Urbana, Ill., 1981), pp. 422–25. Among the signers of the letter were J. Max Barber, Archibald Grimke, William Pickens, Harry C. Smith of the Cleveland *Gazette,* Bishop Alexander Walters, and, of course, William Monroe Trotter, editor of the Boston *Guardian,* and Washington's major antagonist.

8. Harlan, *BTW: The Wizard of Tuskegee,* p. 371.

9. For a recent discussion of "black escatology," see Gayraud Wilmore, *Last Things First* (Philadelphia, 1982).

10. For discussions of the self-determinist values that underpin black religious congregations, see James Washington, "The Origins and Emergence of Black Baptist Separation, 1863–1897" (Ph.D. diss., Yale University, 1979). For AME work with freedpeople, see Clarence Walker, *A Rock in a Weary Land: The African Methodist Episcopal Church During the Civil War and Reconstruction* (Baton Rouge, La., 1982).

11. Cf. John W. Cell, *The Highest Stage of White Supremacy: The Origins of Segregation in South Africa and the American South* (New York, 1982), and Norman L. Crockett, *The Black Towns* (Lawrence, Kan., 1979). See also Rodney Carlisle, *The Roots of Black Nationalism* (Port Washington, N.Y., 1975), pp. 93–101; and Raymond L. Hall, *Black Separatism in the United States* (Hanover, N.H., 1978), pp. 21–37.

12. BTW was not the only black leader and intellectual who opposed the mass migrations, and this and a number of other related issues will be addressed in "Masses and Intellectuals in Afro-American History" in preparation.

13. For a discussion of a predominant "core value" of peoples of European descent in the United States and South Africa, see George Fredrickson, *White Supremacy: A Comparative Study in American and South African History* (New York, 1981). See also Gerald H. Gaither, *Blacks and the Populist Revolt: Ballots and Bigotry in the New South* (University, Ala., 1977).

14. Quoted by John Hope Franklin, *From Slavery to Freedom: A History of Negro Americans,* 4th ed., (New York, 1974), p. 356. See also Allen D. Grimshaw, ed., *Racial Violence in the United States* (Chicago, 1969), pp. 58–63; V. P. Franklin, "The Philadelphia Race Riot of 1918," *Pennsylvania Magazine of History and Biography* 99 (July 1975): 336–50.

15. Marcus Garvey to BTW, 8 September 1914; reprinted in *The Marcus Garvey and Universal*

Negro Improvement Association (UNIA) Papers, Robert A. Hill, 2 vols. to date (Berkeley, Calif., 1983), 1: 66–67.

16. Marcus Garvey, "West Indies in the Mirror of Truth" *Champion Magazine* (January 1917); reprinted in ibid., I, pp. 197–201.
17. R. A. Hill, "Introduction," *Marcus Garvey and UNIA Papers,* 1: xxxix.
18. For discussions of NAACP membership figures during these years, see Charles F. Kellogg, *NAACP: A History, 1909–20* (Baltimore, 1967), pp. 137 and 292; and Eugene Levy, *James Weldon Johnson: Black Leader, Black Voice* (Chicago, 1973), pp. 228–30.
19. See Theodore L. Kornweibel, *No Crystal Stair: Black Life and the Messenger, 1917–1928* (Westport, Conn., 1975); and William H. Harris, *Keeping the Faith: A. Philip Randolph, Milton P. Webster and the Brotherhood of Sleeping Car Porters, 1925–37* (Urbana, Ill., 1977).
20. For information on Cyril V. Briggs and the African Blood Brotherhood see Tony Martin, *Race First: The Ideological and Organizational Struggles of Marcus Garvey and the Universal Negro Improvement Association* (Westport, Conn., 1976), pp. 236–43; *Marcus Garvey and UNIA Papers,* 1: 521–32; and John Henrik Clarke, ed., *Marcus Garvey and the Vision of Africa* (New York, 1974), pp. 174–79.
21. Tony Martin provides important insights into the literary and educational programs of Garvey and the UNIA in *Literary Garveyism: Garvey, Black Arts, and the Harlem Renaissance* (Dover, Mass., 1983).
22. For discussion, see Randell K. Burkett, *Black Redemption: Churchmen Speak for the Garvey Movement* (Philadelphia, 1978), esp. pp. 3–18; and *Garveyism as a Religious Movement: The Institutionalization of a Black Civil Religion* (Metuchen, N.J., 1978), esp. pp. 45–70.
23. *The Philosophy and Opinions of Marcus Garvey,* ed. Amy Jacques Garvey, 2 vols. (1923; reprint ed., New York, 1969), 1: 44.
24. Burkett, *Black Redemption,* pp. 7–15; Martin, *Race First,* pp. 67–80; and Hill, "Introduction," *Marcus Garvey and UNIA Papers,* 1: xli–1.
25. Hill, "Introduction," *Marcus Garvey and UNIA Papers,* 1: 1–li.
26. The "Garvey Must Go" campaign is discussed in Kornweibel, *No Crystal Stair,* pp. 132–75, and Martin, *Race First,* pp. 324–33.
27. Some of these federal documents are reprinted in *Marcus Garvey and UNIA Papers,* vols. 1 and 2.
28. See Martin Luther King, Jr., *Stride Toward Freedom* (New York, 1958), and idem, *Why We Can't Wait* (New York, 1964). The studies of the civil rights movement are already numerous. See, for example, Pat Watters, *Down to Now: Reflections on the Southern Civil Rights Movement* (New York, 1971); Howell Raines, *My Soul Is Rested: Movement Days in the Deep South Remembered* (New York, 1977); Howard Zinn, *SNCC: The New Abolitionists* (Boston, 1971); A. Meier and E. Rudwick, *CORE: A Study in the Civil Rights Movement* (New York, 1973); Harvard Sitkoff, *The Struggle for Black Equality, 1945–1980* (New York, 1981); Clayborne Carson, *In Struggle: SNCC and the Black Awakening of the 1960s* (Cambridge, Mass., 1981); Malcolm X, *Malcolm X Speaks,* ed. George Breitman (New York, 1965); idem, *By Any Means Necessary: Speeches, Interviews, and a Letter of Malcolm X,* ed. George Breitman (New York, 1970); idem, *The Autobiography of Malcolm X* (New York, 1965); Stokeley Carmichael and Charles V. Hamilton, *Black Power: The Politics of Liberation in America* (New York, 1967); Floyd Barbour, ed., *The Black Power Revolt: A Collection of Essays* (New York, 1967).
29. See, for example, Bernard Sternsher, ed., *The Negro in Depression and War: Prelude to Revolution, 1930–1945* (Chicago, 1969); R. Wolters, *Negroes and the Great Depression: The Problem of Economic Recovery* (Westport, Conn., 1970); Harvard Sitkoff, *A New Deal for Blacks: The Emergence of Civil Rights as a National Issue: The Depression Decade* (New York, 1978); Louis Kesselman, *The Social Politics of the FEPC: A Study in Reform Pressure Movements* (Chapel Hill, 1948); Louis Ruchames, *Race, Jobs, and Politics: The Story of the*

F.E.P.C. (New York, 1953); Herbert Garfinkle, *When Negroes March: The March on Washington Movement in the Organizational Politics for F.E.P.C.* (Glencoe, Ill., 1959); and Genna Rae McNeil, *Groundwork: Charles Hamilton Houston and the Struggle for Civil Rights* (Philadelphia, 1983).

30. The most comprehensive surveys of the contemporary social and economic conditions for Afro-Americans are those published annually by the National Urban League. For information on specific problems of the late 1970s and 1980s, see Robert B. Hill, "The Economic Status of Black Families," in James D. Williams, ed., *The State of Black America, 1979* (New York, 1979), pp. 25–39; Robert B. Hill, "The Economic Status of Black Americans," in J. D. Williams, ed., in *The State of Black America, 1981,* (New York, 1981), pp. 1–59; Barbara A. P. Jones, "The Economic Status of Black Women," in J. D. Williams, ed., *The State of Black America, 1983,* (New York, 1983), pp. 115–45; Denys Vaughn-Cooke, "The Economic State of Black America—Is There a Recovery?" in J. D. Williams, ed., *The State of Black America, 1984* (New York, 1984), pp. 1–24.

31. Jesse Jackson's earliest triumph was the proposed "withdrawal of enthusiasm" from Coca-Cola Corporation in July 1981; it netted $30 million for black business over several years. Jackson went on to confront other major corporations that had previously been unresponsive to black capitalist demands for access to advertising funds and economic projects aimed at the black community. In many ways Jackson's crusade was inspired by my paper, "Blackouts: A Strategy for Black Self-Determination in the 1980s" (1 May 1981), which was distributed broadly. The paper, however, emphasized the collective benefits that an entire black community could gain in the form of jobs, improved educational programs, and other objectives through participation in well-organized "blackouts."

32. The best early treatments of the presidential candidacy of Jesse Jackson were Andrew Kopkind, "Black Power in the Age of Jackson," *The Nation* (26 November 1983): 521, 534–41; "What Makes Jesse Run"? *Newsweek* (14 November 1983): 50–56; and David Moberg, "Here Comes Jesse Jackson," *In These Times* 8 (29 February–13 March 1984): 8, 9, 15. See also Clayborne Carson, "From Garvey to Jackson," *The Nation* (31 March 1984): 389–92.

33. Harold Cruse, in "Behind the Black Power Slogan," argued that "Black Power is nothing but the economic and political philosophy of Booker T. Washington given a 1960's militant shot in the arm and brought up to date." But he also stated that "Washington had a mass following among Negroes that Du Bois never had in his life." Cruse provides no evidence (and I have found none) that suggests Washington had a "mass following." He was greatly admired by the masses of Afro-Americans for his achievements at Tuskegee, but when it came to accepting his positions or following his advice, the black masses acted according to their interests and cultural values. See Harold Cruse, *Rebellion or Revolution?* (New York, 1968), pp. 201, 208, 224.

34. Cornel West, *Prophesy Deliverance! An Afro-American Revolutionary Christianity* (Philadelphia, 1982), pp. 18–19.

35. Ibid., pp. 116–17. See also James H. Cone, *The Black Church and Marxism: What Do They Have to Say to Each Other?* (New York, 1980); and Amiri Baraka, "Nationalism, Self-Determination, and Socialist Revolution," *The Black Nation* 2 (Winter 1982): 5–10; and Philip S. Foner, *American Socialism and Black Americans: From the Age of Jackson to World War II* (Westport, Conn., 1977), and Cedric J. Robinson, *Black Marxism: The Making of the Black Radical Tradition* (London, 1983).

NOTES TO EPILOGUE

1. Thomas Sowell, *Race and Economics* (New York, 1975); *Ethnic America: A History* (New York, 1981); *Markets and Minorities* (New York, 1981); *The Economics and Politics of Race: An International Perspective* (New York, 1983); *Civil Rights: Rhetoric or Reality?* (New York, 1984); and *A Conflict of Visions* (New York, 1987).
2. Thomas Sowell, *Affirmative Action Reconsidered: Was it Necessary in Academia?* (Washington, 1975) and *Preferential Policies: An International Perspective* (New York, 1990); Walter E. Williams, *The State Against Blacks* (New York, 1982), and *All It Takes Is Guts: A Minority View* (Washington, D.C., 1987); and Shelby Steele, *The Content of Our Character: A New Vision of Race in America* (New York, 1990).
3. Elizabeth Wright and Robert Woodson quoted in Peter Applebome, "Black Conservatives: Minority Within a Minority," *The New York Times*, July 13, 1991.
4. This criticism of the civil rights leadership was also the central argument in Harold Cruse's *Plural but Equal: A Critical Study of Blacks and Minorities and the American Plural Society* (New York, 1987). For a detailed criticism of these black conservatives, see Adolph Reed, "Steele Trap: An Essay Review of Shelby Steele's *The Content of Our Character*," *The Nation* (4 March 1991): 274–81.
5. William H. Harris, *Keeping the Faith: A. Philip Randolph, Milton P. Webster and the Brotherhood of Sleeping Car Porters, 1925–1937* (Urbana, Ill., 1977); Jervis Anderson, *A. Philip Randolph: A Biographical Portrait* (New York, 1973).
6. Mark Naison, *Communists in Harlem During the Depression* (New York, 1983), pp. 177–92; Paula Pfeffer, *A. Philip Randolph: Pioneer of the Civil Rights Movement* (Baton Rouge, La., 1990), pp. 32–44.
7. A. Philip Randolph quoted in Anderson, *A. Philip Randolph*, pp. 248–49; see also Herbert Garfinkle, *When Negroes March: The March on Washington Movement in the Organizational Politics for the F.E.P.C.* (Glencoe, Ill., 1959).
8. Only a few labor historians have discussed the significance of self-determinist cultural values in explaining the history of the black organized labor movement in the United States. See Charles Wesley, *Negro Labor in the United States, 1850–1925* (New York, 1927); and William H. Harris, *The Harder We Run: Black Workers Since the Civil War* (New York, 1982).
9. Sociologist Aldon Morris refers to these early all-black protest organizations as "local movement centers," which "mobilize, organize, and coordinate collective action aimed at

attaining the common ends of the subordinate group." See *The Origins of the Civil Rights Movement: Black Communities Organizing for Change* (New York: The Free Press, 1984), p. 40.

10. Martin Luther King, Jr., "The Rising Tide of Racial Consciousness" (1960), in James M. Washington, ed., *A Testament of Hope: The Essential Writings of Martin Luther King Jr.,* (New York, 1986), pp. 147–48.

11. Several recent surveys of the civil rights era mentioned Dr. King and other predominantly black civil rights groups growing commitment to integration. See Taylor Branch, *Parting the Waters: America in the King Years, 1954–63* (New York, 1988), pp. 874–75; 916; and Robert Weisbroth, *Freedom Bound: A History of the Civil Rights Movement* (New York, 1990), pp. 170–78.

12. C. Eric Lincoln, *The Black Muslims in America* (1961; revised ed., Boston, 1973); E. U. Essien-Udom, *Black Nationalism: The Search for an Identity in America* (Chicago, 1962); and Weisbrot, *Freedom Bound,* pp. 170–78.

13. For important examinations of the significance of Malcolm X's leadership, see John Henrik Clarke, ed., *Malcolm X: The Man and His Times* (New York, 1969); James H. Cone, *Martin and Malcolm and America: A Dream or a Nightmare* (Maryknoll, N.Y., 1991); and Bruce Perry, *Malcolm X: A Man Who Changed Black America* (Barrytown, N.Y., 1991).

14. Paul Burstein, *Discrimination, Jobs, and Politics: The Struggle for Equal Employment Opportunity in the United States Since the New Deal* (Chicago, 1985), pp. 69–96; Donald G. Nieman, *Promises to Keep: African Americans and the Constitutional Order, 1776 to the Present* (New York, 1991), pp. 162–76.

15. David Garrow, *Protest at Selma: Martin Luther King, Jr. and the Voting Rights Act of 1965* (New Haven, 1978); Donald G. Nieman, *Promises to Keep,* pp. 170–72.

16. Steven F. Lawson, *Black Ballots: Voting Rights in the South, 1944–1969* (New York, 1976); H. Ball, D. Krane, and T. Lauth, *Compromised Compliance: The Implementation of the 1965 Voting Rights Act* (Westport, Ct., 1982), pp. 35–63.

17. Weisbrot, *Freedom Bound,* pp. 222–34; Rhoda L. Blumberg, *Civil Rights: The 1960s Freedom Struggle* (Boston, 1991), pp. 135–56. Martin Luther King, Jr. eventually came to support Black Power when its objective was economic justice for African Americans, see *Where Do We Go From Here: Chaos or Community?* (New York, 1967), pp. 23–66.

18. Stokely Carmichael and Charles V. Hamilton, *Black Power: The Politics of Liberation in America* (New York, 1967); Blumberg, *Civil Rights,* pp. 144–48; Theodore L. Cross, *Black Capitalism: Strategy for Business in the Ghetto* (New York, 1969); Maulana Karenga, *Introduction to Black Studies* (Inglewood, Calif., 1980); Abdul Alkalimat, *Introduction to Black Studies: A Peoples College Primer* (Urbana, Ill., 1984); Molefi Kete Asante, *The Afro-Centric Idea* (Philadelphia, 1987).

19. The March 1972 Gary political convention is discussed in Manning Marable, *Race, Reform, and Rebellion: The Second Reconstruction in Black America, 1945–1982* (Jackson, Miss., 1984), pp. 137–41; see also, Steven F. Lawson, *In Pursuit of Power: Southern Blacks and Electoral Politics, 1965–1982* (New York, 1985), pp. 224–53; and Harold W. Stanley, *Voter Mobilization and the Politics of Race: The South and Universal Suffrage, 1952–1984* (New York, 1987), p. 41–56.

20. Marable, *Race, Reform, and Rebellion,* pp. 165–72; Lawson, *In Pursuit of Power,* pp. 254–81.

21. Books on the "Reagan Revolution" in the 1980s include Stanley Weintraub and Marvin Goodstein, eds., *Reaganomics in the Stagflation Economy* (Philadelphia, 1983); Charles Hulten and Isabell Sawhill, eds., *The Legacy of Reaganomics: Prospects for Long-term Growth* (Washington, D.C., 1984); David Stockman, *The Triumph of Politics* (New York, 1986); Michael J. Boskin, *Reagan and the Economy: The Successes, Failures, and Unfinished Agenda* (San Francisco, 1987); and William Niskanem, *Reaganomics: An Insider's Account of the Policies and the People* (New York, 1988).

22. Kevin Phillips, *The Politics of Rich and Poor: Wealth and the American Electorate in the Reagan Aftermath* (New York, 1990), pp. 8–10.

23. Ibid., pp. 14–23; see also Thomas D. Edsall, *The New Politics of Inequality* (New York, 1984), pp. 67–106; and Frank Levy, *Dollars and Dreams: The Changing American Income Distribution* (New York, 1987), pp. 192–204.

24. Statistical information from William P. O'Hare, et al., *African Americans in the 1990s* (Washington, D.C., 1991); see also Alphonso Pinkney, *The Myth of Black Progress* (New York, 1984); William J. Wilson, *The Truly Disadvantaged: The Inner City, the Underclass, and Public Policy* (Chicago, 1987).

25. For discussion, see Manning Marable, "Black America in Search of Itself," *The Progressive* (November 1991), pp. 18–23.

INDEX

INDEX *to the* EPILOGUE